Continuity and Change in
Soviet–East European Relations

This book is also in the
Studies in International and Strategic Affairs Series
of the Center for International and Strategic Affairs,
University of California, Los Angeles.

A list of the other titles in this series can be found at the back of the
book.

Continuity and Change in Soviet–East European Relations

Implications for the West

EDITED BY

Marco Carnovale
and William C. Potter

Westview Press
BOULDER, SAN FRANCISCO, & LONDON

This Westview softcover edition is printed on acid-free paper and bound in softcovers that carry the highest rating of the National Association of State Textbook Administrators, in consultation with the Association of American Publishers and the Book Manufacturers' Institute.

Copyright © 1989 by Westview Press, Inc.

Published in 1989 in the United States of America by Westview Press, Inc., 5500 Central Avenue, Boulder, Colorado 80301, and in the United Kingdom by Westview Press, Inc., 13 Brunswick Centre, London WC1N 1AF, England

Library of Congress Cataloging-in-Publication Data
Continuity and change in Soviet–East European relations : implications
  for the West / edited by Marco Carnovale and William C. Potter.
    p. cm.—(Studies in international and strategic affairs
series of the Center for International and Strategic Affairs,
University of California, Los Angeles)
  Contains rev. and updated papers from an international conference
held in Rome, co-sponsored by the Center for International and
Strategic Affairs at the University of California, Los Angeles, and
the Istituto affari internazionali in Rome.
  ISBN 0-8133-7526-6
  1. Europe, Eastern—Foreign relations—Soviet Union—Congresses.
2. Soviet Union—Foreign relations—Europe, Eastern—Congresses.
3. Soviet Union—Foreign relations—1975-   —Congresses.
I. Carnovale, Marco. II. Potter, William C. III. University of
California, Los Angeles. Center for International and Strategic
Affairs. IV. Istituto affari internazionali. V. Series: Studies in
international and strategic affairs series.

DJK45.S65C66 1989
327.47—dc19   87-22942
                                                                         CIP

Printed and bound in the United States of America

The paper used in this publication meets the requirements of the American National
Standard for Permanence of Paper for Printed Library Materials Z39.48-1984.

10   9   8   7   6   5   4   3   2   1

Contents

Preface

This book is the product of a conference on "Soviet-East European Relations: Implications for the West," held in Rome on December 16-17, 1985. The conference was sponsored by the UCLA Center for International and Strategic Affairs and the Istituto Affari Internazionali.

The authors wish to thank Michael Intriligator (UCLA) and Cesare Merlini (IAI) for their assistance in organizing the conference and in facilitating publication of this volume. They also wish to acknowledge the editorial assistance provided by Ann Florini. They are grateful to Carol Butcher for her care in typing the manuscript and preparing it for publication.

List of the Contributors

WOLFGANG BERNER is affiliated with the Bundesinstitut für Ostwissenshaftliche und Internationale Studien.

MARCO CARNOVALE is a Research Associate at the Istituto Affari Internazionali.

KEITH CRANE is a Senior Researcher at the Rand Corporation.

DONATO DI GAETANO is affiliated with the Research Center of the Banco di Roma.

ANDRZEJ KORBONSKI is Professor of Political Science and Director, Center for Russian and East European Studies, University of California, Los Angeles.

JOACHIM KRAUSE is a Senior Researcher at the Stiftung Wissenschaft und Politik.

WOLFGANG PFEILER is Professor of Political Science at the University of Bonn and is affiliated with the Konrad Adenauer Stiftung.

WILLIAM POTTER is Executive Director at the Center for International and Strategic Affairs.

EBERHARD SCHULZ is affiliated with the Deutsche Gesellschaft für Auswaertige Politik.

1

INTRODUCTION

William C. Potter

I t is fashionable today to emphasize the dynamic character of communist political systems. *Perestroika* and *novoye myshlenie* ("new thinking") are now common words in the vocabulary of Soviet and East European watchers. Most scholarly attention to change, however, has tended to focus on domestic economic, political, and social developments rather than on foreign relations. Those studies that have looked at the evolution of Warsaw Pact state external affairs generally have focused on Soviet relations with the United States, Western Europe, and the Third World. Much less attention has been directed at the evolving state of Soviet-East European relations.

In order to redress this situation, at least in part, a conference on "Soviet-East European Relations: Implications for the West" was held in Rome, Italy, December 16-17, 1985. The conference was sponsored jointly by the UCLA Center for International and Strategic Affairs and the Istituto Affari Internazionali and sought to explore the elements of continuity and change in Soviet-East European relations with respect to political, economic, and military affairs. Particular attention was devoted to the implications for the West of the observed trends in intra-Warsaw Pact relations. The chapters in this book are revised versions of the papers presented at the Rome conference.

In his opening chapter, Andrzej Korbonski examines the continuity and change in three dimensions of the Soviet-East European relationship--multilateral institutional ties, bilateral agreements, and informal arrangements--over a twenty-year time span. Although he discerns important elements of change, especially with respect to economic institutional relations, he is inclined to emphasize continuity over change and to forecast "more of the same."

One issue that has always been central to Soviet-East European relations and often has served as a barometer of the state of East-West relations is the "German question." Wolfgang Pfeiler examines the evolution of Soviet and

East European views with respect to *Westpolitik* and the German question. He discerns not only major differences between the Soviet Union and the German Democratic Republic over the appropriate *Westpolitik*, but notes a striking change in Soviet and East German policy over the past two decades. While in the late 1960s and early 1970s the GDR sought to impede the Soviet Union's policy of rapprochement with the Federal Republic, in the mid-1980s it attempted to exploit the leadership disarray in Moscow to pursue its own intra-German dialogue. Differences in Soviet and East German *Westpolitik* have diminished under Gorbachev, Pfeiler believes, less because of a retreat on the part of the GDR and more due to a change in Soviet policy. This shift in Soviet policy, which Pfeiler attributes primarily to a rise in the priority Gorbachev assigns to domestic issues, should enhance the prospects for the improvement of both intra-German and East-West relations.

The chapter by Eberhard Schulz also addresses the issue of East Europe's *Westpolitik*, but with a more narrow focus on the sources and substance of East German behavior. Schulz discerns six major phases in the evolution of East German policy toward the Federal Republic between late 1979 and the end of 1986. Most striking is the persistence across these phases of East German efforts to restore a measure of detente in Europe after the deterioration of superpower relations. Although Schulz's chapter was completed prior to Erich Honecker's historic visit to West Germany in 1987, his analysis of the factors underlying East German interest in *Westpolitik* remains valid and foreshadowed the trip.

The Soviet Union has long utilized economic policy, in conjunction with political and military instruments, in pursuing its objectives vis-à-vis Eastern Europe. Keith Crane, in his chapter, examines the costs of Soviet economic policies toward Eastern Europe, explains why the Soviet Union in the past chose to subsidize the other CMEA states, and analyzes the reasons why the Soviets want a change. Trade subsidies, he argues, have most often been used in the past to bolster states in political turmoil, rather than to extort political concessions. Slow economic growth in the Soviet Union, the large opportunity costs incurred from trade credits to other CMEA states, and the limited effectiveness of Soviet trade policies in curbing unrest in Eastern Europe have contributed to a Soviet reassessment of its economic relations with its East European allies. This change was apparent at the 1984 CMEA summit meeting which called for, among other things, improved Soviet terms of trade and a restructuring of East European economies to better serve the Soviet Union. The prospects for achieving these changes, and accelerating East European economic growth, Crane concludes, are not bright and the long-term implications of slow growth are continued or increasing political unrest. Recent Soviet efforts at reform, however, do provide East Europeans leaders with more room for maneuver, including increased trade with the West.

The issue of East-West trade and the economic complementarity of Eastern and Western Europe is the focus of the chapter by Donato Di Gaetano. According to his analysis, the high expectations for East-West trade at the beginning of the 1970s were not realized in the 1980s as the East European states acquired substantial hard-currency indebtedness to the West and curtailed their imports from the EEC. East-West trade was also negatively affected, he maintains, by the divergence of U.S. and West European perspectives on the use of export controls for political and security objectives. Nevertheless, Di Gaetano perceives a basic complementarity in East and West European economies and is cautiously optimistic that economic relations will improve.

One important element of continuity in Soviet-East European relations is the central place that East Europe has occupied and continues to occupy in the minds of Soviet decisionmakers for national security. The region has paramount importance for military-strategic reasons and for over thirty years the Warsaw Treaty Organization (WTO) has been used to pursue Soviet security objectives. Soviet and East European interests in the WTO, however, have changed over time. As Marco Carnovale points out in his chapter on "The Warsaw Pact at Thirty," what was initially an organization dominated by Soviet military considerations has increasingly acquired a political component in which Soviet interests must contend with not always compatible East European objectives. The politicization of the WTO and the increasing political voice of the East European states, Carnovale contends, should be viewed by the West as a favorable trend and its further development should be encouraged.

An important component of Soviet foreign policy has been the extension of military assistance toward the Third World. Joachim Krause, in his chapter, examines the contribution of the East European states to Warsaw Pact military aid diplomacy and how it has changed over time. He observes considerable variation across the East European states, both in terms of the nature of their assistance and their policy incentives. Unlike Czechoslovakia and Poland, for example, which have been mainly interested in the economic benefits of arms sales, the GDR has viewed military assistance as a means to develop its own international identity. Krause also points out the divergence between Soviet interests in the provision of military aid and that of the East European states. One consequence of this divergence has been the general lack of Soviet success in persuading its Warsaw Pact partners to provide military assistance on economic terms that are very favorable to the recipient states. These intra-Pact differences, Krause cautions, do not automatically translate into more benign Warsaw Pact policy or advantages for the West. They may, however, provide a limited opportunity for decision-maker's incentives and disincentives influencing the calculus of East European foreign policy.

A significant but poorly understood area of Soviet-East European relations concerns the role of the Council of Mutual Economic Assistance (CMEA or Comecon). Wolfgang Berner, in his chapter, analyzes the evolution of Comecon relations in the 1980s with special reference to the issue of the organization's size and membership. He details the dramatic change from the policy of organizational expansion to one of "closed doors," in which "socialist-oriented" LDCs were effectively barred from membership because of the economic strains their admission would impose on present Comecon members. Soviet and East European perspectives tend to converge on this issue, Berner argues, and are unlikely to change in the near term.

Marco Carnovale, in his concluding chapter, focuses on Soviet-East European relations during the first three years of the Gorbachev era. He notes that while responses in Eastern Europe to Gorbachev's initiatives vary significantly from country to country, they exhibit a number of common features. Perhaps most interesting is the unusual support they have generated among East European dissidents.

Carnovale also assesses some of the economic and political implications for the West of recent developments in Soviet-East European relations. He discerns a number of risks as well as opportunities for the West and attaches particular importance to the management of the German question. A safer Europe, he concludes, is not necessarily a Europe without blocs. Moreover, care must be exercised to insure that change in Soviet-East European relations is both gradual and peaceful.

2

SOVIET-EAST EUROPEAN RELATIONS IN THE 1980s: CONTINUITY AND CHANGE

Andrzej Korbonski

Introduction

The growth of interest in the problem of continuity and change in the context of Soviet-East European relations is a relatively recent phenomenon. While Western specialists in the general area of Soviet and East European affairs have been aware, at least since the death of Stalin, that Communist political systems are subject to change just like other polities, there has been a rather strange reluctance to address the issue in a systematic fashion.

Several reasons have accounted for the time lag in acknowledging the fact that both the Soviet Union and its East European allies have been changing. One of them was clearly the long-lasting love affair between Western scholars and the so-called "totalitarian" model or syndrome, which dominated academic thinking on the subject of Communist states during and even beyond the early post-World War II period. The basic premise of the totalitarian model was its aversion to change: it was assumed *a priori* that the main objective of a totalitarian system was total control aimed at the preservation of the status quo. Ironically, the classical treatment of the syndrome, which became a bible to successive generations of graduate students in the social sciences, appeared at a time when the Soviet political system itself, on which the model was partly based, began to change.[1] As a result, there was a considerable delay in starting a thorough examination of the process of systemic transformation. Even those scholars who gradually became persuaded that such a transformation was actually taking place were reluctant to jettison the totalitarian baggage in the belief that perhaps the

5

system was irreversible after all.

The second reason was the continuing difficulty in conceptualizing the notion of change. It must be kept in mind that the first generation of Soviet and East European specialists was predominantly recruited from the so-called area studies which were not distinguished by their concern for, or emphasis on, modern social methodology and theory. Moreover, many of the experts were natives of the countries they were studying; most of them were trained in the classical disciplines of law and history, which at that time at least, tended to stress legal-institutional arrangements at the expense of other approaches. This meant that when the field of political science began to undergo its own process of change, especially in the sub-fields of comparative politics and international relations, the community of "Communist" scholars was largely left out of the process of reappraisal.[2]

As a consequence, it took a long time to break through the curtain of academic parochialism and to try to integrate Soviet and East European studies with mainstream political science. The process itself was further delayed somewhat by two factors: one, by the difficulties encountered by scholars trying to come up with an unambiguous definition of such concepts as "change," "modernization," and "development," and two, by a continuing belief expressed by many experts claiming that Communist political systems were so utterly different from the rest that conventional political science analysis was not applicable in their case, and that anyone attempting to utilize it in the Soviet and East European context was bound to generate erroneous conclusions that would provide a distorted image of the Communist political systems, covering up its true nature.[3]

It is difficult to pin down exactly the beginning of a serious study of the process of change in the Soviet Union and its junior partners in Eastern Europe. The early 1960s witnessed a rise in the number of articles analyzing that process. Not surprisingly, scholarly attention was focused almost exclusively on Soviet domestic politics, partly because of a much greater body of available knowledge, and partly because the USSR was still perceived at that time as a model to be closely emulated by the smaller East European countries. It took about a decade for the realization that the process of post-Stalinist de-satellization loosened the previously close links with Moscow and that at least some East European countries became active as autonomous entities, worthy of scholarly attention on their own merits.[4]

While much work was being done with regard to internal changes within the individual East European countries, the subject of Soviet-East European relations, and of changes therein, remained essentially a *tabula rasa*. To be sure, the topic itself attracted growing attention and a number of excellent studies were published in the late 1970s and early 1980s, but the fundamental assumption underlying the analysis was that despite various changes in the domestic arena, the Kremlin managed, by and large, to retain its hegemonial position and to maintain its domination over the region, Romania's deviant behavior notwithstanding.[5] To put it differently, the USSR was still in the position of monopolizing decision-making in the bloc and, at the same time, was able to defuse or minimize the impact of outside influence on the area. Influence transmission was viewed as unidirectional, from East to West, with Eastern Europe being on the receiving end of influences generated in or by the Kremlin.

The relatively recent growth of interest in the problem of domestic or internal determinants of Soviet international behavior persuaded some scholars to challenge the conventional wisdom of unilateral and unidirectional influence transmission within the Moscow-led alliance. Some of them concluded that for a variety of reasons the Kremlin's allies in Eastern Europe have been able for some years to exert influence on the USSR.[6] While there is no convincing or concrete evidence that Eastern Europe managed to force the Soviet leaders to change their policy on a fundamental issue, there is considerable circumstantial evidence suggesting that influence transmission within the alliance has now become mutual, with Eastern Europe as a whole as well as the individual countries in the region not only being listened to but also influencing policymaking in Moscow.[7] It was also becoming increasingly clear that the Kremlin was less and less able to prevent Western and other non-bloc influences penetrating the East European perimeter. Both these phenomena represented a considerable change as compared not only with the state of affairs at the time of Stalin's death but also with the situation within the Soviet alliance at the end of the 1960s. The purpose of this essay is to highlight some of the most important areas and turning points in the process of change in the Soviet-East European relations from the mid-1960s until the present.

Since the topic of Soviet-East European relations has not been neglected in the literature, it is difficult to come up with some original insights into that relationship. The major problem was to choose an approach that would be both parsimonious and yet rich enough to allow us to reach some interesting conclusions. The approach used here is that of comparative statics, which involves contrasting the Soviet-East European relationship at two points in time--1968 and 1988--focusing on a few key variables and examining the way they have changed in the interval.

The starting point in the examination is the state of affairs within the "Communist camp" in the second half of the 1960s, as discussed by Zbigniew Brzezinski.[8] The terminal point is the situation within the Soviet-led alliance twenty years later in the second half of the 1980s, which will be analyzed with the help of the same variables chosen by Brzezinski in his investigation of the Soviet bloc twenty years earlier.

The Soviet Alliance System in 1968

In his analysis of the Soviet alliance in the mid-1960s, Brzezinski focused on three of its aspects: formal institutional ties; bilateral agreements; and informal arrangements.

At that time, the two most important multilateral organs providing institutional links between the USSR and the smaller East European countries were the Warsaw Treaty Organization (WTO) and the Council for Mutual Economic Assistance (CMEA). WTO, which celebrated its tenth anniversary in 1965, was conceived at the initiative of Khrushchev, eager to replace the largely discredited Stalinist "informal" control mechanisms with a formal institutional framework, legitimating, at least *de jure* if not *de facto*, the Soviet hegemony in the region.[9] In the course of the first ten years of its existence, WTO created a number of structures which were supposed to provide a platform for regular mutual consultations and exchange of views among the Treaty members, but which, in fact, provided a convenient cover-up for Soviet monopoly of policy-making in the alliance. WTO was mentioned prominently during the Hungarian Revolt of 1956, but no WTO troops, except for the Soviet, actually participated in the invasion of Hungary. The only other WTO accomplishment worth mentioning was the initiation of joint military exercises in 1961, which subsequently have been conducted annually on the territory of different member-countries.

This facade of seeming stability and cohesion was shattered as a result of the Czechoslovak crisis of 1968. Three events, in particular, were responsible for focusing attention in both East and West on the Warsaw Pact. First, the summer of 1968 witnessed the first open criticism of the Soviet domination of the Treaty's command structures, voiced by a high-ranking East European officer. What General Prchlik said was public knowledge ever since the creation of the Treaty, but the fact that a general in the Czechoslovak army, long considered the most loyal component of the Pact's armed forces, was willing openly to condemn Soviet practices in WTO, testified to the growing dissatisfaction and restiveness among Moscow's junior allies.[10]

Secondly, roughly at the same time, the unity which characterized the Treaty's activities during its first decade was broken as a result of Romania's refusal to join in the collective WTO action against Czechoslovakia. Although this was not surprising in light of Bucharest's defiant behavior within CMEA, Ceausescu's readiness openly to challenge the Kremlin over this critical issue illustrated a certain disarray in the seemingly impregnable alliance.

The impact of Moscow's apparent inability to control its allies was soon offset by the armed intervention in Czechoslovakia in August 1968, which involved the participation of all WTO members except for Albania and

Romania. It was clear that the Kremlin succeeded in persuading its allies to provide military contingents for the first (and so far the only) joint military action in the Treaty's history. Little if anything is known about the methods used by the Soviet leadership to force its allies to participate, but even though the latter, with the exception of Poland, were represented only by token detachments, the invasion was still a rather impressive example of Moscow's ability to mobilize the Treaty's forces.

The following year the Kremlin took some precautionary steps to defuse its allies' dissatisfaction with the *modus operandi* of the Treaty's decision-making mechanisms. Beginning in 1969, a number of new structures were added to WTO's institutional framework, presumably in order to provide the junior allies in Eastern Europe at least symbolically with greater access to the Pact's policymaking bodies.[11] Whether the East European countries did actually take advantage of this opportunity to make their wishes heard remains unknown.

In sharp contrast to the generally stagnating WTO, its economic counterpart, CMEA, was showing considerably more dynamism in the second half of the 1960s.[12] The organization was largely dormant during the first few years of its existence and could not point to any major accomplishments. Together with the Warsaw Pact, it turned out to be a major beneficiary of Moscow's decision, taken after Stalin's death, to institutionalize the Soviet-East European relationship in the economic sphere and to eliminate the system of informal control arrangements responsible for the crass Soviet exploitation of the East European economies in the early postwar period.

The 1960s witnessed a rapid institutional growth of the Council, reflected in a proliferation of CMEA commissions dealing with a variety of specific economic tasks. It may be assumed that the main purpose of this was not only to offer the junior partners greater opportunity to participate in CMEA decision-making but also to erase the memories of the heavy economic burden carried by the East Europeans during Stalin's rule. There is considerable evidence suggesting that unlike WTO, which was seen strictly as Moscow's preserve, CMEA did allow greater access for the East Europeans, who were actually able now and then to influence Soviet decisions affecting the region.

The best known case of such an influence transmission was Khrushchev's decision in 1964 to abandon his cherished idea of creating a supra-national planning agency within CMEA. There were also other examples of intransigence on the part of some individual East European countries which managed to affect Soviet decisions in such areas as product specialization, intra-CMEA trade and payments, and others. Despite the difficulties in achieving a higher degree of economic integration or collaboration, Moscow, on the one hand, appeared to tolerate deviant behavior of such countries as Romania, and on the other, attempted to engineer closer coordination under CMEA's auspices. The crowning achievement of the latter process was the "New Comprehensive Program for Further Intensification and Improvement of Collaboration and Development of Socialist Economic Integration of CMEA Countries," made public in 1971, which was intended to propel the Council into an era of tighter economic integration at all levels.[13]

To sum up, despite high hopes entertained by Moscow, by the mid-1960s the progress on the road to the institutionalization of Soviet-East European relations proved to be rather uneven. Both major multilateral organizations-- WTO and CMEA--presented impressive outside appearances but contained little substance. This was particular true for WTO; CMEA, for reasons discussed above, attempted at least to lay foundations for a more equitable participation on the part of the junior partners.

The second aspect of the Communist alliance, discussed by Brzezinski, was the network of bilateral agreements between the Soviet Union and its East European allies on the one hand, and among the individual East European countries on the other. Most of the treaties of friendship and mutual assistance were concluded shortly after the end of the war and were part and parcel of the process of the Communist seizure of power, aided and abetted by the Kremlin. Until the signing of the Warsaw Treaty in 1955, they provided the sole formal underpinning of the Soviet hegemony in the region. In theory, the comprehensive character of the treaties' network made WTO unnecessary but, apparently, the creation of the latter, supplemented by several "Status of Forces" treaties legitimizing the presence of Soviet troops on the territory of Poland, East Germany, Hungary and Romania, was viewed by Moscow both as strengthening Soviet control over the area and also providing the smaller East European countries with a feeling that they could have some voice in influencing their own fate within the alliance. In fact, it soon became clear that the East European participation in WTO decision-making was mostly symbolic.

In his discussion of the bilateral treaties in Eastern Europe, Brzezinski left out one category of treaties which, in retrospect, had a powerful impact on the future of Moscow-led alliance. I have in mind here the bilateral treaty between Romania and West Germany, signed in 1967, which succeeded in accomplishing several objectives. First, it was the only visible success in the otherwise abortive *Ostpolitik*, initiated by Willy Brandt, that also spelled out the doom of the Hallstein Doctrine which until then put serious constraints on Bonn's policy vis-à-vis Eastern Europe.[14] Secondly, the break in the hitherto solid WTO front with respect to West Germany not only suggested a certain weakening of Soviet control over the alliance but also encouraged West Germany to proceed with the second round of *Ostpolitik* despite initial setbacks.

The final aspect of the Communist alliance given a prominent place by Brzezinski was the growing importance of informal arrangements. To be sure, Stalin had shown strong preference for informal contacts, but during his rule the latter consisted of the individual East European leaders being summoned to Moscow and given their marching orders by the aging dictator. There is no record of Stalin ever visiting an East European country. Khrushchev changed all this. Until his ouster in 1964 he not only met fairly regularly with his East European counterparts, either as a group or individually, but also travelled extensively throughout the region. As a result, he developed close personal relationships with several of his East European colleagues, who did not hide their unhappiness when Khrushchev was removed and replaced by Brezhnev. Even though the new Soviet leader continued the rather benign policy of his predecessor, at least until the Czechoslovak crisis, he never quite succeeded in developing the same kind of rapport with his opposite numbers in the alliance.

In an earlier analysis of the Soviet bloc, Brzezinski made two important observations.[15] First, he felt that the Communist camp in the post-Stalinist period was reasonably well equipped to deal with conflicts and rifts that were bound to occur in any multinational organization, since it was able to develop a system of shock absorbers capable of defusing both elite and mass discontent. The price of greater flexibility and adaptability was a threat of ideological erosion.

Secondly, while Eastern Europe during the Stalinist era was effectively a national empire run for the benefit of the Soviet Union, thus resembling, in a sense, the Roman, French or British empires, by the mid-1960s the camp was increasingly becoming an international Communist empire, held together not only by Soviet military and economic power but bound also by the ambitions and preferences of the ruling East European elites.

The Soviet Alliance System in 1988

Are the above conclusions valid in the second half of the 1980s? The answer is both yes and no. It must be kept in mind that Brzezinski reached his conclusions before the "Prague Spring," the growing challenge to the alliance's cohesion posed by Romania, and the three successive crises in Poland, culminating in the birth of "Solidarity." In light of these developments, his assumption about the alliance's ability to deal with shocks appears over-optimistic, although he was certainly correct about ideological erosion. Yet, it may also be argued that although the various crises represented a major disappointment if not an outright defeat for the Kremlin, for all practical purposes Moscow's hegemony over the region remained essentially unimpaired in the second half of the 1980s.

To be sure, until Stalin's death the camp clearly resembled a Soviet colonial empire, but to equate it in the early 1960s with an international Communist empire, supported by local East European elites, does not square with the facts. If anything, the camp has never reached that exalted stage but instead began to resemble the Ottoman empire. At the height of its power, the latter was a rather decentralized yet effectively managed multinational state, and it was only in the course of the seventeenth century that it began to show the fissures and strains that ultimately earned it the dubious distinction of being called the "sick man of Europe." At the risk of overstatement it may be said that although Nikita Khrushchev could hardly be compared with Suleiman the Magnificent, Leonid Brezhnev, especially during the last few years of his rule, easily resembled the line of inept and corrupt sultans who eventually brought an end to the empire. The verdict on Mikhail Gorbachev is still open.

If the Communist alliance in Europe in the second half of the 1980s is neither an international Communist empire nor a quasi-Ottoman empire, what is it? An observation made more than twenty years ago by a well-known British authority in the field of international relations may help us to answer this question:

> Alliances are a means to an end, whether it is primarily to increase the security of a group of sovereign states in the face of a common adversary, or to increase the diplomatic pressure which they can bring upon him, or to share the economic cost and the political risk with either objective.[16]

Starting with the military sphere, after thirty years of existence WTO has neither shown greater cohesion nor greatly strengthened the security of its East European members. Despite an impressive institutional growth and the holding of regularly scheduled military exercises on the territory of some of its members, the Treaty is largely a paper organization, an "empty shell" rather than an "entangling alliance."[17]

I am well aware that I represent a minority view. Several respected specialists in Soviet and East European affairs consider WTO to be an efficient, well-organized and well-managed military alliance which ought to be taken seriously as representing a major threat to NATO forces in Central Europe. One of them has even viewed WTO as "a vital institution for the management of Soviet-East European political affairs" that "has become so important that its sudden disappearance would, to paraphrase Voltaire, force Pact members to invent another structure to take its place."[18] I beg to differ. As suggested earlier, the creation of WTO and the reasons for its establishment are not entirely clear some thirty years later. While WTO is not likely to disappear, its military-strategic utility and value to Moscow has clearly been limited, especially in the late 1980s, when the repercussions of the "Solidarity" crisis are still being felt.

This has been equally true for the other two aspects of the Treaty: diplomatic and political. The record shows that during the series of East-West meetings in the past decade or so, including the meetings of the Conference on Security and Cooperation in Europe (CSCE) in Helsinki, Belgrade and Madrid, as well as the lengthy and largely abortive Vienna sessions dealing with the Mutual and Balanced Force Reductions in Europe (MBFR), none of the East European countries showed any independent initiative that would have enhanced either the Soviet or their own negotiating posture. On the contrary, with the possible exception of Romania, they tended faithfully to toe the Moscow line which, if anything, resembled their past behavior as Soviet satellites, and created a rather poor impression on the Western participants in the negotiations.

On the political scene, the demise of the U.S.-Soviet detente in the early 1980s generated surprisingly wide cracks in the alliance. This rather unexpected development was triggered by Moscow's withdrawal from the INF talks in Geneva and the Kremlin's decision to deploy additional SS-20s in Czechoslovakia and East Germany.[19] The negative reaction from both East Berlin and Prague, hitherto considered most loyal and submissive to the Soviet Union, testified to the inability of the Soviet leaders to maintain proper discipline in the alliance. Admittedly, they were able, at least temporarily, to slow down the rapprochement between East and West Germany, but at the price of being faced with an unusual coalition of East Germany, Hungary and Romania which insisted on playing a role in attempting to same the East-West detente from total demise. The fact that only Czechoslovakia, and hesitatingly at that, took the Soviet side in the dispute, spoke for itself.

Perhaps the only relative success achieved by Moscow was in mobilizing its junior allies in support of Soviet policies in the Third World as suppliers of military and economic aid. However, even in this case, the performance of the East European countries has been uneven and in most cases it appeared that the Soviet allies have been motivated less by Moscow's orders and more by purely economic calculations.[20]

It can also be argued that from the economic standpoint the value of CMEA to the USSR has been limited.[21] The fact that the Council has existed now for almost 40 years might suggest that the Soviet Union has found it useful and even profitable. Yet a good case can be made that

CMEA has not fulfilled any of the Soviet expectations which accompanied the Council's creation and which spurred the impressive institutional buildup and ambitious plans of increased cooperation.

I would further suggest that the Council peaked in 1971, at the time of the proclamation of the previously-mentioned "New Comprehensive Program." The announcement of the Program coincided with the entry of most of the CMEA members, with apparent Soviet blessing, onto the arena of East-West trade. Helped by generous credits from the West, ostensibly intended for the modernization of their increasingly obsolete industrial plant, the East European Six became much more concerned with developing various economic links with the United States and members of the European Economic Community than with strengthening economic integration under CMEA's auspices. Interestingly enough, even when the East-West trade bubble burst in the early 1980s, leaving most of the East European countries saddled with a heavy hard-currency debt, none of them urged total withdrawal from the new international economic order in favor of redirecting their trade in the Easterly direction. This clearly suggested that the economic links between Eastern and Western Europe were stronger than Moscow anticipated and that CMEA, even if rejuvenated, was not seen as a viable substitute. The fact that at the same time several East European countries were undergoing a process of economic reforms which emphasized decentralization in decision-making militated against the revival of CMEA, which favored central controls.

Even though by the mid-1980s CMEA has lost a good deal of its earlier dynamism, it did not mean that as a result the Kremlin was deprived of its economic leverage over Eastern Europe. Far from it. In fact, it may be argued that Moscow's economic clout over the region has actually been strengthened, although it took a different form. It was represented by a network of bilateral commercial agreements between the USSR and its junior partners that seemed to benefit both sides. While the Soviet Union was providing "implicit trade subsidies" to Eastern Europe by exporting raw materials, including energy, at below world market prices and importing manufactured goods from the region at above world market prices, in return it derived "unconventional gains" from that trade in the form of military bases, transit rights, diplomatic support, etc.[22] Until recently, however, the arrangement clearly benefited Eastern Europe, which ultimately became transformed from a Soviet economic asset into a growing burden.[23]

The most recent period witnessed significant changes in this respect, mostly as a result of falling oil prices. The worldwide decline hurt both the Soviet Union and Eastern Europe. The former was no longer able to reap windfall profits from its energy exports to Western Europe and, in fact, had to export more in order to generate sufficient hard currency to pay for food and capital equipment, to feed the Soviet people and modernize its industry. This could have been achieved if Soviet oil production were growing, but since in the mid-1980s the oil output was either stagnating or declining, exports to Western Europe could be maintained or expanded at the cost of either cutting Soviet domestic consumption or reducing exports to the East European Six. Not surprisingly, CMEA countries received less oil and, adding insult to injury, had to pay more for it because of the peculiar CMEA pricing formula adopted in 1975.[24]

Despite all this, however, Eastern Europe continued to be economically heavily dependent on the USSR for the simple reason that, by and large, it had no other place to go to in order to acquire the vital supplies of energy and raw materials. At the same time, CMEA was gradually becoming less and less useful as an instrument of Soviet economic hegemony over the region.

Both of the two remaining aspects of the alliance as it existed in 1968--bilateral agreements and informal arrangements--were still present twenty years later, albeit in a somewhat different form. The bilateral treaties of friendship and mutual assistance between the USSR and its junior allies, signed in the late 1940s and duly extended in the mid-1960s, were once again extended in the mid-1980s, but played little if any role in reinforcing Soviet control over the region. Far more important were the previously discussed bilateral trade agreements which strengthened Moscow's economic leverage. They were further supplemented by economic agreements between the USSR and some of the East European Six, such as Poland, in which the Soviet Union promised to deliver raw materials in return for finished goods produced by industries which otherwise would have to either shut down or operate at reduced capacity for lack of raw materials. Needless to say, such agreements in effect tied these countries closer to, and made them more dependent on, the Soviet Union.

Whereas in 1968 it was only Romania that decided to break the alliance's unity by establishing diplomatic relations with West Germany and concluding a bilateral treaty to that effect, twenty years later all of the East European countries signed similar treaties, recognizing the existence of two separate German states.

The practice of informal meetings between the Soviet leaders and their East European counterparts, initiated by Khrushchev, was maintained by Brezhnev until the last few years of his life. For years the East European leaders used to gather each summer in Brezhnev's home in the Crimea, presumably for an informal exchange of views, which all sides presumably found useful.[25] Neither Andropov nor Chernenko ruled long enough to revive the practice and so far there is no record of similar meetings being held between Gorbachev and his East European colleagues, although the new Soviet leader has met with them several times on more formal occasions.

Soviet-East European Relations, 1968-1988: Continuity or Change?

In comparing the state of Soviet-East European relations in the twenty-year period 1968-1988, we can easily discover elements of both continuity and change. The three aspects of the Moscow-led alliance singled out for discussion--multilateral institutional ties, bilateral agreements and informal arrangements--remained roughly unchanged in 1988, at least on the surface, exhibiting a high degree of continuity. This, in itself, was not surprising in light of the traditional Communist penchant to stress form over content and an equally traditional reluctance to tamper with established institutions and procedures in the belief that any major change in any of them might be interpreted as an acknowledgement of their failure.

However, under the impressive and seemingly impregnable facade of formal and informal arrangements, some major changes have taken place. Perhaps fewest of them occurred in the strategic-military sphere, where the Warsaw Pact remained essentially unchanged as an instrument of Soviet control over the East European military establishments. In contrast, the Council for Mutual Economic Assistance has become almost irrelevant, despite retaining its rather elaborate institutional structure. At the same time, Moscow's economic leverage has been strengthened. Although in the political arena both the bilateral agreements and informal arrangements remained in place, their character and content have clearly changed, and they no longer could be viewed as strengthening the Soviet position in the alliance.

At this stage a question ought to be raised regarding the reasons for the change in Soviet-East European relations in the past twenty years. In providing a tentative answer to this question, we may view the Soviet-East European relationship between 1968 and 1988 as a function of three more or less independent variables: the Soviet perception of Eastern Europe, the domestic situation in the region, and the state of East-West relations.

There is little doubt that the Soviet hierarchy's perception of the region has been and continues to be a major factor in influencing the Kremlin's priorities and options which, in turn, determine Moscow's behavior toward Eastern Europe. Of the various factors and forces affecting these perceptions, personal idiosyncrasies of the Soviet leaders play an important role, especially insofar as the individual East European countries are concerned. In general I agree with James F. Brown that Moscow's stakes in

Eastern Europe can be subsumed under the two broad headings of cohesion and viability.[26] Cohesion in this context implies general conformity of East European domestic and foreign policies to Soviet prescriptions and the rough identity of institutional arrangements between the USSR and its junior allies. Viability suggests the presence of confident, credible, efficient and legitimate regimes in Eastern Europe that obviate the need for continuous Soviet preoccupation with, and intervention in, the region.

The main conflict that has faced Moscow's leaders in the region ever since the end of World War II has been that between cohesion and viability. The early postwar period, characterized by the presence of "domesticism," might be seen as reflecting Stalin's preference for viability of the newly-formed Communist states in Eastern Europe, which still faced many problems connected with the process of takeover. In the late 1940s, this rather benign attitude was drastically transformed into Moscow's policy of "one road to socialism" which implied strict cohesion. Throughout most of his rule Khrushchev adhered to the principle of viability and so did Brezhnev, at least until the "Prague Spring," whereupon his perception of Eastern Europe changed dramatically in favor of cohesion. It was only toward the end of his rule, when his capacity to make decisions was clearly impaired, that the Soviet grip over the region began to show signs of relaxation, which was again interrupted by the crisis in Poland.

The four-year period 1981-1985, which saw four successive occupants of the Kremlin, is obviously hard to describe: Andropov was viewed, at least by the East Europeans, as essentially sympathetic to the region, and the opposite appeared to be true for Chernenko. The early signals out of Moscow suggested that Gorbachev might assume a tough stance vis-à-vis Eastern Europe, but as of the middle of 1988 the predictions of a more cohesive Soviet policy had not come true.

In fact, the record of the last three years has shown rather clearly that there has been an unmistakable change in the Kremlin's behavior vis-à-vis Eastern Europe, especially in the style and manner of policy-making by the Soviet leadership, particularly on the bilateral level, and in the general atmosphere of conducting business in the Warsaw Treaty Organization and CMEA.

Moreover, questions have been raised in both East and West challenging the continuing validity of the "Brezhnev Doctrine" which was generally assumed to determine Soviet-East European relations since 1968. Although Gorbachev himself has rather carefully avoided making unequivocal statements about the "Doctrine," his advisers and spokesmen have attempted to create an impression the the "Brezhnev Doctrine" is essentially dead, and Gorbachev himself, by formally denying the Soviet primacy in the Warsaw alliance, has at least implicitly confirmed that view.[27]

It can be assumed that the perceptions and expectations of successive Soviet leaders were influenced by both their knowledge of Eastern Europe and the personal relationships they might have established with their counterparts in the area. Here again the differences were quite striking. Thus Stalin had no personal knowledge of Eastern Europe and there is no evidence of his developing a special relationship with any of the local leaders. In contrast, Khrushchev travelled widely throughout Eastern Europe, initiated the practice of regular multilateral and bilateral meetings with his junior colleagues, and managed to establish close personal relationships with some of them. Brezhnev continued the practice of personal travel and regular meetings but there is no record of his favoring anyone in particular from among his East European opposite numbers. Neither Andropov nor Chernenko ruled long enough to indicate their personal preferences.

Gorbachev's "new thinking" in Soviet foreign policy also affected the relationship between the USSR and the individual East European countries. A truly striking change, for example, could be observed in the relationship between Moscow and Warsaw: Jaruzelski, who only a short time before was viewed by Moscow as a black sheep in the East European flock, has now become Gorbachev's strongest supporter and closest friend. Kàdàr also continued as Gorbachev's close ally (although he was removed from office in 1988), while Honecker, who under Brezhnev assumed a leading role in the alliance, seemed to have lost that position in the mid-1980s. There has been no change in Gorbachev's attitude toward Ceausescu and Husàk, which continued to be cool on both sides, and it may be assumed that it was that coolness that contributed to Husàk's recent ouster from party leadership in Prague. Zhivkov, the perennial survivor, who lagged behind the Poles and Hungarians in embracing *perestroika* as the new dogma, ultimately saw the light and accepted Gorbachev's reformism as the new creed.

In contrast to Moscow's seeming indifference in the military, political and ideological spheres, Gorbachev right from the start indicated his strong interest in tightening economic cooperation within the alliance. It is not inconceivable that the main reason for it has been his belief that an economically viable Eastern Europe would also be a politically stable region and that, in turn, economic efficiency, well-being and interdependence would most likely strengthen the cohesion of the bloc.[28]

To conclude, the above summary points to changes in the perceptions and attitudes of top Soviet leaders with respect to Eastern Europe, which oscillated between the goals of viability and cohesion throughout the postwar period. If one were to consider also the views of the other members of the Soviet ruling oligarchy, such as Suslov or Gromyko, which presumably counted for something in the era of collective leadership, as well as the reports of Soviet ambassadors to the individual East European countries, it could be argued that the emphasis on cohesion tended to take precedence over, and proved stronger and longer-lasting than, the stress on viability. Still, it would be incorrect to conclude that the Kremlin has always preferred tighter rather than looser control over Eastern Europe.

Turning to the internal situation within the region, limitation of space precludes a full discussion of individual countries. Only some generalizations, which tend to be risky, can be made. This riskiness is best illustrated by trying to generalize about Eastern Europe as a whole when the region has been going through a process of political and economic differentiation that has made it increasingly hard to view as a single entity.

In the second half of the 1980s it is clear that in the political arena the East European Six often show less similarity with each other than with some of their counterparts in Western Europe: a neo-Stalinist Romania has little in common with a relatively liberal Hungary and the same can be said about the conservative government in Czechoslovakia being quite different from the reasonable relaxed military regime in Poland. The political differentiation was the end result of a series of gradual adjustments in the institutional structures and the political style of the ruling elites, who had to deal with a plethora of economic difficulties and social tensions experienced by the individual countries.

Considering the multiplicity of problems faced by the region, it is rather surprising that only two countries went through systemic crises-- Czechoslovakia in 1968 and Poland in 1970 and 1980-1981--both of which generated considerable concern in the Kremlin. Since the crises have been analyzed in great detail in the West, little purpose would be served by going over them again. A more interesting question concerns the ability of the remaining East European regimes to weather the storms sparked in Prague and Warsaw and to remain in full control of their respective societies, to the considerable relief of Moscow.

One of the reasons was undoubtedly the leadership skills exhibited by most of the powerholders in the area, notably by Kàdàr, Zhivkov and Ceausescu, who managed to survive the critical year 1968 and the potentially more serious "Solidarity" crisis in Poland.[29] Husàk (until December 1987)[30] and Honecker also succeeded in retaining a firm grip on their societies, leaving only Poland as the single flagrant example of its leaders' ineptitude, with the possible exception of General Jaruzelski who assumed power at the height of the 1980-1981 crisis.

Thus, from a purely political viewpoint, the domestic situation in Eastern Europe appeared remarkably stable during most of the twenty-year period prior to 1988. In light of this, it is perhaps not surprising that at some point in the mid-1970s Moscow began to take Eastern Europe for granted and turned its attention to other areas around the world, only to be rudely awakened by the Polish upheaval. By hindsight, however, even the latter appeared less troublesome for the Kremlin than it was initially perceived, at least in the West. The failure of the Polish crisis to spill over to other countries was obviously greeted with relief by the Soviet leaders, who were most likely afraid of a repetition of the situation in 1968 when the "Prague Spring" managed to cross national boundaries and to start blooming in East Germany and Poland. That nothing of this sort happened in 1980-1981 was due to several factors, including the previously-mentioned ability of the individual East European leaders to isolate their respective countries from the threat of the Polish disease. Possibly for that reason, despite signals to the contrary, Gorbachev did not remove any of the top leaders in Bulgaria, Czechoslovakia, East Germany and Hungary, who were duly re-elected at their party congresses held in the spring of 1986.

It can be speculated that the political stability in the alliance may be more apparent than real, as there are numerous signs suggesting that the region is about to face major economic difficulties which would require making several hard choices that ultimately might affect its relations with the USSR. The main problem stems from the close dependence of Eastern Europe on the Soviet Union in the fields of raw materials and energy. There are indications that the lengthy period of Soviet economic largesse and support for the region in the form of "implicit trade subsidies" is about over. Already, because of the previously-mentioned CMEA pricing formula, the East European Six are forced to pay higher prices for Soviet oil than those charged on the world market, which means a *de facto* elimination of subsidies. Moreover, as suggested earlier, there is a very real possibility of Soviet oil deliveries to Eastern Europe being cut rather drastically in order to compensate for larger exports to Western Europe and to offset the worldwide decline in energy prices. How the East European countries will handle this unprecedented crisis is anybody's guess, but it is clear that whatever solution is finally chosen, it is going to be painful for most of the countries, already burdened with heavy hard-currency debt repayments.

This brings me to the third variable in the Soviet-East European matrix: the state of East-West relations. By now it is generally agreed that Eastern Europe has been a major beneficiary of East-West detente from its earliest days in the late 1960s. The highlights of detente are well known: the normalization of relations between Eastern Europe and West Germany; the start of the MBFR negotiations; the Helsinki Conference and its follow-ups; expansion in East-West trade helped by Western credits; the signing of SALT II Treaty and, finally, the arms control negotiations in Geneva. For that reason, Moscow's junior allies were clearly chagrined by the Soviet intervention in Afghanistan and even more unhappy with Moscow's decision to withdraw from the INF negotiations, followed by the deployment of additional Soviet missiles in the region. The damage caused by both of these events, which signaled the end of detente, was made worse by Western reaction to the imposition of martial law in Poland in December 1981, which took the form of harsh sanctions directed against the region as a whole that further aggravated the already difficult economic situation.

The sanctions illustrated the dilemma faced especially by Western Europe. The latter was clearly sympathetic to the plight of Eastern Europe, hoping to see the region slowly gain even a modicum of autonomy from the USSR and improve its economic well-being. It was strongly supportive of "Solidarity" in Poland in the vain hope that it might be accepted and tolerated by the Kremlin. The imposition of martial law by Warsaw was greeted with considerable anger mixed with disappointment, and Western Europe had little choice but to follow the U.S. lead in imposing the sanctions on both the Soviet Union and the rest of the alliance, in sharp contrast to its indifference vis-à-vis the Soviet action in Afghanistan. In time, however, the West Europeans concluded that the sanctions were proving counterproductive and the mid-1980s witnessed an attempt to re-establish normal relations with Eastern Europe, with lukewarm approval on the part of the United States.

The Soviet Union has also been facing a dilemma. On the one hand, one of the cherished goals of the Kremlin has been to weaken NATO by decoupling Western Europe from the United Sates, using Eastern Europe as a sort of a Trojan horse. On the other hand, Eastern Europe can only prove useful in this respect if it appears to Western Europe as a relatively free region, which means in practice Soviet willingness to emphasize the alliance's viability at the expense of its cohesion. Thus Moscow must sooner or later choose between its desire to flirt with Western Europe and reduce its links with the United States, and the fear of relaxing the Soviet grip on Eastern Europe. What the ultimate choice is going to be, is still too soon to tell.

Conclusion

There have been some voices in the West claiming that for various reasons, some of which were summarized above, the Soviet-dominated alliance in Europe is near collapse. I am more inclined to borrow a phrase from Charles Gati, who described the alliance as "alive but not well."[31] The view that the Soviet imperium has been ailing has been shared by many authorities in the field and, by and large, I have no quarrel with their analysis.[32] Where I do part company with them is in their conclusions, which range from the hope that the crisis in Eastern Europe would force the Kremlin to grant more autonomy to the individual countries, to the belief that the new leadership in Moscow would have to, sooner or later, impose tighter control over the region. My own feeling is that neither is likely to happen and that Soviet policy toward Eastern Europe in the near future would continue on its present course, which for a lack of a better word might be termed "muddling through" or "more of the same."

I base this prediction on the fact that the current critical situation in the alliance is not unprecedented, and that Eastern Europe has faced worse crises before. Each of the previous crises was followed by some institutional changes accompanied by appeals, promises and exhortations from Moscow, and once the dust has settled things returned back to the normal *Schlamperei*, so characteristic of Communist systems in the region and, one should add, of the Ottoman empire in the latter stages of its existence. Thus, other things being equal, I see little difference between the situation in 1988 and that twenty years ago, and hence I do not expect radical changes in Soviet relations with Eastern Europe, at least in the foreseeable future.

Notes

1. Carl J. Friedrich and Zbigniew K. Brzezinski, *Totalitarian Dictatorship and Autocracy* (Cambridge, MA: Harvard University Press, 1956).

2. The significant exception was Zbigniew Brzezinski, *The Soviet Bloc*, Revised and Enlarged Edition (Cambridge, MA: Harvard University Press, 1967).

3. See, for example, Andrzej Korbonski, "Prospects for Change in Eastern Europe," and comments by Melvin Croan and William E. Griffith, *Slavic Review*, vol. 33, no. 2, June 1974, pp. 219-258. See also William Taubman, "The Change to Change in Communist Systems: Modernization, Postmodernization, and Soviet Politics," in Henry W. Morton and Rudolf L. Tökés, eds., *Soviet Politics and Society in the 1970s* (New York: The Free Press, 1974), pp. 369-394.

4. The two representative works are Charles Gati, ed., *The Politics of Modernization in Eastern Europe* (New York: Praeger, 1974); and Jan F. Triska and Paul M. Cocks, eds., *Political Development in Eastern Europe* (New York: Praeger, 1977).

5. Morris Bornstein, Zvi Gitelman and William Zimmerman, eds., *East-West Relations and the Future of Eastern Europe* (London: George Allen & Unwin, 1981); Karen Dawisha and Philip Hanson, eds., *Soviet-East European Dilemmas* (London: Heinemann, 1981); and Robert L. Hutchings, *Soviet-East European Relations: Consolidation and Conflict, 1968-1980* (Madison, WI: University of Wisconsin Press, 1984).

6. Zvi Gitelman, *The Diffusion of Political Innovation From Eastern Europe* (Beverly Hills, CA: Sage Publications, 1972) and "The Impact on the Soviet Union of East European Experience in Modernization," in Gati, *The Politics of Modernization in Eastern Europe*, pp. 256-274; Paul Marer, "The Economies of Eastern Europe and Soviet Foreign Policy," and Andrzej Korbonski, "Eastern Europe as an Internal Determinant of Soviet Foreign Policy," in Seweryn Bialer, ed., *The Domestic Context of Soviet Foreign Policy* (New York: Praeger, 1980), pp. 271-332; and Sarah M. Terry, ed., *Soviet Policy in Eastern Europe* (New Haven and London: Yale University Press, 1984).

7. Andrzej Korbonski, "Soviet Policies in the Communist Alliance: The Role of Eastern Europe," (Paper Presented at a Conference on "Domestic Sources of Soviet Foreign Policy," University of California, Los Angeles, October 1985).

8. Brzezinski, *The Soviet Bloc*, pp. 456-484.

9. The literature on the Warsaw Pact is by now quite extensive. In 1985-1986 alone the following studies were published: Jeffrey Simon, *Warsaw Pact Forces: Problems of Command and Control* (Boulder, Colorado: Westview Press, 1985); *The Warsaw Pact and the Question of Cohesion* (Washington, D.C.: Kennan Institute for Advanced Russian Studies, 1985); Robert L. Hutchings, "Foreign and Security Policy Coordination in the Warsaw Pact," *Berichte des Bundesinstituts für ostwissenschaftliche und internationale Studien*, no. 15, 1985; and Douglas A. Macgregor, "Uncertain Allies? East European Forces in the Warsaw Pact," *Soviet Studies*, vol. xxxvii, no. 2, April 1986, pp. 227-247.

10. For details, see Condoleezza Rice, *The Soviet Union and the Czechoslovak Army 1948-1983* (Princeton, NJ: Princeton University Press, 1984), pp. 139-144.

11. For details, see Lawrence Caldwell, "The Warsaw Pact: Directions of Change," *Problems of Communism*, vol. xxiv, no. 5, September-October 1975, pp. 1-19; and Dale R. Herspring, "The Warsaw Pact at 25," *ibid.*, vol. xxix, no. 5, September-October 1980, pp. 1-15.

12. An extensive bibliography on CMEA, comprising 142 items, can be found in an Appendix to Paul Marer and John Michael Montia, "CMEA Integration: Theory and Practice," in *East European Economic Assessment, Part 2, Regional Assessments*, A Compendium of Papers Submitted to the Joint Economic Committee, 97th Congress, 1st Session (Washington, D.C.: U.S. Government Printing Office, 1981), pp. 189-194.

13. For a detailed discussion, see Henry W. Schaefer, *Comecon and the Politics of Integration* (New York: Praeger, 1972).

14. For details, see Fritz Ermarth, *Internationalism, Security and Legitimacy: The Challenge to Soviet Interests in Eastern Europe, 1964-1968* (Santa Monica, CA: RAND RM-5909-PF, March 1969).

15. Zbigniew Brzezinski, "The Organization of the Communist Camp," *World Politics*, vol. xiii, no. 2, January 1961, pp. 206-208.

16. Alistair Buchan, "The Future of NATO," *International Conciliation*, no. 565, November 1967, p. 5.

17. Andrzej Korbonski, "The Warsaw Pact After Twenty-five Years: An Entangling Alliance or an Empty Shell?" in Robert W. Clawson and Lawrence S. Kaplan, eds., *The Warsaw Pact: Political Purposes and Military Means* (Wilmington, DE: Scholarly Resources, 1982), pp. 3-25.

18. Herspring, "The Warsaw Pact at 25," p. 1.

19. Hutchings, "Foreign and Security Policy Coordination in the Warsaw Pact," pp. 1-6.

20. Andrzej Korbonski, "Eastern Europe and the Third World, or 'Limited Regret Strategy' Revisited," in Andrzej Korbonski and Francis Fukuyama, eds., *The Soviet Union and the Third World: The Last Three Decades* (Ithaca and London: Cornell University Press, 1987), pp. 94-122.

21. Luba Fajfer, "Does the Soviet Union Need the Council for Mutual Economic Assistance?" (Unpublished Paper, Winter 1985).

22. Michael Marrese and Jan Vanous, *Implicit Subsidies and Non-market Benefits in Soviet Trade with Eastern Europe* (Berkeley, CA: University of California Institute of International Studies, 1983).

23. For an interesting discussion of this issue, see Valerie Bunce, "The Empire Strikes Back: The Evolution of the Eastern Bloc from a Soviet Asset to a Soviet Liability," *International Organization*, vol. 38, no. 1, Winter 1985, pp. 1-46.

24. Vladimir Sobell, "The Impact on the CMEA of Declining Oil Prices," Radio Free Europe Research *RAD Background Reports/15 (Economics)*, 28 January 1986.

25. Hutchings, "Foreign and Security Policy Coordination in the Warsaw Pact," pp. 18-21.

26. James F. Brown, *Relations Between the Soviet Union and Its East European Allies: A Survey* (Santa Monica, CA: RAND Report R-1742-PR, 1975).

27. Jackson Diehl, "Gorbachev Calls on Eastern Europe to Change but Not to Mimic," *Washington Post*, and Elizabeth Teague, "Gorbachev Addresses Prague Rally," Radio Liberty, *Research Bulletin*, no. 16, 22 April 1987.

28. Andrzej Korbonski, "East European Political and Ideological Perceptions and Concerns," (Paper presented at a conference on the "The Soviet-East European Relationship in the Gorbachev Era: The Prospects for Adaptation," University of Toronto, Toronto, Canada, October 1987.)

29. Kàdàr was replaced as General Secretary by Karoly Grosz in May 1988.

30. Husàk was replaced as General Secretary by Milos Jakes in December 1987.

31. Charles Gati, "Soviet Empire: Alive But Not Well," *Problems of*

Communism, vol. xxxiv, no. 2, March-April 1985, 73-86.

32. For a comprehensive treatment, see John Van Oudenaren, *The Soviet Union and Eastern Europe* (Santa Monica, CA: RAND R-3136-OF, March 1984).

3

TRENDS IN SOVIET AND EAST EUROPEAN WESTPOLITIK AND THE GERMAN QUESTION

Wolfgang Pfeiler

Introduction

During the discussion about NATO's dual-track decision, there were deep-rooted concerns in both parts of Germany as to whether the positive achievements of *Ostpolitik* could be maintained, given the deterioration in U.S.-Soviet relations. Would not the growing intensity of the East-West conflict in some way or another affect the intra-German relationship? Or could it be expected that the intra-German connection would be undisturbed by storms in the East-West atmosphere? The latter assumption became known in Germany as the so-called *Windschattentheorie* (theory of leeway).

At the time, both Soviet and East German rhetoric intensified, indicating severe repercussions in intra-German relations if the dual-track decision were implemented. Accordingly--so at least it appeared at first glance--the GDR reacted after deployment of missiles began. It declared that it had no choice but to go along with the deployment of new Soviet short-range missiles on East German soil. But at the same time there were many hints that this was more a matter of demonstrating solidarity with the USSR than a matter of conviction. Moreover, the Politburo of the East German communist party, the SED (Sozialistische Einheitspartei Deutschlands), quickly moved to make *Schadensbegrenzung* (limitation of damage) a primary aim of the GDR's *Westpolitik*.[1]

In 1985 there were again Soviet and East German declarations and indications that West Germany's participation in the SDI program could seriously affect the intra-German relationship. At the same time, SED General Secretary Erich Honecker showed no inhibitions about reiterating his intention to visit West Germany in the near future.

What is the state of affairs now with regard to the relationship between the two German states? Will the GDR leadership continue its efforts to improve this relationship, or is a deterioration to be expected? The answer to this question cannot be given without regard to the international setting in which the German problem is embedded, the most salient component of which is the Soviet Union's policy toward the two German states. Therefore, the first part of this chapter deals with respective Soviet perceptions and attitudes. The second part outlines divergencies of opinion in Moscow and between Moscow and its European allies. The third section describes what is known about the USSR's position concerning the German question and the German nation at large. The fourth section deals with the GDR's perception of all these problems. The next part, then, tries to explain what all this could mean for the *Westpolitik* of the USSR, the East European countries and the GDR. Here, particular emphasis is given to the foreign policy priorities of Mikhail Gorbachev. The final section outlines some policy implications for the West.

Soviet Perceptions

In the view of all Soviet and East European leaders, the Federal Republic of Germany is the most influential political factor in Western Europe. Beyond that, the FRG is the most important European trade partner in the Western world. The German Democratic Republic occupies a similar position with respect to the Eastern bloc. Accordingly, the policies of both German states, and the German question at large, play a significant role in Soviet foreign policy considerations, including the field of security policy.

In the past, the USSR's foreign policy attitude toward West Germany has been and continues to be determined by two major considerations:

1. An alliance between the United States and West Germany is highly undesirable.

2. Existing contradictions between these two capitalist powers can be exploited to the Soviet Union's advantage. Accordingly, since the end of World War II, the USSR has done everything in its power to destabilize the U.S.-German alliance, mainly relying on a carrot-and-stick policy vis-à-vis the Germans, with the ultimate goal of rolling back or at least reducing the U.S. presence and influence in Europe.[2]

This attitude changed somewhat after the Nixon administration had proved its propensity to come to terms with Moscow on a basis of strategic equality. The conclusion of a series of bilateral treaties and agreements (particularly those of May 1972 and June 1973) seemed to herald a new, worldwide Soviet-American accord. Something like a cohegemony or condominium appeared to be in the offing: "The Soviet Union is convinced that the USSR and the USA...can and must actively cooperate in the settlement of all unresolved and international problems and in the elimination of all dangerous hotbeds of tension and conflict."[3] By implication, such an accord promised the long-term control of both Germanies. However, from 1976 on, the Soviet leaders came to the conclusion that such an overall agreement with the U.S. was not feasible because the Americans were not prepared to accept the Soviet Union as an equal. Consequently, they fell back on their earlier stance. They attempted to draw the West Germans into some cooperative kind of relationship, while at the same time doing all they could to exert pressure on West Germany's government by mobilizing the public against the government's pro-American policy.[4]

This policy, however, did not lead to a decoupling of the Federal Republic from the Atlantic alliance. On the contrary, by the end of the 1970s, Soviet policy had only contributed to a further consolidation of NATO opinions and actions. Nor did the USSR succeed in strengthening its influence on West Germany. Rather, its own position in West Germany became weaker.[5] The failure of Soviet efforts to prevent the deployment of U.S. medium-range missiles on German territory and the collapse of the Communist party of Poland may be assessed as significant political defeats.

In the course of the subsequent leadership crises in the early 1980s, it once again became apparent that the Soviet position is hampered by three fundamental liabilities:

1. Unlike the United States, the Soviet Union does not have strong allies or friends;

2. Soviet economic power is still insufficient with respect to its status as a global power;

3. Soviet political elites seem to be totally insensitive to the fact that many of their actions (e.g. the deployment of SS-20 missiles, the build-up of a blue-water navy, armament policy, and interventions around the world) have had negative repercussions by enhancing threat perceptions in the West.

In order to overcome these weaknesses and in order to reduce the costs of their empire and improve their own economic position, the Soviet leaders have increased hard currency exports while at the same time curbing support for several CMEA countries. Lest this decreased support lead to destabilization or further unrest in the bloc, the Soviet leadership has had to give more leeway to its clientele. In a way, this meant the renunciation of total control and allowed for not entirely predictable implications in the political domain. One of the consequences of this was that most of the countries belonging to the Soviet hegemonial sphere became "self-assured vassals" whose interests could not be neglected by the hegemonial power.[6]

Two essential ingredients of the so-called Brezhnev doctrine, however, remain unchanged: (1) none of these countries is allowed to renounce its membership in the Warsaw Treaty Organization; and (2) the power monopoly of the Communist party in each country must never come into jeopardy. In order to alleviate the Soviet dilemma between bloc cohesion, stability of the region, and viability of the East European regimes,[7] however, the allies were given a particularly free hand in economic affairs. As one observer points out, "To preserve the calm and the stability of its empire the Kremlin is prepared to let the various nomenclatures play their cards themselves."[8]

With respect to the German Democratic Republic, this policy has had another far-reaching implication. Since the internal stability of the Communist German society is to a certain extent dependent upon the intra-German connection, the East German leadership had also to be granted limited leeway in this regard.[9]

It now appears that this policy got somewhat out of hand. In the summer of 1984, the Western public witnessed a series of foreign policy declarations by several officials in East Germany, Hungary, and Romania that seemed to come close to a "ganging up" on the Soviet Union. The variety of problems the USSR has had to face within its own orbit developed to such an extent that some analysts even spoke of a "communist encirclement" of the Soviet Union.[10] In reality, the situation was less dramatic. The core of the problem was to be found in the leadership of the CPSU. After the 1983 walk-out from the arms control talks and following the death of Yuri Andropov, the previous foreign policy consensus apparently fell apart. It was to be restored--albeit not completely--only after Mikhail Gorbachev succeeded in systematically installing his own people in the decisive posts.

Divergencies in the East

During this period, diverging interests and diverging opinions became visible between the Soviet Union and its allies. The media, particularly in the GDR and in Hungary, openly contradicted some Soviet declarations and took sides with those groupings in Moscow that favored a more moderate foreign policy. They also claimed a special role for the smaller countries: "The small and medium-sized European states in both alliance-systems can have a favorable impact on the international atmosphere by dialogue and constructive relations, whereby more possibilities also with regard to the relationship between the Soviet Union and the U.S. may be opened. This may have a decisive impact on the process of detente."[11] Articles like this were regularly reprinted by the GDR press, while at the same time some opposing Soviet views were not. East Germany started an extensive campaign propagating a worldwide "coalition of reason and realism,"[12] a conception which by now has become the centerpiece of the GDR's *Westpolitik*.

Much more than in the Soviet Union's official declarations, both the GDR and Hungary emphasized the necessity of keeping peace, and they downgraded the importance and the meaning of "Proletarian, Socialist Internationalism." In this way they expressed their disapproval of Moscow's hard-line policy and their expectations that eventually a more moderate course in the Kremlin might and should prevail. Erich Honecker even traveled to Bucharest to hail the Romanian Olympic delegation, which had not joined the boycott imposed on the GDR by the USSR. The gap in foreign policy attitudes also became apparent in the slogans regarding the celebrations of Mayday and the anniversary of the October revolution.[13]

In the past, rifts between Moscow and its European allies occurred "...when East Europeans sense division and drift in Moscow; when they believe that they can get away with 'more'--usually more independence--than they might be able to do when the Soviet leadership appears less preoccupied with the struggle for power."[14] So it happened this time. The Soviet leadership was deeply split not only in different factions and clienteles but also with respect to perceptions of the West and, accordingly, to the appropriate way of action in its *Westpolitik*.[15]

These differences, too, became apparent in Soviet journals and papers. And they were not confined to *Westpolitik* alone but also concerned the USSR's global strategy. Particular arguments arose with regard to policy in the Soviet bloc and toward Third World countries and so-called liberation-movements. The bloc issue was reflected by the debate on "contradictions in Socialism."[16] The other issue was reflected by the discussion over what precisely "Proletarian Internationalism" means with respect to the "revolutionary process" in the Third World, (i.e., what kind of Soviet support should it be given?)[17] Differences in the *Westpolitik*, similarly, were reflected by the debate over whether small countries in Europe could play a role of their own in the field of security policy, as Hungary and the GDR had maintained.

On the one hand, there was the position of the Central Committee's Department of Relations with Communist and Worker's Parties of Socialist Countries, headed by Konstantin Rusakov and his First Deputy Oleg Rakhmanin, which was summarized in a famous article in *Pravda* under the pseudonym O. Vladimirov.[18] In it, the notion that small states could play a special role as a kind of mediators between the great powers was bluntly rejected. Such notions were declared to be associated with "nationalism," which in turn were connected with "Russophobia" and "anti-Sovietism" in covert and sometimes even in overt form. These ideas would only play into the hands of Western imperialism. On the other hand, this article was rejected by two subsequent pieces of writing--one by Oleg Bogomolov, head of the Institute of Socialist World Economy, and a second one by Nikolai Shishlin, who most likely represented the view of Mikhail Gorbachev.[19] Herein a much cooler and more moderate attitude is reflected. The same holds true for the new Program of the Communist Party of the Soviet Union (CPSU), which does not present statements in the sense of the Vladimirov article.[20]

The available evidence allows the cautious conclusion that Gorbachev's views seem to prevail in all of the three above-mentioned ramifications of foreign policy. Of course, perceptions do not disappear merely on the strength of a shift in power. They remain with the beholder. So it is hardly a surprise that some of Gorbachev's perceptions and conceptions in this field have been implicitly criticized. For instance, immediately after he had delivered his inauguration speech as General Secretary of the Central Committee, he obviously was opposed by the CC's declaration regarding the support of Third World countries and national movements. Similarly, some of the statements Gorbachev made in his two speeches before the Central Committee's plenary session in January 1987 were not endorsed by the plenum's ensuing resolution.[21]

As to the majority of foreign policy issues, a new consensus in the CPSU leadership has evolved, which is also reflected in the new Party Program. Many questions, of course, have never been contested, at least not in public. One of these issues is what is largely referred to as the German Question, i.e., the partition of the German nation and the Soviet Union's responsibilities as one of the four Great Powers. The following section depicts what is known of this position.

Soviet Perceptions of the German Problem

From the Soviet point of view, the concept of nationhood is a basic category in history and in international affairs. National consciousness is seen as much more steady and stable than so-called class-consciousness.[22] Statehood, on the other hand, is not considered as a necessary characteristic of a nation. From this, the inference can be drawn that dividing a nation into two states will not necessarily lead to the creation of two nations.

This principle becomes very clear in the Soviet attitude toward the reunification of Korea:

> The Soviet people very well know and understand that fundamental national problem for the solution of which the Korean people stubbornly struggles. This is the problem of the reunification of the country, having been divided by the guilt of U.S. imperialism. The Soviet Union consequently stands up for the reunification of Korea by peaceful means on a democratic basis, after the withdrawal of American forces from South Korea. This is our firm and unchangeable position.[23]

The contention, however, that there are two Koreas is declared as a doctrine of the United States and South Korea. "Progressive peoples" of the world are said to be in favor of the reunification of the Korean people, of a confederation "Koryo."[24]

In the case of Germany, however, the Soviet leaders maintain that the division of the nation is final and not open to negotiations. Yet in some cases, the principle of nationalism reappears in Soviet references to Germany. The anniversary of the founding of the GDR is usually celebrated as a victory for socialism on "German soil", and from time to time there are references to the Germans or to the German people in the Federal Republic *and* the GDR.[25]

Although the Soviet Union does not openly use the German option in the sense of an operative policy, it is hidden in the background and could be reactivated any time this is considered appropriate. Thus, both German states were accepted as members of the United Nations only under the proviso that the Four-Powers' responsibility for Germany "as a whole" remains valid. Also, in Article 10 of the treaty the USSR concluded with the GDR in October 1975, there is a clause, not included in any of the other treaties, which indicates that the Potsdam agreement remains untouched and that the military missions of the three Western powers can do their work unimpeded by East German authorities.

Finally, the Soviet leadership is extremely careful in its use of semantics regarding the GDR. For example, Soviet troops deployed in the GDR are called the "Group of Soviet Forces in Germany" and not "in the GDR". When East Berlin's leading party paper *Neues Deutschland* in April 1985 twice attempted to improve the GDR's status by renaming those 19 divisions "Soviet forces in the GDR," the Soviet Union immediately reacted. The commander of the troops, Army General Zaitsev, intervened and up to the present no further incidents of this kind have occurred.[26] Moreover, while West Germans refer to their country always in the nominative case, the Soviets refer to it in the genitive. This underscores by implication that the Federal Republic is understood to be part of a broader entity known as "Germany". Russian language usually employs the nominative, for instance, "Sotsialisticheskaya Federativnaya Respublika Yugoslaviya" or "Narodnaya Respublika Bolgariya". This sort of semantics is taken very seriously and is practiced without exception. Even when the West German chancellor used the nominative in a speech given in Moscow, the Soviet media printed it in the genitive.[27] The Soviet Union, therefore, very carefully keeps the German option open for itself.

There is evidence that the Gorbachev leadership does not see fundamental changes in this regard during the next decade or so. On the contrary, some Soviet experts on Germany have only recently expressed the opinion that Germany's partition will continue for a long time to come. Former ambassador Valentin Falin, for instance, has depicted the possibility of a reunited neutral Germany as one of the specters which do not exist in real life. While Germany in the past aspired to a hegemonial millennium in Europe, what it got was probably a millennial partition.

As far as Mikhail Gorbachev is concerned, he has only once addressed the German problem. Asked by an Italian journalist at a press conference whether he did not feel the necessity after forty years to cope with the problem of Germany's unity, he answered that this problem had been dealt with at the Helsinki Conference on Security and Cooperation in Europe (CSCE). The results of this Helsinki conference, both of the negotiation process and of the final act, were the answer to this question.[28] What Gorbachev thus did not exclude is the statement in the final act of the Helsinki conference that existing European borders may be changed a) peacefully, b) with mutual agreement, and c) observing international law. The inference to be drawn from the general secretary's response is that even the existing border between the two states in Germany may be changed peacefully, considering international law, on the basis of a mutual accord.

Interests of the GDR Leadership

The importance and the role of the German Democratic Republic have increased in the last decade, both worldwide and within the Eastern bloc. Concerning economic growth, it has been one of the most successful economies of the world. In particular its 'Kombinate' has become the model to be followed by the USSR's efforts to improve the performance and efficiency of its own economy. Unchanged, however, remains the SED's dependence upon Soviet protection. Therefore its leeway in foreign-policy matters is limited. Nevertheless the GDR, as represented by the SED leadership, has its own particular national interests.

As a consequence of its geostrategic position, the GDR is extremely vulnerable, should war break out. Its territory would be a battlefield, and it would suffer very high casualties. Therefore, the GDR leadership emphasizes repeatedly that there is no objective more important than the prevention of a war.[29] Avoiding war has been declared "the categorical imperative of international relations" in our time. In the face of the destructive effects of nuclear weapons, "war...can no more be a rational means of politics, because afterwards there would exist no more politics whatsoever."[30] Representatives of the GDR continuously stand up for "peaceful coexistence," "the rebirth of detente," and for a "security partnership" or a "partnership in peace" with the Federal Republic. They speak in favor of a "coalition of reason and realism" and the continuation of the East-West dialogue.[31] Erich Honecker even took up the slogan of the West German government, "Frieden schaffen mit immer weniger Waffen" (create peace with fewer and fewer weapons).[32] The two German states were given a special responsibility for the improvement of the international situation.[33]

That last objective is especially remarkable since, before the deployment of U.S. medium-range missiles on West German territory, the GDR had joined the Soviet campaign against the missiles, warning that such action would seriously affect East-West relations in Europe. After deployment began, the GDR then made clear that it had no choice but to go along with the deployment of new Soviet short-range missiles on East German soil. But there were many hints that this was more a matter of demonstrating solidarity with the USSR than a matter of conviction. *Neues Deutschland* published two letters from church groups in East and West Germany "expressing their horror over the prospect of the deployment of such missiles in the GDR and their fear of a possible 'ice age' in East-West relations."[34] Moreover, the Politburo of the East German Communist party quickly moved to make *Schadensbegrenzung* (limitation of damage) a primary aim of the GDR.[35] And while the Soviet side used NATO's beginning deployment as a pretext to break off the Geneva negotiations, the GDR continued to negotiate with West Germany in fourteen different forums.[36] *Schadensbegrenzung*, subsequently, became the basic rationale of its policy vis-à-vis Bonn.

To many observers in the West, the new rhetoric of the SED leadership came as a surprise. But in fact this orientation, caused by specific security interests, is not totally new. A comparison of speeches by Soviet and East German leaders, printed in the Soviet press, shows that the East Germans had early on emphasized much more than the Soviets the importance of preserving peace and avoiding war.[37] Beyond that, Erich Honecker joined the Hungarian notion of a special role for smaller European countries and conveyed this message to the readers of *Pravda*: "As the big countries have to make their contribution to the common cause of preserving peace, so have the medium-sized and small ones down to the very smallest."[38]

Somewhat later, the GDR again raised the topic of its *Westpolitik* by joining Soviet warnings that West Germany's participation in the U.S. Strategic Defense Initiative might jeopardize what had been achieved in *Deutschlandpolitik*. And Erich Honecker's reluctance to agree definitely to a visit to the Federal Republic must also be seen in this context. The results of the Geneva summit in 1985 and of subsequent summits had a calming effect on the deep-rooted apprehensions as to whether the achievements of German-German relations could be safeguarded, given the previous trend of deterioration in U.S.-Soviet relations. Since the GDR's security interests are not directly affected by SDI, this encumbrance seems to have been cleared for the time being.

Another key factor that the SED leadership must take into account is the so-called *Machtfrage* arising from the fact that there is still a "legitimacy gap" due to the lack of democratic assent on the part of the population of the GDR. In order to overcome this gap, the party has attempted in its domestic policy to make itself more acceptable. This demands a certain standard of living and of contentment on the part of the population. Ultimately, however, the party's power rests on the Leninist concept of "democratic centralism" and on its tight alliance with the Soviet Union. Moreover, the safeguarding of the political rule of the SED has also created a strong interest in keeping the Soviet bloc together.

The prevailing issue, however, in this respect is the bilateral relationship with Moscow. The SED therefore has a much stronger interest than the USSR has in preserving and strengthening this alliance. That is why the SED again and again declares that Soviet-GDR friendship is indissoluble and of eternal duration.

In external trade affairs, the GDR, like the Federal Republic, is highly dependent upon the export of industrial products and the import of raw materials and energy, and this again means a great deal of dependence upon the Soviet Union. The USSR provides a market for the bulk of East Germany's industrial output and is at the same time its main supplier of oil, natural gas, uranium and other raw materials. In this manner there is a strong economic background for the alliance between the two countries. The same also holds true for their scientific-technological collaboration.

But while the USSR would like to raise mutual economic relations "on a qualitatively new level of...economic *integration*," the GDR prefers to maintain at least a certain degree of economic self-determination. Therefore, it has declared itself as being in favor of a "single economic strategy" with only the "*coordination*" of economic policies.[39] In order not to discard totally the Soviet notion of integration, the concept is sometimes used to mean the bilateral relationship. For instance, Gunther Mittag (member of the SED Politburo) used the word "integration" in an article in *Pravda* in such a way that mutual Soviet-GDR shipments became the basic criterion for the level of integration. In this respect there were "no comparable example in the whole world" for such a kind of integration.[40]

Another important issue for the GDR is its trade with Western countries and particularly with Western Germany. Although minor in size as compared to the Comecon trade, it is nevertheless of high qualitative importance. The goals set by the SED's party congress with respect to economic growth could not have been achieved without this trade and this also holds true for the goals of the current Five-Year plan. They will be achievable only under conditions of undisturbed and--if possible--increasing trade with the West.

Above all, trade with the West means trade with the Federal Republic of Germany. Notwithstanding the above-mentioned "integration" with the USSR and the CMEA, several circumstances have contributed to the GDR's decision in the early 1980s to strengthen this connection: deteriorating terms of trade with the Soviet Union; the inability of other CMEA states to respond adequately to the GDR's needs; slowing of investment growth; and general difficulties in making the "technological shift to the new electronics-based industries."[41] Moreover, by means of the regime of intra-German trade, the GDR has a certain--albeit limited--access to the Common Market of the European Community. Therefore, there is a strong incentive to cultivate and to extend this relationship.

East Germany's special relationship with the Common Market always has been and still is observed by the East European countries with some suspicion. It is true that there are no open discussions on this topic within the CMEA; rather, it seems that this connection is treated as a kind of socialist taboo.

As regards the political and social intra-German connection, the East

German leadership is also in favor of preserving and strengthening the status quo between the two Germanies. Although it contends that there are no special intra-German relations whatsoever--only normal relations between two distinct states--it is nonetheless no secret that this relationship is the most salient issue for the East German population and even the SED. For them the Federal Republic is the standard by which the GDR evaluates its own achievements. So the GDR leadership has met many of the West German proposals for improving this relationship.

On the other hand, the SED has to be very careful in handling these affairs on two grounds. First, the extent of intra-German rapprochement and collaboration is watched carefully by Moscow. Therefore, the GDR wishes to avoid the appearance of any kind of "special relations" with the FRG. The leadership knows for sure that the decoupling of intra-German relations from overall East-West relations is only possible for a limited period of time. This is another reason that GDR politicians unconditionally support every possible improvement of U.S.-USSR relations. Additionally, they try by all means to eschew the impression that their Western trade connection is conducted at the expense of heightened demands for economic and technological contributions to the Soviet Union.[42] Secondly, the SED has to be concerned with safeguarding the power of the party against the destabilizing risks arising out of the improved intra-German connection. For instance, more than four million Germans from the West and all together almost six million Western visitors annually come to the GDR with its seventeen million inhabitants. (A comparable figure for the United States would be about 85 million convinced communist visitors a year.) The SED here speaks of a socialist state "open to the world" (*Weltoffenheit*).

This is the key motivation behind East Germany's so-called *Abgrenzungspolitik* (policy of demarcation or delimitation). It means that some of the aspirations of West Germany and of the populations of the GDR will remain unfulfilled for the time being. For instance, there will be no unrestricted travel from the GDR to West Germany and no West German newspapers will be allowed in East Germany.

So far the GDR leadership has been rather successful in dealing with Western influences and also with internal dissent. It appears "to have overcome many of its early trepidations over socio-political instability resulting from its forced opening to the West, having proved far more adept at managing domestic disaffection and Western 'contaminations' than many observers ever expected."[43] It has established a series of measures within the framework of *Abgrenzungspolitik* that are designed to counteract possible Western influence. The most outstanding of these has been the campaign to use German and Prussian history in order to aid the creation of a new, separate GDR-consciousness.[44]

With respect to the issue of intra-German communication and especially intra-German travel, the SED has followed a certain pattern. In all German-German agreements concerning this issue, it refuses to enter into binding obligations. Ultimately, therefore, all the decisions on intra-German travel rest with East German authorities. Moreover, time and again, the SED has brought up the demands Erich Honecker first made in his famous Gera speech in October 1980:

1. Recognition of GDR citizenship;

2. Upgrading of permanent diplomatic representation to ambassadorial levels;

3. Liquidation of the 'Recording agency' in Salzgitter; and

4. Final determination of the Elbe border.[45]

Germany's destiny in the long term, as viewed by the SED party leaders, is characterized by two expectations. On the one hand, the partition of Germany into two states is seen as final: "Unification of the socialist GDR and the capitalist FRG will never be possible"; there "can be and will be no unity whatsoever"; the question has been declared as "not real", since "one cannot unite socialism with capitalism."[46] On the other hand, it does not preclude the possibility of a united socialist Germany in the distant future. As the precondition, the Federal Republic is supposed to become a socialist state: "The question, whether later on, after the working class of the FRG...will have obtained the socialist transformation of society, a unified socialist nation may arise, will be decided by history after the requisite conditions for this have evolved."[47] The question will not be solved as the consequence of an agreement of the great powers but only "when in the Federal Republic of Germany the societal structure has been changed too, and the claim will be made that two socialist Germanies should then unite."[48] In this sense, the SED has not entirely given up the German option.

GDR Policy

This configuration of interests, as depicted above, has policy ramifications. Given its dependence upon the Soviet guarantee, the GDR leadership will always attempt to contribute to a reduction of East-West tensions and will always plead for a moderate policy toward the West. It will do so much because the GDR will always be the first among the communist states to be asked to make financial sacrifices whenever and wherever the Soviet Union gets involved in a conflict. That is why East Germany welcomes every indication of an improvement in the political dialogue between the superpowers. This policy attitude has become increasingly evident in recent years, and it has become obvious that there was a gap between the positions of the GDR and the USSR in the first half of the decade.

This has not been the first time that such a rift has occurred. In 1970/71, then-General Secretary Walter Ulbricht had attempted to oppose the Soviet Union's policy of detente. While at that time the reason for the divergencies between Moscow and East Berlin was Ulbricht's fear that Soviet concessions to the West would be detrimental to the GDR, in the beginning of the 1980s it was the other way around. Now it was East Germany in favor of more moderation, more dialogue, more negotiations and agreements.[49] While the Soviet Union still emphasized the importance of "Proletarian, Socialist Internationalism," the GDR leaders in their declarations have tended to underline the need for peace and "Peaceful Coexistence". Some of them even went so far as to admonish the Soviet leadership by insisting that the assistance to revolutionary movements abroad must not include military means. In this sense, Gunter Schabowski, chief editor of *Neues Deutschland*, wrote in *Pravda*: "V. I. Lenin has pointed out that internationalism in fact means 'unselfish work for the development of revolutionary movements and the revolutionary struggle in its own country, and support (by propaganda, empathy, materially) of this struggle, of this line, and solely of this line, in all countries without exception."[50] Most recently, Harald Neubert, director of the Institute for the International Worker's Movement at the Academy of Social Sciences of the Central Committee of the SED, declared that socialism would do everything in its power to prevent people from being forced to conduct just wars.[51]

From East Berlin's point of view, peaceful coexistence and the prevention of war has to be given absolute priority over the policy of "Internationalism" and over the support of revolutionary movements abroad. At best, the policy of "Internationalism" was declared "a matter of our hearts."[52] This is not only a declaratory policy. It is also deeply rooted in the GDR's policy of education. For instance, the value of "Internationalism" is almost totally absent in the more popular literature of the GDR.[53]

These divergencies of opinions were underscored in the slogans for the May Day celebrations for 1984 and 1985. A comparison shows that the policy of "Proletarian, Socialist Internationalism," which was given highest priority in *Pravda*, ranked last in *Neues Deutschland*. The salience the SED gives to the continuation of the East-West dialogue is also demonstrated by the promotion of two men to full membership in the Politburo who have been most outspokenly in favor of such a course of action: Herbert Häber and Gunter Schabowski.[54]

It goes without saying that the planned visit in September 1984 of General Secretary Honecker to the Federal Republic would have crowned this policy. This visit--a few days before the 35th anniversary of the founding of the GDR--would have been a special episode in Honecker's *"Schadensbegrenzungspolitik."*[55] Obviously the SED was even prepared to take some risk with regard to the official Soviet line:

1. In the late summer of 1984, *Pravda* published three articles full of warnings against West Germany's alleged policy of revanchism. The FRG was said to use intra-German economic levers and intra-German connections at large in a combined plot of reactionary forces with the ultimate goal of changing the territorial status quo in Europe; the relations between both German states could *not* make a contribution to limit damage done by the beginning deployment of U.S.-medium-range missiles on German territory. For its part, the GDR was initially very reluctant to join Moscow's official campaign against revanchism and actually did so only after several months of foot-dragging. The East German press omitted reprinting some official articles from *Pravda* while at the same time reprinting articles from *Izvestiya* and from the Hungarian press that were more in line with the SED's policy. In an interview on August 17, 1984, Honecker even declared that West German revanchism had already suffered its historical defeat 35 years ago. And he spoke of the "rusted trumpet of revanchism,"[56] making clear, in this manner, that at least East German communists did not perceive a genuine threat.

2. Another author, Central Committee institute director Harald Neubert, wrote in the East German foreign policy journal *Horizont* that each communist party should rely on its own experiences and its own achievements. It should be taken into consideration that different experiences may lead to different assessments and to different inferences and this in turn occasionally may even lead to divergencies of opinion between individual communist parties. After all, his article concluded, the international communist movement was and would remain a voluntary community of equal and independent parties.[57]

3. In July 1984 East Berlin honored a second credit, granted by West German banks, by some reciprocity in the field of humanitarian affairs although it was not, by any means, in need of new credit.

4. The telegram sent by the SED on the occasion of Chernenko's birthday in

September 1984 obviously did not satisfy the Kremlin's expectations. *Pravda* published a text praising Chernenko's merits in reducing the danger of war and in strengthening the alliance of CPSU and SED, a text which was not contained in the original German version as published in *Neues Deutschland*.[58]

5. In November 1984 the GDR authorities closed a bridge between West Berlin and Potsdam (GDR), which gave access to the Western powers' military mission in Potsdam. Even though the bridge was reopened very quickly after Western protests, from Moscow's point of view this must have appeared as just another high-handed East German attempt to improve its status.[59]

Of course, the SED leadership would not have dared to let these divergencies become public unless it knew for sure that some support could be expected from within the Soviet Union. It may be assumed that Erich Honecker was reassured in this conviction by the Soviet ambassador to the GDR, Vyacheslav Kochemasov.[60] In view of Chernenko's illness and the ensuing succession crisis, a positive change in Moscow's inflexible *Westpolitik* was being anticipated.

The eventual postponement of Honecker's visit may likewise be attributed to the preceeding developments in the Kremlin and to East Berlin's wishes to stick to its policy of detente without upsetting the establishment in Moscow. The conspicuousness of a visit to West Germany and to Chancellor Kohl had to be sacrificed in order to keep the basic policy line unchanged. Since the Geneva summit changed at least some negative trends in U.S.-USSR relations, this policy by now has found its justification. The SED Politburo demonstrated excellent hibernating abilities during the East-West winter.

The GDR leaders have successfully used this time for the improvement of their international standing: After the breakdown of the German-German summit, Honecker visited the Finnish president, the Italian president, the Italian prime minister and the Pope, while Prime Minister Horst Sindermann went to Madrid and Paris. Something like a breakthrough were the visits of the British foreign minister and the French prime minister to the GDR in the first half of 1985.[61] Although it is quite clear that all this contributes to the international reputation of the GDR and thus to its internal stability as well, it should not be overlooked that from East Berlin's point of view this is also a contribution to a lessening of tensions between East and West and serves to consolidate the whole socialist bloc.

The same may be said with respect to the GDR's economical performance: "It is well understood with us that the strength (*moshch'*) of socialism has a decisive impact upon the preservation of peace. ...By strengthening the republic the common potential of the socialist community is increased," Erich Honecker wrote in *Pravda*.[62] He boasted of the achievements of his economic policies and recommended them--particularly the institution of '*Kombinate*'--as a model for the Soviet economy.

Something similar had happened already between 1968 and 1971. At that time then-SED General Secretary Ulbricht declared in his new constitution of 1968 the GDR's new economic system to be "*das ökonomische System des Sozialismus*." At the XXIVth congress of the CPSU in April 1971, he even implicitly recommended to his Soviet comrades that they should learn from their German comrades how to build up an efficient organization. A few days later he was removed from his post and put on pension. What now is the reaction of the Gorbachev leadership?

New Priorities under the Gorbachev Leadership

The answer to this question can best be given in the context of Mikhail Gorbachev's overall foreign-policy attitudes. An analysis of his speeches from 1983 to 1985 indicates the following priorities:[63]

1. Gorbachev is above all interested in domestic policy, economic policy, and social policy. It has become obvious that he holds economic factors in the competition between East and West as having decisive importance. He has only mentioned the military factor in the context of the security of his own country and that of the "Socialist Community."

2. The Soviet leadership is in agreement that the cohesion of the alliance system, adherence of the alliance relationships and the future development of the "Socialist Community" are the primary foreign policy priorities. In this sense, the concept of "Proletarian, Socialist Internationalism" is now used primarily for the Eastern bloc. It has become apparent that Moscow gives increased attention to the institutions of the CMEA. The socialist countries will be more closely controlled and at the same time their interests will be given greater consideration.

3. Gorbachev is attempting to reduce the active "internationalist" involvement of his country in the Third World. His "hearty support" for the so-called liberated countries and liberation movements has relegated them to the back-burner. The available evidence after the XXVIIth party congress speaks for a success of the general secretary's line: the triumphal tone of the Brezhnev era has been replaced by Soviet analyses

which emphasize the costs of a further expansion of Soviet activism in the Third World.[64] The new rhetoric is given particular support by social scientists. For instance: "The Soviet Union is molding its relations with the Afro-Asian and other developing countries on the basis of peaceful coexistence and the principles of anti-imperialistic solidarity which are in accord with the most basic interests of these countries." The author then repeats Gorbachev's statement of March 1985: "Today as well our empathy is with the countries of Asia, Africa, and Latin America which are attempting the consolidation of their independence and social renewal. They are our friends and partners in the struggle for a permanent peace."[65]

"Internationalism" was approached in a similar sense in an unsigned *Pravda* article: It was of utmost importance that the existence of civilization and of life on earth be secured. In this struggle, the states of the "Socialist Community" as well as the communist and worker's parties of the world, the developing countries and the "democratic forces" were on their side.[66] In the long term, an increase in Soviet restraint in its "internationalist" policy is becoming obvious. This, of course, does not mean that the USSR will not adhere to its already-existing commitments.

4. Gorbachev's *Westpolitik* is based on the expectation of increasing contradictions in the Western world, particularly contradictions between the U.S. and the Europeans. Obviously, however, he is not disinclined to make another attempt to come to terms with the United States. For this purpose he met Reagan in Geneva, in Reykyavik, in Washington, and in Moscow. But he is oriented toward "Europe--our common house."[67] He seems to believe that the existing "capitalist contradictions" can be exploited to the Soviet Union's advantage. For this purpose, he intends to improve the relationship with the West European countries. All his actions before the Geneva summit have underlined this inclination.[68]

In this context an important role is given to the collaboration between the European Community and the Council of Mutual Economic Cooperation.[69] He also mentioned the possibility of "establishing contacts in some form between the Warsaw Treaty and the North Atlantic Union as organizations."[70]

With regard to the exploitation of Western contradictions, he several times mentioned the "lessons of the Anti-Hitler coalition." In a broader sense this referred to the possibility of an alliance of capitalist and socialist countries which is directed against the "main enemy." The "lessons to be drawn from history" could possibly refer to a Soviet attempt to isolate the United States, unless it desists from its policy of "threatening world peace." Eduard Shevardnadze, Gorbachev's foreign minister, however, also mentioned the "experience of the Anti-Hitler coalition" but without mentioning the U.S. explicitly. This had been done by a Soviet historian a few weeks earlier speaking about the necessity to struggle against this "main enemy": "Today such an enemy most of all are the militaristic circles of the U.S. and NATO."[71]

5. Gorbachev's preference for Western Europe does not justify, however, any expectations that the Soviet Union again might play the famous "German card." As before, the German question is declared not to be open for revision. Moreover, in spite of West Germany's economic potential and political salience in Europe, it seems to rank low in the general secretary's European conception. "Without a doubt and probably for a longer period of time, the Federal Republic has lost its role as a preferential partner in the West, a role which Brezhnev and Andropov emphasized."[72] Since Soviet attempts in the past have failed to produce the desired results with regard to the exploitation of U.S.-German contradictions, Bonn became somewhat less important to Moscow.[73]

In Gorbachev's policy toward Western Europe, France, Italy, Great Britain, the EEC, and also Spain were given primacy. Within Western Germany, the Social-Democratic Party (SPD) and the Greens are the political factors which are being given increased positive attention on Moscow's part.

Only after the West German government had declared that it would by no means impede an American-Soviet INF-agreement and, therefore, was prepared to scrap the Pershings Ia did a normalization of Soviet-West German relations take place.

6. As mentioned in point no. 2, the bloc countries will be more strictly under Soviet control. At the same time, they will be given more leeway in their internal affairs. Also, the role small states can play on the international level is not forgotten in Moscow.[74] But individual bloc countries are not affected to the same extent and limits do exist for all three principles. Gorbachev obviously perceived a necessity to repeatedly stress that Hungary will stick to socialist principles.[75] On the other hand, the economic successes of the German Democratic Republic are now considered as an example to be followed by the USSR.[76] Thus, the Soviet leadership's reaction to East German apprehensions in the economic field today is totally different from that of 1971. The economic system of socialism, rejected 15 years ago, has now become accepted as a model for the Soviet Union. And when Shevardnadze in February 1987 visited East Berlin, he eventually even endorsed the GDR's "policy of dialogue with all the forces of reason, realism and good will."[77]

Implications for the West

In a recent publication, Christoph Royen of the *Stiftung Wissenschaft und Politik* came to the following conclusions:[78]

- The Soviet Union's political system is not totally unchangeable.
- There is at least some Western potential by which a Soviet "Aggiornamento" could be influenced.
- The Soviet leadership must not be confronted with the alternative "confrontation or capitulation." This would be detrimental to Western attempts to bring about a more constructive role for Moscow in its global and regional policies.
- From this the inference is to be drawn that the West has no other choice than to accept the Soviet challenge and at the same time strive for mutual cooperation.
- Thus a combination of three basic policy elements--containment, detente, and confrontation--would best serve Western interests.
- Such a triple track policy also would offer a long-term perspective to the East European countries.

The shifts in Soviet foreign policy priorities which this chapter has dealt with may be seen as a confirmation of this conclusion. Doubtless the Reagan administration's firm position has to some extent contributed to Gorbachev's more restrained attitude toward Third World developments. If the CPSU endorses this shift in priority, the chances for an improvement in superpower relations would rise. And that, in turn, would constitute a better setting for the intra-German relationship.

For the foreseeable future, West Germany's *Deutschlandpolitik* will continue to attempt to mitigate the consequences of the German partition and to improve the existing modus vivendi. This requires the cooperation of the German Democratic Republic and the general acceptance of such a policy by the Soviet Union. In this sense, the Federal Republic of Germany will proceed with its policy of communication and cooperation between the two states on all levels.

Regarding the international framework, it will try, as before, to shield the achievements and developments of the intra-German connection as much as possible from any heightening of East-West tensions. West Germany feels it can best serve its interests by gaining its allies' support or at least their acceptance of this policy. In this sense, the statement still seems to be justified that *Ostpolitik* must stay *Westpolitik* in the first instance, and, again in this sense, the endorsement of *Deutschlandpolitik* is tantamount to an encouragement of West German efforts, as President Reagan did in his speech before the United Nations General Assembly: "We take heart from progress by others in lessening tensions, notably the efforts by the Federal Republic to reduce barriers between the two German states."[79]

48

Notes

1. See for instance the address of Politburo member Herbert Häber to the Eighth Session of the Central Committee of the SED, *Deutschland-Archiv* 7 (1984), pp. 777-779.

2. Wolfgang Pfeiler, "Die Deutsche Frage in der Sicht von UdSSR und DDR," *German Studies Review*, May 1980, pp. 230-237.

3. E. Baskakov and Y. Kornilov, *Soviet-American Relations: New Prospects* (Moscow, 1975), p. 90.

4. Cf. Gerhard Wettig, *The Role of West Germany in Soviet Policies Toward Western Europe* (Sonderveroeffentlichung des Bundesinstituts für ostwissenschaftliche und internationale Studien Köln: June 1982), p. 6.

5. Cf. Eberhard Schulz, "Weltpolitische Burden der Sowjetunion," Wolfgang Wagner, et al., eds., *Die Internationale Politik 1979-80* (Munchen-Wien, 1983), p. 163.

6. Boris Meissner, "Wandlungen in den Bundnisformen und der Vormachtpolitik der Sowjetunion in Ostmittel-und Sudeuropa," *Sudosteuropa* 3/4 (1985), p. 166; Magarditsch A. Hatschikjan, *Der Ostblock und Gorbacov 1986. Zur Block-und Westpolitik der kleineren Warschauer-Pakt-Staaten*, Sankt Agustin, February 1987.

7. Cf. Charles Gati, "The Soviet Empire: Alive But Not Well," *Problems of Communism 2* (1985), p. 81.

8. Leopold Unger, "Plot Against Moscow or a Ginger 'De-Satellization'?" *International Herald Tribune*, 3 September 1984, p. 4.

9. Cf. Rupert Scholz, "Perspektiven der Deutschlandpolitik," *Deutschland Archiv* 3 (1984): 266.

10. Seweryn Bialer and Joan Afferica, *Andropov's Burden: Socialist Stagnation and Communist Encirclement*, Adelphi Paper No. 189 (IISS: London, Spring 1984), pp. 13-25.

11. CC Secretary Matyas Szuros, as quoted by Gyula Jozsa, "Ungarn im Kreuzfeuer der Kritik aus Prag und Moskau. Part I: Die Aussenminster-konferenz der WP-Staaten (April 1984) und die Polemik zwischen Prag und Budapest," *Berichte des Bundesinstituts fur ostwissenschaftliche und internationale Studien* 5 (1985, p. 20). See also Gati, "The Soviet Empire," p. 79.

12. See at length Max Schmidt/Gerhard Basler, "Koalition der Vernunft

und des Realismus. Zusammenwirken fu die Bewahrung des Lebens," *IPW-Berchte* 5 (1985), pp. 1-7.

13. For a comparison see *Pravda*, 15 April 1984, 13 April 1985; 11 October 1984, 13 October 1985.

14. Gati, "The Soviet Empire," p. 86.

15. I have dealt with these diverging perceptions in the Soviet leadership in: Wolfgang Pfeiler, "Intra-German Relations in a Period of East-West Tensions," *CISA Working Paper* No. 50 (Los Angeles: Center for International and Strategic Affairs, University of California, Los Angeles, June 1985), pp. 17-20.

16. See at length: Hannes Adomeit, "Widerspruche im Sozialismus: Sowjetpolitik in Osteuropa im Kontext der Ost-West-Beziehungen," (SWP-paper SWP-Az 2412), Ebenhausen 1985.

17. See at some length: Wolfgang Pfeiler, "Die Sowjetunion und ihr europaisches Bundnissystem. Neue Prioritaten unter der neuen Fuhrung," Sankt Augustin, July 1985.

18. O. Vladimirov, "Vedushchii faktor mirovogo revolyutsionnogo protsessa," *Pravda*, 21 June 1985, p. 4.

19. Oleg Bogomolov, "Soglasovanie ekonomicheskikh interesov i politiki pri sotsializme," *Kommunist* 10 (1985). Nikolai Schischlin, "Das Erste Gebot," *Neue Zeit (New Times)* 35 (1985), pp. 9-11. See also: Fred Oldenburg, "Das Verhaltnis UdSSR - Bundesrepublik Deutschland," *Sowjetunion 1984/85.* Ereignisse, Probleme, Perspektiven, (ed. by BIOst), Munchen/Wien 1985, p. 271.

20. See for complete text: *Pravda*, 26 October 1985.

21. "Materialy vneocherednogo Plenuma Tsentral'nogo Komiteta KPSS," *Mirovaya ekonomika i mezhdunarodnye otnosheniya*, 4, 1985, p. 7 and p. 13. See also speech of Mikhail Gorbachev, "O perestroyke i Kadrovoy politike partii," *Pravda*, 29 January 1987, pp. 1-5; Mikhail Gorbachev's concluding address, *Pravda*, 30 January 1987, p. 1; Resolution of the Central Committee, "O perestroyke i Kadrovoy politike partii," *Pravda*, 29 January 1987, pp. 1-2.

22. Cf. G. E. Glezerman, *Klassy i natsii* (Moscow, 1974), pp. 10, 16; IML CC CPSU (ed.), "Leninizm i natsional'nyy vopros v sovremennykh usloviayakh," (Moscow, 1972), p. 40.

23. K. U. Chernenko, speech of May 23, 1984, *Pravda*, 24 May 1984, p. 2.

24. Andrei Krusinsky, *Pravda*, 12 February 1978; E. A. Shevardnadze,

Pravda, 21 January 1987, p. 4 and *Pravda*, 24 January 1987, p. 4.

25. *Pravda*, 9 October 1974; *Pravda*, 7 October 1983, p. 1.

26. "General Saizew nimmt es mit Statusfragen genau. Es gibt "Streitkafte in Deutschland" - nicht in der DDR," *Frankfurter Allgemeine Zeitung*, 18 April 1985.

27. Speech of Chancellor Helmut Kohl as printed in *Pravda*, 5 July 1983, p. 4.

28. M. Gorbachev, *Pravda*, 22 November 1985, p. 2.

29. Erich Honecker in his answer to Yuri Andropov, *Pravda*, 4 May 1983, p. 2. See also: Erich Honecker, "Novaya glava v istorii nashego naroda," *Pravda*, 5 October 1984, p. 4f. Gerhard Hahn, "Friedenssicherung - Hauptziel der Aubenpolitik der DDR," *IPW-Berichte* 5 (1985), pp. 8-13.

30. Max Schmidt, "Bedingungen und Moglichkeiten zur Fortsetzung der Politik friedlicher Koexistenz in Europe," *IPW-Berichte* 9 (1984), pp. 1, 3.

31. Ibid., pp. 1, 3, 6. See also Henry Tanner, "Honecker is Viewed as Prime as 2 Germanies Improve Relations," *International Herald Tribune*, March 20, 1984, p. 1f.; and Peter Jochen Winters, "Personalentscheidungen und ihr politischer Hintergrund: Die 8. Tagung des SED-Zentralkomitees," *Deutschland Archiv* 7 (1984): 676. See also: Schmidt/Basler, "Koalition der Vernunft und des Realismus," p. 30.

32. *Neues Deutschland*, 14 March 1983, p. 5.

33. Winters, "Personalentscheidungen und ihr politischer Hintergrund," p. 676, quotes Kurt Hager in this sense. See also Schmidt, "Bedingungen und Moglichkeiten," p. 5.

34. Ronald D. Asmus, "The Dialectics of Detente and Discord: The Moscow-East Berlin - Bonn Triangle," *Orbis* 4 (Winter 1985), p. 748.

35. See for instance the address of Politburo member Herbert Haber to the Eighth Congress of the Central Committee of the SED, *Deutschland Archiv* 7 (1984): 777-779.

36. Asmus, "Dialectics of Detente and Discord," p. 748.

37. See for instance the speeches by Honecker and Zimyanin in *Pravda*, 12 April 1983, p. 4; and by Honecker and Andropov in *Pravda*, 4 May 1983. See also Erich Honecker, "S Sovetskim Soyuzom--po puti uspekhov," *Pravda*, 7 October 1983, p. 4f.; see "Das Honecker-Interview vom 17 August 1984," *Deutschland Archiv* 10 (1984): 1103-1113. See also Erich

Honecker, "Vsemirno-istoricheskaya pobeda vo imya mira i schastlivogo budushchego chelovechestva," *Pravda*, 7 May 1985, p. 4f.

38. Ibid., p. 5.

39. TASS, "Krepit' edinstvo," *Pravda*, 21 October 1983, p. 4. Emphasis added.

40. Gyunter Mittag, "Istoricheskoe dostizhenie," *Pravda*, 9 August 1983, p. 4.

41. John Garland, "Recent Developments in Inter-German Trade and Economic Relations," Paper Presented at the III World Congress for Soviet and East European Studies, Washington, D.C., Oct. 30 - Nov. 4 1985, p. 1.

42. Cf. Bernard von Plate, "Interessen und aussenpolitische Handlungsmoglichkeiten der DDR in ihrer deutschlandpolitischen Bedeutung," (SWP-paper SWP - AP 2444), Ebenhausen, August 1985, p. 9. See also: Jackson Diehl, "Soviet Bloc Watching for Signals from Gorbachev," *International Herald Tribune*, 19 November 1985, p. 5.

43. Ronald D. Asmus, "East Berlin and Moscow: the Documentation of a Dispute," (RFE Occasional Papers No. 1.), Munich 1985, p. 17.

44. See Gunther Heydemann, *Geschichtswissenschaft im geteilten Deutschland: Entwicklungsgeschichte, Organisationsstruktur, Funktionen, Theorie-und Methodenprobleme in der Bundesrepublik Deutschland und in der DDR* (Frankfurt/M., 1980); Johannes Schradi, *Die DDR-Gesschichtswissenschaft und das burgerliche Erbe* (Frankfurt/M. 1984).

45. *Neues Deutschland*, 14 October 1980, pp. 3-5.

46. Erich Honecker, *Neues Deutschland*, 1 November 1973; Erich Honecker, *Neues Deutschland*, 17 February 1987; and in the Austrian television program, "Die unruhigen Deutschen," March 8, 1984, as quoted by Wolfgang Venohr, "35 Jahre DDR und die nationale Frage," *Deutschland Archiv* 12 (1984), p. 1271.

47. Georg Klaus und Manfred Buhr (eds.), *Marxistisch-leninistisches Worterbuch der Philosophie*, 10. neubearb. und erw. Aufl., (Reinbek, 1975).

48. Honecker, as quoted by Venohr, "35 Jahre DDR," p. 1271.

49. Bernard von Plate, "Deutsch-deutsche Beziehungen und Ost-West-Konflikt," *Aus Politik und Zeitgeschichte*, Beilage nur Wochenzeitung Das Parlament, B 15/1984, p. 39; see also Dieter Mahncke, *Berlin im geteilten Deutschland*, Schriften des Forschungsinstituts der Deutschen Gesellschaft fur Auswartige Politik (Munchen/Wien, 1973), p. 11f.

50. Gunter Schabowski, "Dviszhushchaya sila," *Pravda*, 3 April 1982, p. 4. In the meantime Schabowski has been elevated to full membership in the SED Politburo.

51. Harald Neubert, "Der 8. Mai und das Vermachtnis der Anti-Hitler-Koalition," *Horizont* 4 (1985), p. 3f.

52. Erich Honecker, as quoted in *Pravda*, 17 April 1983, p. 4; see also *Pravda*, 12 April 1983, p. 4; and Franz Loeser, "SED: Die meisten Genossen denken wie ich," *Der Spiegel*, 6 August 1984, p. 120.

53. Cf. Anita M. Mallinckrodt, "Das kleine Massenmedium. Soziale Funktion und politische Rolle der Heftreihenliteratur in der DDR," Koln 1984, p. 277.

54. Cf. Winters, "Personalentscheidungen und ihr politischer Hintergrund," p. 657; Wolfgang Seiffert, "Jetzt ist Honecker gefordert," *Der Spiegel*, 6 August 1984, p. 38.

55. Wolfgang Seiffert, "Eine verlorenc Schlacht," *Der Spiegel*, 10 September 1984, p. 20.

56. "Das Honecker-Interview vom 17. August 1984," *Deutschland Archiv*, 10 (1984), p. 1110f. See also Honecker's articles in *Pravda*, 5 October 1984, p. 5 and 7 May 1985, p. 5.

57. Harald Neubert, "Aktuelle Aufgaben der Kommunisten," *Horizont* 8 (1984), p. 10.

58. Cf. for the differing wording *Neues Deutschland*, 25 September 1984; and *Pravda*, 25 September 1984.

59. Cf. Peter Danylow, "Der aussenpolitische Spielraum der DDR. Wechselnde Grenzen der Handlungsfreiheit im ostlichen Bundnissystem," *Europa Archiv*, 14 (1985), p. 438.

60. Editorial, *Der Spiegel*, 13 August 1984, p. 24.

61. See at some length Fred Oldenburg, "Die DDR - Partner in Europa," *DDR-Report*, 8 (1985), p. 435f.

62. Erich Honecker, *Pravda*, 7 October 1985, p. 4f.

63. Pfeiler, "Die Sowjetunion und ihr europaisches Bundnissystem," pp. 26-40.

64. Heinz Brahm/Heinrich Vogel, "Gorbatschow vor groben Aufgaben," *Aus Politik und Zeitgeschichte* (Beilage zur Wochenzeitung Das Parlament), B 21-22 (1985), p. 13.

65. Yu. Alimov, "Svyaz' vremen i sobytiy (K 30-u godovshchine Bandungskoy konferencii)," *Mirovaya ekonomika i mezhdunarodnye*

otnosheniya 6 (1985), p. 47.

66. "Internatsionalizm v deystvii," *Pravda*, 15 June 1985, p. 4; See also the recent article by Yuri Zhdanov, "Klassovoye i obshchechelovecheskoye v yadernom veke," *Pravda*, 6 March 1987, p. 3f.

67. M. S. Gorbachev, *Pravda*, 19 December 1984, p. 4; see also headline in *Pravda*, 13 December 1985, p. 4.

68. Cf. Scott Sullivan, "Gorbachev as a 'Europeanist': The Challenge for NATO: Fending off Soviet wedges," *Newsweek*, 1 April 1985, p. 6f; ;see also "Sowjetisches Werben um Osteuropa," *Neue Zurcher Zeitung*, 23/24 June 1985.

69. "Internatsionalizm v deystvii," *Pravda*, 15 June 1985, p. 4; see also Christian Meier, "Vor neuen Verhandlungen zwischen RGW und EG?," *DDR-Report* 9 (1985), pp. 506-509; see also the round-table discussion between V. Zagladin, A. Yakovlev, F. Burlatskiy, "Vostok - Zapad: tsivilizovannoe otnosheniya. Neobkhodismot'? Real'nost'? Utopiya?" *Literaturnaya Gazeta*, 26 June 1985, p. 2.

70. M.S. Gorbachev, "Za mirnoe, svobodnoe, protsvetayushchee budushchee Evropy i vsekh drugikh kontinentov," *Pravda*, 4 October 1985, p. 2.

71. E.A. Shervardnadze, "Luchshiy mir - eto mir dlya vsekh," *Pravda*, 25 July 1985, p. 4.

72. Fred Oldenburg, "Sowjetische deutschlandpolitik - von Breshnew zu Gorbatschow," *Osteuropa* 5 (1985), p. 318.

73. See also Hannes Adomeit, "The German Factor in Soviet Westpolitik," *The Annals of the American Academy of Political and Social Science*, September 1985, p. 26f.

74. See for instance Boris Ponomarev, "Za sotrudnichestvo v bor'be protiv yadernoj ugrozy," *Pravda*, 18 October 1985, p. 4.

75. Cf. "Druzheskaya vstrecha," *Pravda*, 18 October 1985, p. 4.

76. Cf. A. Grabovskiy, "Obshchim kursom k yedinoy tseli (K itogam 40-go sessii SEV)," *Mirovaya ekonomika i mezhdunarodnye otnosheniya* 9 (1985), p. 9.

77. *Pravda*, 4 February 1987, p. 4.

78. Christoph Royen, "Wandel in Osteuropa. Osteuropas Rolle in der sowjetischen Politik und die Chancen westlicher Einflussnahme," (SWP-paper, SWP-2400), Ebenhausen, October 1984, p. 49.

79. President Reagan's address to the U.N. General Assembly, *Wireless Bulletin from Washington*, 24 September 1984.

4

RECENT CHANGES IN THE POLICY OF THE GERMAN DEMOCRATIC REPUBLIC TOWARDS THE FEDERAL REPUBLIC OF GERMANY

Eberhard Schulz

For more than thirty years, conventional wisdom has held that the German Democratic Republic is the most loyal ally and obedient satellite of the Soviet Union. The numerous reasons for this perception sometimes obscure the fact that it was also the East German state where the first revolt occurred after the communist take-over in Eastern Europe. This was only three months after Stalin's death and three years before Khrushchev's secret speech at the twentieth congress of the CPSU that preceded the uprisings in Poland and Hungary. In June 1953, the workers of the Stalinallee in East Berlin rallied for a demonstration against the Ulbricht regime. Within a few days the rebellion spread over the whole of East Germany and the Soviet leaders resorted to tanks in order to smash the resistance of the unarmed people. It is true, though, that after the last loophole had been closed by the erection of the Berlin wall, the GDR became the most reliable member of the Warsaw Pact and observed the Soviet line in foreign policy more closely than any other East European country.

But it is in East Germany that the most notable changes have taken place in foreign policy since the early 1980s. Before trying to explain the reasons for Erich Honecker's unexpected initiatives, this paper will cast a glance at the genesis of East Germany's *Westpolitik* until the break-down of the detente policy of the 1970s. It will shed some light on the factors determining the foreign policy of the GDR and the reasons why the Soviet Union lost the capability of tight control. After a short description of the steps taken by Honecker, the rationale of the GDR's policy overtures towards the Federal Republic of Germany will be discussed.

Detente as an Ice-breaker
for East German Westpolitik

For a long time after the foundation of the two German states in 1949, the Federal Republic of Germany, with the loyal help of its Western allies, had succeeded in preventing other nations from formally recognizing the German Democratic Republic.[1] Thus, the international activities of the communist German state were confined to the crypto-diplomatic level of trade missions or ping-pong diplomacy. While in the course of time the GDR skillfully managed to expand its visible presence in quite a few countries of the Third World, *Westpolitik* proper remained unimportant. GDR initiatives not originating in Moscow were unthinkable.

This changed at the end of the 1960s, when the United States and the Federal Republic of Germany engaged in their new Ostpolitik. Curiously enough, it was the East German leader, Walter Ulbricht, who initially refused to join the corresponding new Soviet *Westpolitik*. Did not the Erfurt meeting between the two German prime ministers Willy Brandt and Willi Stoph in March 1970 demonstrate how fragile the East German regime was and how dangerous uncontrolled inter-German contacts could be?[2] Ulbricht painfully remembered Stalin's initiatives of the early 1950s, which, at the expense of the East German communists, played with the idea of a German reunification in order to prevent the Federal Republic from joining NATO.[3]

Indeed, in 1971, when Ulbricht had been removed, it was the GDR which had to pay the price for the quadripartite agreement on Berlin and the consolidation of the European status quo by the treaties of Moscow, Warsaw, etc. The East German ruling Socialist Unity Party (SED) had to finally bury its hopes for a separate peace treaty with the Soviet Union, an SED demand since the mid-1950s. Such a treaty, Ulbricht had hoped, would provide for full international sovereignty, removing all rights of the victorious Four Powers of 1945 over Germany as a whole and over Berlin. Instead, the Soviet Union brushed aside the "Ulbricht doctrine" of the 1960s, according to which no member state of the Warsaw Pact would resume diplomatic relations unless Bonn allowed for full national recognition of the GDR. Brezhnev even did not formally dismiss the disclaimer in the "letter on the unity of Germany" which the FRG attached to the Moscow treaty. The rights of the Four Powers were confirmed in the Quadripartite Agreement (in

Berlin) to the effect that the Soviet Union no longer supported the claims of the GDR that West Berlin was located "on the territory of the GDR." The GDR was forced, in a treaty with the FRG, to guarantee free access to West Berlin, and to sign a "basic treaty" with the FRG which did not provide for recognition of the GDR as a foreign state nor for separate East German citizenship. Thus, the Soviet Union subordinated the "national" interests of the GDR to its own desire to establish a relationship of detente vis-à-vis the Federal Republic of Germany. So did all other member states of the Warsaw Pact. Poland went so far as to conclude a treaty with the Federal Republic, attempting to obtain FRG recognition of Poland's western border line--which is a border with the GDR, not the FRG, and which was formally recognized by the GDR as early as 1950.

In the longer run, however, it became apparent that the GDR benefited substantially from detente. The Soviets could not deny the GDR immediate contacts with Western governments, since detente was considered to correspond to the interests of the East as well as of the West. In particular, German-German relations, though watched by Moscow with growing suspicion, could not be interdicted, especially as Bonn became the only motor in the West of detente policy. In this respect, Brezhnev's new *Westpolitik* weakened the quasi-monopoly the Soviet Union had exercised in the relations of the Warsaw Pact states with the West. It even turned out that under conditions of detente, the Soviets sometimes had difficulties merely coordinating Eastern approaches towards the West.

Thus, in the early 1970s there was a firm belief that the freedom of maneuver of the East Central European states and the GDR in particular largely depended on detente. As soon as strong tensions between the two superpowers re-emerged it was assumed the Russians would draw in the reins. This idea was quite logical and corresponded to former Russian attitudes, yet this assumption did not hold true in the early 1980s. In spite of rapidly growing tensions between the United States and the Soviet Union, the freedom of maneuver of the East European countries actually grew. What was the reason for this novel experience?

The Limits of Detente

During the period of detente, it was generally supposed that in the East-West relationship ideological factors were in recess and that pragmatism was growing. There was a visible inertia in Brezhnev's last years, at least as far as political leadership was concerned, while the unprecedented Soviet military build-up continued. It was, however, generally held that the contacts between

East and West were to the benefit of all--the participating countries as well as their governments and their people. But apparently it was overlooked that detente could flourish only under certain conditions, notably that it was controlled by the leading powers of the two alliances, that it was considered by those two powers as beneficial for themselves, and that a certain threshold of military superiority on one side was not transgressed.

In the 1970s these conditions vanished. Tensions between the two blocs had been growing since the mid-1970s, but after the shock created by two almost simultaneous events--the Iranian seizure of American hostages and the Soviet occupation of Afghanistan--political links between the two superpowers virtually broke down. The crisis in Poland added to conditions where the use of force seemed to be the only political instrument the Soviet leadership was in a position to apply. An unprecedented fear of war spread over the whole of Eastern Europe and the danger was primarily attributed to the adventurous use of force by the Soviet Union. At the same time, incompetent management led the East Europeans into a deep economic crisis with zero growth or even reccssion. The indebtedness of the East European countries vis-à-vis the West reached a degree which could not be settled in an atmosphere of political hostility. Last but not least, the Soviet Union lost its capacity for political leadership due to inertia and factionalism in the Politbureau and the age and sickness of the General Secretary. East European countries were confronted with a situation in which they no longer received unambiguous directives from Moscow on how to resolve their economic problems and maintain domestic stability, let alone being protected by the Soviet military and financial umbrella. For the first time since they came to power with Soviet assistance after World War II, the East European communists had to act on their own and at their own risk.

However, their new freedom of maneuver is not unlimited. In summer 1984 it became apparent that there is a threshold of Soviet tolerance: Honecker was not allowed to pay the visit to the Federal Republic he so often had announced. The "Group of Soviet Armed Forces in Germany" is still deployed in the GDR. The fact that its official denomination carries the notion of Germany and not that of GDR reminds the East German leaders of their inferior status.[4] But the Politbureau in Moscow has had to recognize that within the Warsaw Treaty Organization national interests are more and more diverging. There are also differences in ideological fervor. Some of the more pragmatic East European leaders tend to neglect the sacred class standpoint, while the Soviet leaders are keen to keep to this ideological prescription in order not to jeopardize the legitimacy of their rule and stability in their country. In addition, the long-concealed distrust of the Germans---this time of the communist German state within the Warsaw Pact--re-appeared.[5]

Since Mikhail Gorbachev took over, at least two elements of Soviet weakness have been eliminated: the immobility of the old leadership and the factionalism occasionally visible since the last years of Brezhnev. But important questions remain. Is the new Soviet leader really prepared to return to a policy of detente, and if so, would such a decision be matched by his American counterpart?

At this point some reflections on detente are indispensable.[6] For many in the West, the notion of detente has a negative connotation, which is easily understandable as there has never been agreement on what detente really means. Detente is not a value in itself, nor does it solve contradictions. One might rather say that detente makes political decision-makers relax, so that they do not tend to worst-case analyses and therefore do not overreact in political crises. In a state of psychological relaxation, if shared by public opinion, they might be in a position to engage in fair compromises with the other superpower, which otherwise are considered too risky. In this sense detente may facilitate reaching agreements on complicated issues such as international security.

It was in this state of relaxation that the Soviet leaders, after strengthening their European glacis by the occupation of Czechoslovakia in 1968, took up American and West German initiatives regarding compromises on the control of strategic weapons, on the situation in central Europe (including the complicated Berlin issue), and on a settlement in Vietnam. The peak of this policy, from their point of view, was reached with the Nixon-Brezhnev agreement on "strategic parity" in 1972. Soon afterwards, for a variety of reasons, tensions between East and West reappeared. This experience taught the world an important lesson: Detente is not a permanent state. It cannot be reached except in the rare coincidence of favorable predispositions on both sides and is therefore a very vulnerable and volatile phenomenon.

An indispensable precondition for detente is a feeling, on either side, that one is strong. Nothing is more harmful to detente than doubts in public opinion as to the toughness of one's own political leaders. On the other hand, the Soviet policy of excessive armament and exploiting opportunities in the Third World during the 1970s fatally hit detente. On the Western side, doubts in public opinion as to American strength have largely been overcome under President Reagan. Whether self-confidence in the Soviet Union can be restored by Gorbachev after the period of frail leadership and whether Soviet elites can be convinced that the Reagan administration really wants peace and can be trusted remains to be seen.

Gorbachev's Choices

The 27th Party Congress of the CPSU in February/March 1986 did not give clear signals about future Soviet foreign policy. Will Gorbachev give priority to bloc cohesion as a price for semi-autonomy of the East European states? What about the financial and technological strains which affect not only the Soviet Union but also all East European nations? Will Gorbachev proceed with pragmatism and a technocratic approach, which would mean that the East European governments are in a position to continue their *Westpolitik* in economic as well as in political respects? Or will Gorbachev tend to an unconditional seclusion of the Soviet bloc under Soviet hegemony and thereby re-introduce the method Stalin had applied in the late 1940s and the 1950s? Will Gorbachev pursue a confrontational policy which needs enormous resources for improving the correlation of forces vis-à-vis the West? Will the Soviet Union try to tighten control over the Germans and will it even resort to hitting the West German achilles heel, which is West Berlin? Will the generational gap between the relatively young Soviet leader and the older East European leaders play a role? Will personal antipathies between those leaders have an impact on Soviet-East European relations? Or, last but not least, will ambiguity and contradictory policies or counterproductive steps be continued?

Gorbachev's situation has to be seen in the context of world-wide or at least all-European developments. In many respects the post-war era of stability seems to have come to an end. The "results of Yalta"--whatever the true intention of the participating leaders and political changes in the late 1940s--are not accepted by all nations. Simply sticking to the status quo is no longer considered a matter of course. People begin to realize that what they had been accustomed to for the past four decades is not necessarily forever. Some ideas are re-emerging which had been popular before the nuclear age. In Eastern Europe as well as in the West intellectuals have begun discussing "the future of Yalta."[7] Such ideas imply dangers. Russian leaders more than anybody else are suspicious of people who are *novarum rerum cupidi*, as the ancient Romans would say. They rather try to keep what they have.

These factors might also affect Germany, which for so long has been one of the few stable regions in the world. In strategic terms the two Germanys are the center-pieces of their respective alliances. It is here where the prerogatives of the four victorious powers of World War II are still visible and it is in Germany where all of the four allies of World War II still have a similar interest in control. But the basis of this structure seems to be crumbling away. The Germans have ceased to be the political outcasts. The victorious rights of the four powers have become disputed and cannot be maintained indefinitely. Technological change diminishes the strategic importance of Germany and Central Europe in global politics. While the East-West antagonism in the late 1940s had superseded traditional national interests of the European nations, international developments now seem to tend in different directions.

Speculations about future possibilities are always questionable, but it might be worthwhile to look at the events of the early 1980s, when the GDR for the first time in its existence appeared as an individual actor on the East-West scene. This actor did not just play the part prescribed by the actor in Moscow. What were the driving forces in the GDR'S policy? What were the steps Honecker took on his own? To what extent did they deviate from Moscow's line and where did they lead him--back in the circle to the Moscow camp, to a crossroads or simply into a blind alley?

Bridge-building After Afghanistan and the Polish Threat

The more or less normal but not very substantial intercourse of the leaderships of the two German states which had been developed during the 1970s became complicated after the Soviet invasion of Afghanistan.[8] Federal Chancellor Helmut Schmidt was to visit Honecker in February or March 1980, but at the end of January, apparently as a reaction to pressure from Moscow, the invitation was canceled by Honecker. In mid-April, however, the GDR again took the initiative. Günter Mittag, East Germany's chief economist and a member of the Politbureau, for the first time took the opportunity of the Hanover Fair to see Helmut Schmidt in Bonn. Soon afterwards, at the funeral of Yugoslav President Josip Tito, Schmidt and Honecker met in Belgrade. Honecker made it plain afterwards that he and Schmidt had agreed to co-operate in order to maintain East-West communications in Europe. At the 12th plenary session of the Central Committee on May 22, Honecker referred to the "sacrifice" the GDR had to make in order to match the deployment of American missiles in West Germany, if the NATO decision of December 1979 was realized and negotiations failed. On the same day he met with Brezhnev on the Crimea, August 11, Honecker's representative in Bonn formally renewed his invitation to Schmidt for the end of the month. This time it was Schmidt who, in view of the developments in Poland one week before the planned event, had to withdraw.

This ended a sequence of events which had begun after Brezhnev on October 6, 1979 had tried in vain to prevent the NATO decision of December on the deployment of Pershing II and cruise missiles, to begin in late 1983 unless an agreement with the Soviet Union were reached on the mutual and balanced reduction of intermediate-range missiles.[9]   It is worthwhile mentioning that on December 4, 1979, Schmidt had announced his visit to Honecker, one day before the Party Congress of the SPD approved the social-liberal government line endorsing the forthcoming NATO decision. Honecker, on the other hand, announced Schmidt's visit and his own plan of a countervisit to West Germany on December 14--two days after the NATO decision. Thus, both sides chose a risky timing of their announcements. The Soviet invasion of Afghanistan and the American reaction forced the two German leaders to be more circumspect. At the end of January the mutual visits were canceled. However, both sides continued their efforts to maintain the East-West dialogue on a regional level after the Soviet leaders had interrupted all meaningful political talks with the United States.   As mentioned above, GDR Politbureau member Günter Mittag used the Hanover Fair in April 1980 to call on Helmut Schmidt in Bonn. Other European leaders joined these efforts. Thus, Poland's Edward Gierek arranged a meeting between Brezhnev and Giscard d'Estaing in Warsaw in May 1980. At the end of June, Schmidt even went to Moscow in order to persuade the Russians to resume the dialogue with the Carter administration. Although he received a Soviet commitment, in this final phase of the Carter administration effective results could not be reached.

The evolving crisis in Poland confronted the GDR with a new situation. Not only did Honecker have to react to Soviet apprehensions that they might lose their Western glacis, he was first of all concerned lest the Polish bacillus might infect the GDR. Hundreds of Polish workers were employed at the dockyards in Rostock. Would they behave like their colleagues in Gdansk and Szczecin? Would the East German workers join them, if they demanded the same rights the *Solidarnosc* fought for in Poland? Honecker acted very cautiously. On October 13, 1980 he publicly raised demands which he could be sure were unacceptable to the Federal Government,[10] but he avoided any confrontation and communication continued, if with lower profile.[11] At his regular meeting with Brezhnev on the Crimea, Honecker got Brezhnev's consent to continuing the dialogue with the West. At the same time he faced criticism within his own party leadership. The East Berlin party secretary and Politbureau member Konrad Naumann came out with a public demand for toughness vis-à-vis the tiny peace movement which had developed in some parts of the GDR.[12] Naumann was ousted from the Politbureau in November 1985.

In November 1981 Brezhnev paid his last visit to Bonn. The substance of the talks was minimal. Except for a new gas-pipe deal, which included deliveries to West Berlin,[13] no substantial results were achieved. But at least Brezhnev did not oppose Honecker's invitation to Schmidt and less than three weeks later Schmidt met with Honecker in the GDR. The atmosphere of the talks and of the official statements showed a remarkable improvement. For the first time Honecker agreed to the sentence that never again from German soil war should originate.[14] He spoke of "good-neighborly relations" with the Federal Republic and stressed that the achievements of past agreements should be maintained.[15]

Schmidt's visit ended in the small town of Güstrow on the day Jaruzelski in Poland proclaimed martial law. The town of Güstrow presented a ghostly picture. All streets were cleared of people except plain-clothes men. With respect to the situation in Poland, Honecker more than ever was concerned that people might rally around Schmidt as it happened in 1970 with Brandt in Erfurt. But the meeting produced some minor concessions by the GDR in exchange for financial cooperation by the Federal Republic, signaling the wish on both sides to continue a modest form of intra-German detente.

The proclamation of martial law in Poland on December 13, 1981 apparently softened apprehension in East Berlin. In Bonn the Socialist-liberal coalition of Schmidt and Genscher was faltering. When Honecker applied for a government guarantee for a credit by private West German banks, Schmidt was no longer strong enough to comply. Brezhnev's demise on November 10, 1982 made Honecker proceed cautiously.

From Funeral Diplomacy to Security Partnership

The sequence of deaths of political leaders in Yugoslavia (1980) and the Soviet Union (1982, 1984, 1985) produced a new kind of funeral diplomacy. Never before in the history of the Soviet Union were non-communist state and government officials invited as official guests for funerals. It is highly unlikely that Andropov deliberately introduced this new form. It was probably some sort of a routine consequence of Tito's funeral that when Brezhnev died, Western statesmen announced their attendance of the ceremonies in Moscow. This had the curious result that the most prominent Western representatives were received by Andropov for individual talks, while the communist allies, including Honecker, were not. However, the funeral in Moscow in November 1982 provided an opportunity for a meeting between Honecker and the president of the Federal Republic, Karl Carstens. At the Leipzig Fair in March 1983 Honecker talked of his planned visit to the Federal Republic and of the necessity to promote East-West understanding. He took up slogans of the West German peace movement such as "Secure peace with less weapons" ("Frieden schaffen mit weniger Waffen") instead of the former official GDR slogan "Secure peace against NATO weapons." He even used notions such as the social-democratic ones on "security partnership" and on the "common interest in securing peace."

A fatal incident on the transit road to Berlin and the highly emotional overreaction to it by parts of the West German public made Honecker in April 1983 cancel his visit in the Federal Republic. The GDR received, however, a credit of one billion Deutsche Marks from private banks which was guaranteed by the Federal Government in June. One week later on July 4 Chancellor Kohl visited the new General Secretary Andropov in Moscow. In autumn of that same year, the GDR again made some concessions regarding re-uniting separated families and the dismantling of killing machines on the intra-German frontier. Hinting at the forthcoming deployment of medium-range missiles in the Federal Republic, Honecker in a letter of October 5, 1983 addressed to Kohl demanded a "coalition of common sense" ("Koalition der Vernunft") and addressing the Central Committee on November 26 he spoke of the necessity to "limit the political damage" which was to be expected from the mutual deployments of the two (!) alliances.

On February 9, 1984 Yuri Andropov died. This provided the opportunity for a first meeting of Honecker and Kohl in Moscow. While Western media continued to speculate about a forthcoming visit of Honecker to the Federal Republic, Soviet propaganda in April opened a massive offensive against "West German revanchism." The Poles joined this campaign immediately before General Jaruzelski travelled to the Soviet Union in early May to secure Soviet economic assistance. But Honecker kept to his plan of visiting West Germany in spite of unprecedented Soviet reproaches, blaming him inter alia for jeopardizing the socialist system in the GDR by accepting West German credits.[16] In the meantime, influential West German conservatives raised questions about the issues the government could talk about with Honecker, to the effect that the government reduced the possible agenda to less prestigious issues such as environmental protection. The curious interplay between orthodox communists in Moscow and elsewhere and the conservative part of the parliamentary group of CDU/CSU in the Federal parliament in September 1984 made Honecker eventually cancel his plan. But he did so in very conciliatory terms in order to keep his options open.

It was not Honecker, however, who lost from this failure. It had always been regarded as conventional wisdom that the way towards international reputation in the West for the GDR had to be paved by Bonn. By 1984, this no longer held true. The emergence of the peace movement in the Federal Republic and Honecker's political overtures had raised distrust against the two German states in the West as well as in the East. One of the consequences of this development was that the Federal Republic's NATO allies loosened their restraint vis-à-vis the GDR. In summer 1984 there began a very vivid exchange of visits of high-ranking politicians between the GDR and NATO countries, including the United States. Thus, the GDR succeeded in taking a major step towards international reputation and for the first time it did so without the assistance or consent of the Federal Republic of Germany.

Continued *Westpolitik* and Soviet Reactions under Gorbachev

This notwithstanding, the Federal Republic remained the main political counterpart of the GDR in the West. In March 1985 at Chernenko's funeral, Honecker eagerly took the opportunity for a two-hour meeting with Chancellor Kohl. He did not mind that Chernenko's successor Gorbachev only "took notice" of Kohl's invitation to Bonn but did not accept it. In evident contradiction to Soviet propaganda, the East German party newspaper *Neues Deutschland* on February 28, 1985 mentioned that Chancellor Kohl had come out with the inviolability of frontiers in Europe, while Günter Mittag on April 18 again met with Kohl. On May 19, Horst Sindermann, the president of the Volkskammer (the parliament of the GDR), had to cancel his visit to Bonn which was planned for mid-June. On May 4 to 5 Honecker had been to Moscow, but he was shown the minimum of diplomatic politeness. In summer 1985 new economic agreements were reached between the two German states which resulted in concession by the GDR regarding the unauthorized transfer of fugitives from Sri Lanka to West Berlin.[17]

On June 21, 1985 the Soviet party newspaper *Pravda* published an article which did not mention the GDR in so many words but was highly critical of independent political and ideological attitudes of socialist countries.[18] In striking contrast to their normal practice, the GDR media did not reprint this article and did not even mention it. One week earlier the SED published a draft for an international agreement on a zone free of chemical weapons in Central Europe which it had negotiated in several rounds with the West German social-democratic opposition party SPD. In the West the SPD was severely criticized for this kind of unofficial foreign policy. The draft chemical weapons' agreement was precisely in line with Soviet propaganda proposals, although it contained provisions of verification which the Soviets formerly never had conceded. In any case, the SED could boast of having achieved a diplomatic success for the socialist camp by common endeavors with the SPD. It was highly indicative of Russian distrust of these intra-German communications that the Soviet press hardly mentioned the agreement and strictly avoided the notion of "common endeavors" of which the SED and the SPD were so proud.[19]

Other developments must have made the Soviets raise their eyebrows in September 1985. Within three days Honecker officially received the president of the West German SPD, Willy Brandt, on September 18 and a delegation of West German unionists on September 20. Each of these events was publicized on the first page of the official party newspaper, *Neues Deutschland*, with pictures extending across the front page. Never before there had been comparable publications on intra-German events before. *Pravda* published an article by Honecker, commemorating the October Revolution, which was full of pride about GDR achievements and of self-assertiveness. *Neues Deutschland* reprinted it only eleven days later.

Rumors about a forthcoming visit by Erich Honecker in Bonn resumed in early 1986. In February, Sindermann, accompanied by several Volkskammer members, visited Bonn at the invitation of the SPD parliamentary group. While the parliamentary group of CDU/CSU still rejects formal contacts with the Volkskammer, as this body is neither elected according to the rules of a Western democracy nor has any comparable responsibilities, Sindermann was received by the president of the Bundestag and other high officials, including Federal Chancellor Helmut Kohl. Although Sindermann nearly matched Gorbachev's skills in dealing with the Western media, it was difficult to establish what his visit meant to the prospects of the GDR *Westpolitik*.

It was noticed in Bonn that three weeks before Sindermann's arrival, *Pravda* carried an article on "The status of West Berlin."[20] The only reason given for this article was an alleged question of a Soviet reader. Whatever its intention the article clearly hinted at the victorious rights of the ant-Hitler coalition. It reminded the West Germans that "as West Berlin is a chain link of paramount importance nobody will succeed in knocking it out of the chain of European detente." While this was a signal from Moscow to Bonn that the Soviet leaders are aware of their option against the achilles heel of Germany's security, it also contained a message to East Berlin. It is still the Soviet Union that decides on the range of intra-German relations.

One week after the *Pravda* article, the GDR media published a decree on the control of Asian refugees travelling via the GDR to ask for asylum in the Federal Republic.[21] At first glance this looked like a favor to the Federal Republic. However, the decree made it plain that West Berlin, which is the only place really hit by the flood of emigres, is excluded from the regulation. It did also not escape the attention of West German observers that at the 27th Congress of the CPSU in February and March, Soviet relations with the Federal Republic or Western Europe were scarcely mentioned, while the civil rights of ethnic Germans in Kazakhstan, to which they were deported by

Stalin in World War II, were praised to the skies in order to defy Bonn's claims for human rights for these people.[22]

Foreign Developments Influencing Honecker's *Westpolitik*

Six phases may be discerned in GDR policy vis-à-vis the Federal Republic of Germany in the period between the Soviet intervention in Afghanistan in late 1979 and the end of 1986.

First: from January 1980 to autumn 1980. This was a phase in which Honecker and other East European leaders were struck by the fact that the dialogue between the two superpowers had broken down. All of them, Gierek in Poland, Kàdàr in Hungary, Honecker in East Berlin, Zhivkov in Sofia, Ceaucescu in Bucharest and even to some extent Husàk in Czechoslovakia engaged in some sort of bridge-building in order to keep alive a minimum of detente in Europe.

Second: from autumn 1980 to autumn 1981. In this phase it was feared that the developments in Poland would carry grave consequences for stability in the GDR. While this apprehension proved exaggerated, it caused Erich Honecker to keep a low profile in relations with the West. He was careful to insulate the GDR against possible influences from Poland and West Germany, but cautiously cooperated with West Germany's Helmut Schmidt in trying to encourage a resumption of the superpower dialogue.

Third: from end 1981 to spring 1984. After the proclamation of martial law in Poland, the immediate threat for the GDR was over, but the fear of war which gradually had been increasing in Europe since 1980 spread in the GDR and threatened the credibility of the leadership. This was no novel phenomenon in itself; there were other periods in East German history when the regime was even less accepted by the population. The novel phenomenon was a different one: The developments in Poland had shown that in view of its engagement in Afghanistan and the inertia of its leadership, the Soviet Union was no longer in a position to guarantee the stability of communist regimes.

Although it might be argued that in case of instability in the GDR, which is the center piece of their Western glacis, the Soviets would not hesitate to intervene by force, Honecker and his comrades could not take this for granted. In spite of the discouraging experience of Alexander Dubcek, he tried therefore to gain the loyalty of the majority of the East German citizens by actively promoting peace and good-neighborly relations with the Federal Republic of Germany. He tried at least to keep open his options, which were threatened by Soviet announcements that the deployment of the new American INF systems in Germany would put the Germans into a situation in which they could look at each other only across a "fence of missiles."[23] Honecker apparently did not share the optimism of some of the Soviet leaders, who seemed to believe that the peace campaign in West Germany would preclude the deployment.

Fourth: spring of 1984 until summer of 1986. It took some time, after the INF deployment in West Germany had begun and Chernenko had taken over in February 1984, until the Soviet leadership waged a bitter propaganda campaign against "West German revanchism and militarism." In view of their terrible economic situation after May 1984, the Poles had no choice but to join the Soviet propaganda for a year or so. On the diplomatic level and in cultural relations--though not in foreign trade--the Soviet Union in its official relations tried to bypass the government of the Federal Republic. Backed by the Hungarians, and to some extent after summer 1985 also by the Poles, Honecker somehow managed to escape the extreme consequences of this Soviet policy.

Fifth: July to October 1986. There was a short phase after Foreign Minister Hans Dietrich Genscher visited his Soviet counterpart in Moscow. Genscher apparently succeeded in convincing Shevardnadze of Bonn's intentions to restore as much as possible a policy of detente and to achieve meaningful agreements on the reduction of forces between East and West. As the Soviet leaders had realized that Helmut Kohl was very likely to lead the next Federal Government after the elections of January 25, 1987, they rested in kind of a waiting position. So did the GDR.

Sixth: after November 1986. In a delicate phase of West German-U.S. relations, Chancellor Kohl, before visiting President Reagan, in a Newsweek interview referred to both Soviet leader Gorbachev and the former Nazi propagandist Goebbels in one sentence. This was regarded by the Soviets as a grave insult against the Soviet Union and Gorbachev personally. Kohl also compared the summit of Reykjavik with Daladiev's and Chamberlain's appeasement policy in Munich 1938 and mentioned "concentration camps" in the GDR. All this provoked angry responses from the GDR, but, as nobody expected meaningful negotiations during the hot phase of the election campaign, it did not produce visible practical damage. Further developments will largely depend on U.S.-Soviet relations and Moscow's readiness--on a limited scale--to cooperate with the Federal Government in Bonn.

The Rationale of Honecker's Inter-German Policy

The reasons why Honecker engaged in the risky business of not strictly adhering to the Soviet line are manifold. There is first of all the wide-spread, if not clearly articulated, feeling in Europe that the post-Yalta situation is about to change. In the Soviet Union, political leaders have lost the overwhelming prestige they enjoyed in Eastern Europe for some 40 years in comparison with the weakness of the East European regimes. There is a marked generational gap between Gorbachev and nearly all of his East European colleagues. Gorbachev's heavy criticism has exposed the enormous socio-political and economic backwardness of the Soviet Union not only vis-à-vis the highly industrialized countries in the West but also vis-à-vis some of the East European states. With some observers in the West as well as in the East, these factors have provoked the idea that the time is ripe for the Germans to reappraise their situation. Feelings of that kind are indeed growing in both German states. But they cannot be attributed to Honecker and his SED colleagues. The well-experienced GDR leaders know that the Soviet Union will not loosen its grip on its part of Germany. Honecker has realized that his attempt to deprive the East Germans of their national identity has failed. So, he has allowed for a more open attitude towards German history. He is very cautious not to loosen the *Abgrenzung*, the separation of the two German states. When he ordered the dismantling of the automatic killing appliances on the intra-German frontier, which had been deployed in order to prevent people from escaping to West Germany, he tried to evade accusations of cruelty and the reproach of violating international law, but he made sure that the frontier will be as unsurmountable from East to West as ever.

Honecker abandoned the traditional practice of East European communist leaders to wait for directives from Moscow rather than to develop initiatives of their own. He began to argue about the political line of the alliance instead of just executing what had been ordered by the Soviets. He joined the view expressed most articulately by the Hungarians, according to which the smaller and medium states in Eastern Europe have to play a role of their own in East-West relations.[24] When the Soviet leaders stared at their superpower counterpart Honecker pleaded for a more sophisticated and diversified view. He did not share the opinion, which apparently still prevails in Moscow, that the Federal Republic of Germany is fully in line with the "aggressive" policy of the American administration and that the West Germans even instigate American hostility against the Russians in order to restore the German Empire of 1937. Unlike the Soviet propaganda, he did not exclude Bonn's wish to maintain peace in Europe.

The most striking change in Honecker's attitude, however, is his contribution to modifying ideology. The attitude of the Reagan administration vis-à-vis the Soviet Union had enhanced the re-emergence of the theory Zhdanov proclaimed in 1947 about the dichotomy between the two main forces in world politics, socialism and imperialism. Honecker and his advisers promote the overcoming of this sterile interpretation of Marxism-Leninism. While his demand for a "coalition of common sense" is spectacular, his view that endeavors to maintain peace are values which stand above the interests of classes and states is nothing short of sensational.[25]

It is no wonder that Honecker meets with strong opposition from the camp of the orthodox ideologues in Moscow, but as a well-trained communist and experienced political leader Honecker would not have dared such extravagances if he did not know that there are strong forces inside the Soviet Union sharing his views. Indeed, Andrei Gromyko, who used to be one of the young executives of Stalin's foreign policy, was stripped of his authority in international affairs. The same happened to two still more aged gentlemen who lost their seats as candidate members of the Politbureau at the 27th Party Congress, Boris Ponomarev and Vasily Kuznetsov. Gorbachev himself does not excel by ideological imagination, but it is hardly conceivable that the opposition of the hard-liners will easily be overcome.

Thus, Honecker is threatened by a dilemma: On the one hand he might be toppled by the Soviets if he exposes himself too much. In view of their engagement in Afghanistan and their trouble with the Poles this may be unlikely, but it is certainly not impossible. On the other hand Honecker faces the threat of domestic destabilization, as the populace is not ready to accept a Soviet line of total confrontation against the United States. As yet there are no forces visible in the GDR who might try to replace the aged Honecker by another leader, but unexpected developments cannot be totally excluded.

What are the implications for the West? Differences of political cultures and of national interest were always strong within the Atlantic alliance. It would be unrealistic to expect that the alliance will develop a coherent and permanent line vis-à-vis the Soviet Union and Eastern Europe. There will always be people defending the view that one should force the Soviets to their knees and thereby liberate the East European nations. On the other hand, particularly in the Federal Republic of Germany, a proclivity to a policy of detente can be expected to prevail, especially as this is the only way to secure the viability and security of West Berlin.

Notes

1. Peter H. Merkl, *German Foreign Policies, West and East: On the Threshold of a New European Era* (Santa Barbara, Calif./Oxford: Clilo Press, 1974); Philip Windsor, *Germany and the Management of Dètente* (New York/Washington 1971); Hans Siegfried Lamm and Siegfried Kupper, *DDR und Dritte Welt* (Munich 1976).

2. In March 1970, for the first time since the two German states had been established in 1949, Federal Chancellor Willy Brandt met with the East German Prime Minister Willi Stoph in the small town of Erfurt in the GDR. Although the exact time of the meeting had not been announced by the GDR authorities, tens of thousands of GDR citizen rallied in Erfurt and cheered "Willy, Willy." Western reporters easily found out that who they had in mind was not their Prime Minster Willi Stoph, but West Germany's Willy Brandt.

3. In 1952 the SED even received a secret message from Moscow ordering Ulbricht to prepare for the chance that Germany could be reunited and neutralized. Stalin ordered the SED to accept the possibility of playing the role of a loyal opposition in the unified German democratic state but, at the same time, to make provision of forming a clandestine party organization if the communists were outlawed.

4. Several times the GDR leadership tried to introduce the denomination of "Group of Soviet Armed Forces in the GDR" and was forced to recant. The most recent attempts were made in reports of 3, 4, and 13 April 1985. On 14 April the GDR media had to back down.

5. See Eberhard Schulz and Peter Danylow, *Bewegung in der deutschen Frage? Die ausländischen Besorgnisse über die Entwicklung in den beiden deutschen Staaten*, 2nd ed., (Bonn 1985).

6. See Josef Füllenbach and Eberhard Schulz, *Entspannung am Ende?* (Müchen 1980), p. 357 seq.

7. See Zbigniew Brzezinski, "The Future of Yalta," *Foreign Affairs*, vol. 63, Winter 1984, p. 279 seq.; Schulz, Danylow (fn. 4), p. 157 seq.

8. As to the effects of the Soviet occupation of Afghanistan on the freedom of maneuver of the socialist states in a historical context see Eberhard Schulz, "New Developments in Intra-bloc Relations in Historical Perspective," Karen Dawisha and Philip Hanson (eds.), *Soviet-East European Dilemmas: Coercion, Competition, and Consent* (London: Heinemann, 1981).

9. Brezhnev announced the readiness of the Soviet Union to reduce the number of their INF, unless NATO deployed new systems in Europe. He also announced the unilateral reduction of Soviet conventional forces within 12 months by 20,000 soldiers and 1,000 tanks. Besides that he urged some improvements of confidence-building measures in the CSCE framework. In view of his apparent tactical intentions, Brezhnev's move was not taken seriously by the West. Brezhnev's behavior had a striking similarity with the diplomatic maneuver Stalin took by his note to the three Western powers on 9 March 1952, offering the unification and neutralization of Germany in order to prevent the rearmament of West Germany by the Paris treaty which was to be signed in May. Whether Stalin in 1952 and Brezhnev in 1979, in spite of their tactical second thoughts, aimed honestly at a fair compromise with the West remains disputed.

10. Inter alia, Honecker demanded the recognition of GDR citizenship (which is in contradiction to the Basic Law, the provisional constitution, of the FRG providing for only one "German" citizenship for all Germans notwithstanding their residence in West or East), the renaming of the mutual permanent representations in East Berlin and Bonn to "embassies" (which contradicts the West German claim that the GDR must not be considered a "foreign" country) and a final agreement on the inter-German frontier on the Elbe river (which is beyond the competence of the Germans since it is part of the agreements of 1945 among the victorious Four Powers). While Honecker's aides tried to create the impression that meaningful negotiations are excluded unless these conditions were fulfilled, it was obvious that Honecker first of all needed a pretext for an interruption of the contacts.

11. A new GDR regulation drastically increasing the obligatory currency exchange for West German visitors to the GDR became effective of October 13. To large strata--especially of people in West Berlin--this raise was prohibitive. Even persons who just wish to call on a cemetery in the afternoon have to pay the full amount. At the same time East Berliners who regularly receive West Berlin's TV commercials expect their Western relatives to take along consumer goods which in the GDR are in short supply. All this renders visits in East Berlin very expensive. It was obvious that Honecker tried to kill two birds with one stone: On the one hand he aimed at reducing private Western contacts, on the other hand he hoped at least to maintain the level of revenue of hard Deutsch Marks by the obligatory exchange.

12. This was disclosed by a high-ranking GDR professor Herbert Meissner

who was caught in summer 1986 shoplifting in West Berlin. He later escaped into the GDR. The case was mysterious, but Meissner's story on Naumann sounded convincing.

13. The gas pipeline to West Berlin has a substantial impact on the viability of West Berlin. The construction is such that the line cannot be locked without interfering with gas deliveries to the Federal Republic by which West German credits for the pipes are being paid back and hard currency earned. How seriously the Soviet Union is interested in keeping to the deal became clear when the line was completed in 1985 at a time of high tensions between Moscow and Bonn.

14. This sentence is extremely surprising. Formerly the communists (in Moscow as well as in East Berlin) used to say that it is imperialism which is the source of war, and that West Germany is dangerous because--as opposed to the GDR--it did not eradicate nazism and militarism on its territory. Now Honecker put imperialist West and socialist East Germany on the same footing, neglecting the "class standpoint" and thereby committing a deadly ideological sin. No wonder the Soviet media sharply criticized this sentence.

15. Again, the Soviets wondered how Honecker could speak of "good neighborly relations" with a country which by the Soviet media was called "revanchist" and bellicose.

16. In negotiating this credit guarantee, the Bavarian Prime Minister Franz Josef Strauss, often described as a right-wing anti-communist diehard, was instrumental. It is noteworthy that the center-right coalition of Helmut Kohl was ready to provide the guarantee which his predecessor Helmut Schmidt dared not agree to.

17. The GDR authorities tried to conceal the nexus between the two events. On July 5 the FRG announced that the technical swing (an interest-free mutual credit which de facto could be used by the GDR as a long-term credit) in the bilateral trade was raised again to 850 million Deutschmarks. The swing had been reduced in 1983 to 600 million with a proviso that is was to completely expire by 1985 if no new agreement was reached. Then days later, on July 15, the GDR unilaterally announced that transfer to West Berlin via the GDR airport of Schönefeld would be denied to fugitives from Sri Lanka who did not have valid visas (as had been requested by the Federal Republic in order to maintain the viability of West Berlin). As Greater Berlin (in its prewar boundaries) is considered one legal entity by the Three Western Powers and by the Basic Law of the Federal Republic, control of persons crossing over from East Berlin ("capital of the GDR") is not

permitted in West Berlin. This is but one of the many peculiar features of the Berlin situation which make it easy for the Communists to destabilize West Berlin by all kinds of manipulations and which make the viability of West Berlin partly dependent on a minimum of good will from the Communist side.

18. O. Bladimirov on "The leading factor of the global revolutionary process." One of the main conclusions to be drawn from this article was that anything like equidistance in international relations is anathema for socialist countries.

19. In view of the strong Soviet antipathy for common endeavors of the East German Communists with Western social-democrats, SED officials of late have avoided the notion of a common initiative with the SPD when talking about the draft for an agreement on a zone void of chemical weapons in Central Europe. See e.g. Honecker's interview to U.S. News and World Report, 12 January 1987. For details of the Soviet-GDR dispute on this point see Eberhard Schulz, "Neue Nuancen in der sowjetischen Deutschland-Politik," *Deutschland Archiv*, 10/1986, p. 1064 seq.

20. Stanislav Zyubanov, "Status Zapadnogo Berlina," *Pravda*, 21 January 1986.

21. The dissimilarity to the way the case of fugitives from Sri Lanka was handled by the GDR authorities (see above, footnote 18) is striking. While in the former case the Federal Republic and West Berlin were taken together, this time West Berlin was excluded from the regulation.

22. Ethnic Germans in the Soviet Union are rarely mentioned by the GDR. While a great number of them expressed the wish to emigrate to West Germany, few chose emigration to the GDR.

23. Yuri Andropov used this term in his talk with Helmut Kohl in Moscow. See *Pravda*, 6 July 1983.

24. See e.g. Màtyàs Szürös, "Interaction of the National and the International in Hungarian Policy," *The New Hungarian Quarterly*, vol. xxv, no. 93, Spring 1984, p. 8 seq.

25. This idea was developed in a long series of speeches and articles up to a sentence by the director of the East Berlin Institute for International Politics and Economics of the GDR, Max Schmidt, saying: "The present situation enforces recognition of the fact that peace is to be considered the higher-ranking value even taking into account the antagonism of capitalism and socialism." "Neues Denken in Handeln umgestzt," *horizont*, 9/1986, p. 8.

5

SOVIET ECONOMIC POLICY TOWARDS EASTERN EUROPE

Keith Crane

Introduction

T he Soviet Union faces several dilemmas in choosing its policy goals for its relations with its East European allies. It wishes to retain political control over Eastern Europe, yet foster popular support for local regimes. It would like to use Eastern Europe as a security buffer and for military support, as an example pointing to the superiority of its ideology and politico-economic system, and for political support in international forums, yet it simultaneously wishes to maintain tight control.[1] It also faces the economic dilemma of wishing to increase its gains from trade with Eastern Europe, yet prevent further deterioration in the region's economic situation.

The primary source of Soviet influence in Eastern Europe has been military might, the ultimate guarantor that Eastern Europe will remain a Soviet security buffer, but that is an unwieldy instrument for pursuing other Soviet objectives. The traditional political and economic instruments of foreign policy have therefore dominated in recent years. Economic policies, exercised within bilateral relations and under the auspices of the Council for Mutual Economic Assistance (CMEA), have been an important mechanism for making Eastern Europe dependent on Soviet markets and Soviet sources of supply. These policies include trade agreements, credits, joint investment projects, target programs (a way of inducing specialization and thereby, it is hoped, increasing gains from trade), and a plethora of mechanisms for transferring technologies. They have been used to weave a tight web of economic dependence on the Soviet Union.

Unfortunately for the Soviets, these policies have been only partly successful. They have made Eastern Europe economically dependent on the Soviet Union. The Soviet Union is both the primary export market for all the

75

East European countries and the primary supplier of raw materials and energy, especially oil and gas. Yet these policies have failed to produce an alliance that is politically stable, economically dynamic, and militarily strong. The imposition of a Soviet type of system in Eastern Europe has resulted in economies that are slow to adapt to new conditions. Although these systems may have generated satisfactory growth in output, they function inefficiently: They use far more inputs (capital, labor, raw materials, and energy) to generate a unit of output than do Western, and even many Third World, economies. Unsatisfactory economic performance has led to domestic discontent and political instability, and has limited East European military expenditures. Consequently, although Eastern Europe is now closely tied to the Soviet economy, its value to the Soviet Union is much less than had Eastern Europe performed as well as Western Europe.

Not only have Soviet benefits from Eastern Europe probably been less than the Soviets had hoped, but the Soviet Union has paid a high price for these benefits in recent years. The East Europeans frequently state they are eager to engage in trade with the West on "mutually beneficial" terms. With the Soviet Union they seem to drop the adjective "mutually." The Soviets have given the East Europeans more favorable terms of trade than those prevailing on world markets. One estimate of the opportunity cost of this favorable treatment runs 110 billion 1984 dollars for 1970-1984, although this may be excessive.[2] The Soviets have also provided Eastern Europe with trade credits of roughly 14 billion rubles since the mid-1970s, during a period when resource constraints on the Soviet economy have been tightening because of slower rates of economic growth (Table 1).

Given the magnitude of these estimates, why have the Soviets treated Eastern Europe so generously over the past decade, and are they likely to continue to do so? If not, what are the implications for the countries of Eastern Europe of a reduction in assistance, and what policies can the leaderships adopt to cope? How can Soviet leaders resolve the dilemma of reducing Soviet assistance without exacerbating East European economic and political problems?

This chapter provides possible answers to these questions. It presents measures of the costs of current Soviet economic policies with regard to Eastern Europe and discusses the methodology used to compute them. This is followed by a discussion of why the Soviets have adopted their present economic policies toward Eastern Europe. The chapter then assesses Soviet economic policy options for dealing with Eastern Europe and their implications for the East European economies. It concludes with an analysis of three alternatives open to the East European governments for coping with potential Soviet policy changes: restructuring trade toward the Soviet Union, economic reform, and increasing investment.

The Costs of Soviet Foreign Economic
Policies Towards Eastern Europe

Like all countries, the Soviet Union engages in trade to improve its material well-being. Goods in which the Soviet Union has a comparative advantage, such as lumber and oil, are exchanged for goods it finds relatively more expensive to produce. Also, like most other countries, the Soviet Union uses economic policies to pursue noneconomic goals. Soviet officials claim that trade and economic cooperation "strengthen the material basis of detente" with Western countries and explicitly endorse the creation of what they see as politically useful "economic complementarities" between East and West. The Soviet Union also uses economic leverage to exert pressure on other countries. For example, the Soviets totally embargoed trade with Yugoslavia after falling out with Tito and halted economic aid to China after the ideological split with the Chinese leadership. They also provide grants and low-interest long-term loans to Vietnam and Cuba to foster allegiance to the Soviet Union.

The Soviet Union's economic relationship with Eastern Europe is more complex than with any other region of the world. The potential for using economic policies to pursue political or ideological goals is correspondingly greater. Although all these policies entail costs, those involving intra-CMEA terms of trade, bilateral trade balances, and joint investment in the Soviet Union seem to be among the largest or most readily quantifiable. Estimates of costs of policies in these three areas are assessed below and compared with other transfer payments to other areas of the world.

Trade Subsidies

The most noted estimates of the opportunity costs of Soviet ruble trade with Eastern Europe have been computed by Michael Marrese and Jan Vanous (Table 2).[3] They calculate these subsidies by computing dollar/ruble price ratios for Soviet ruble and hard currency exports and imports for six commodity groups: machinery, arms, raw materials, fuels, foodstuffs, and manufactured consumer goods. These ratios are derived by calculating implicit prices for Soviet exports to socialist and nonsocialist countries and taking the ratio to obtain an exchange rate for each commodity group. The same procedure is used for imports. Marrese and Vanous then use these ratios, or exchange rates, to convert trade flows to the CMEA into dollars. For example, Soviet energy exports are converted to dollars by means of the implicit exchange rate for fuels, and machinery exports are converted with a different rate for machinery. Soviet imports in dollars are then subtracted from exports in dollars to obtain a dollar trade balance. If ruble trade is in balance, this dollar balance equals the subsidy, the difference in the dollar value of ruble trade flows. If ruble trade is not balanced, the deficit or surplus has to be factored out of the equation before the subsidy is computed by converting the ruble trade deficit to dollars with the average dollar value of Soviet ruble imports. The dollar value of the deficit is then subtracted from the dollar trade balance; the difference equals the subsidy.[4]

Both Western and East European scholars have criticized these estimates for exaggerating the size of the subsidy.[5] Most of the disagreement centers on the dollar/ruble exchange rate ascribed to intra-CMEA trade in machinery which generates much of the subsidy.[6] A comparison by Dietz of changes in actual Soviet dollar terms of trade and the hypothetical terms of trade with Eastern Europe using Marrese-Vanous exchange rates shows that Soviet terms of trade with Eastern Europe would have improved much more than with the West if the Marrese-Vanous rates would have been used. Because Soviet exports to the West contain a much higher share of energy than to Eastern Europe, this result is implausible; even trading at world market prices, Soviet terms of trade with Eastern Europe should have improved less than they did with the West. Consequently, it appears that that the M-V estimates in Table 2 are significantly biased upward and should be considered a firm upper bound on the size of the implicit subsidy.

Trade Credits

The Soviet Union also incurs large opportunity costs when granting ruble loans. This subsidy is two-fold. First, nominal interest rates on ruble loans run about two and one half to three percent,[7] less than the Soviet discount rate (10 percent), the rate of increase in Soviet export prices to the CMEA (over 9 percent per year since 1980),[8] and market interest rates in the West. Thus, ruble loan recipients receive a large interest rate subsidy.

Second, because of intra-CMEA price ratios, East European countries enjoy a trade subsidy when they repay the loans. At world market prices the goods they use to repay the loans are worth substantially less than the goods they received on credit; the Soviet Union absorbs the difference.

For example, assume the Soviet Union has a trade surplus of 600 million rubles with East Germany (as it did in 1982), covered by a loan. The bulk of Soviet exports that constitute the surplus consist of goods that could easily be sold on world markets for hard currency (petroleum, iron ore, etc.). East Germany agrees to repay the Soviets for these exports in the future, but repayment will primarily consist of "soft" goods, low quality machinery for which the Soviet Union pays a higher relative price than if it purchased similar machinery from the West. The Soviet Union loses twice: once because it exchanges more valuable goods today for less valuable goods in the future, and once because the interest rate the East Germans pay on the loan is less than the rate of return the Soviets could obtain if they sold their exports to hard currency markets and deposited the proceeds in Western banks.

Table 3 contains estimates of the value of these subsidies for Eastern Europe between 1974 and the present. The estimates were calculated by converting estimated new ruble debt into 1984 dollars using the dollar/ruble conversion ratios for Soviet exports and dollar deflators in M-V.[9] Loans were assumed to be granted for a period of ten years at a three percent rate of interest.[10] Annual payments (interest and principal) on the loans were then converted into 1984 dollars using the dollar/ruble conversion ratios for Soviet imports and the deflators cited in M-V.[11] These payments were present-valued using a 3.2 percent discount factor[12] and then subtracted from the value of the original loan. The difference equals the credit subsidy.

Because these figures were calculated using the M-V exchange ratios, they suffer from the same upward bias as the M-V estimates. The estimates for Bulgaria, Czechoslovakia, and East Germany may also be biased, probably upward, because the debts of these countries were estimated from trade data. Czechoslovakia and East Germany have probably run surpluses in service trade with the Soviet Union because of transit charges on Soviet-West European trade. Nevertheless, rankings in terms of credit subsidies are probably correct, as is the conclusion that these subsidies have been large.

Other Potential Economic Foreign Policy Costs

Aside from providing its partners with favorable terms of trade and balance of payments loans, the Soviet Union also uses several other instruments in its economic foreign policy, many of which have been fashioned and are wielded under the umbrella of the CMEA. They include: specialization agreements, target programs, cooperation in planning, joint ventures, and agreements on sharing the results of scientific research and technological development.

Specialization agreements are nonbinding accords directing individual countries to specialize in particular products. Several hundred bilateral agreements have been signed within the CMEA; multilateral agreements numbered over one hundred in 1977.[13] They cover a large portion of machinery trade in the CMEA. These agreements are implemented at the discretion of the participating governments; they often merely formalize the existing pattern of trade.

Although all parties probably benefit from these agreements, an exact calculation of net gains is beyond the scope of this report. The agreements can generate economic losses, however, if a partner fails to uphold its side of the agreement. This has been especially costly for the smaller countries in the bloc, because they often rely completely on imports for particular commodities. For example, the Hungarians agreed to specialize in the production of large buses and the East Germans in small buses. The East Germans failed to fulfill their part of the bargain and Hungary was forced to renew production of uneconomical quantities of smaller buses.[14] The Soviet Union generally uses imports from Eastern Europe to supplement domestic production, so it is better insulated from these shortcomings.

The CMEA also sponsors target programs in which participating countries either coordinate or jointly initiate investments in an economic area of major joint concern. These investments have been concentrated in the Soviet Union and have been designed to provide raw materials to Eastern Europe. They also provide a mechanism for transferring capital in the CMEA. Capital is transferred physically, rather than financially. Contracts stipulate physical quantities of steel, manpower, and machinery to be provided by the Eastern Europeans and the amounts of raw materials the Soviets will ship in return. The East Europeans also often commit themselves to purchasing Western machinery, paid for in hard currency, for these projects.

These projects are expensive and entail a substantial investment commitment on the part of the East Europeans. The most famous and the largest of these projects has been the Orenberg Gas Pipeline with an estimated cost of almost $12 billion. Given the cost of these projects and the need for the Soviets to pressure their partners to participate, one wonders whether the East Europeans have been subsidizing Soviet economic development through these programs.

The answer in the case of the Orenberg pipeline appears to be No. Both the Soviet Union and Eastern Europe have benefited from the transaction; the Soviets obtained the capital necessary to develop gas reserves at a time when pressures on investment were increasing, and the East Europeans obtained annual rates of return of 19.5 to 31.5 percent, comparable to rates of return on similar projects in the West.[15] Nonetheless, few new projects have been undertaken since the Orenberg pipeline, in part because the East Europeans have found it so difficult to determine the payoff from the projects. The distribution of project costs and overruns is not determined ahead of time, and the prices of output are also ambiguous during the period of construction.[16] Moreover, investment has been squeezed in every country in the bloc, so leaders are reluctant to make commitments to large international projects when domestic producers are undergoing cuts.

The Soviets also push the East Europeans to cooperate in planning. Although both parties could conceivably benefit from more integrated investment policies, plan fulfillment has been mixed in all countries and CMEA suppliers tend to be unreliable, so leaders are reluctant to depend heavily on decisions made outside the country. Soviet success has been poor in this area, possibly because the costs of poor decisions would be borne disproportionately by the East Europeans, who are more dependent on sole sources of supply.

The CMEA also encourages transfers of technology between countries. The net beneficiaries of this policy are hard to determine. On the one hand, the less developed members of the bloc, such as Romania and Bulgaria, would benefit from designs and discoveries of the more advanced countries. On the other hand, these designs are supposed to be transferred free of charge, so the inventors have little incentive to make the transfers, and the less developed countries may be denied technologies they would have been willing to purchase were commercial licensing arrangements more widespread in the bloc. Possibly because of this bottleneck, in recent years more licenses have been sold on a commercial basis within the bloc, which has probably facilitated transfers of technologies.

There is little evidence to show that this policy leads to a one- way transfer of Soviet technology to Eastern Europe. In several areas (pharmaceuticals, robotics, computer peripherals, shipbuilding) Eastern Europe is as advanced as the Soviet Union, or more so. The benefits of scientific exchanges flow both ways.

Why Has the Soviet Union Been Subsidizing Eastern Europe?

This section examines a series of hypotheses explaining the Soviet Union's willingness to incur these costs. These hypotheses are in general found wanting. A better explanation for the subsidies, explored in the next section, appears to be Soviet preferences for the present CMEA trading system coupled with the desire to temper the cost of East European economic adjustment to higher energy prices.

Soviet Perceptions of the Size of the Subsidies

One possible explanation for Soviet willingness to absorb these large opportunity costs is that the Soviets and the East Europeans have not perceived a subsidy; therefore there has been little pressure to eliminate it. Dietz notes that the Soviets made no complaint about the costs of inferior terms of trade until 1979, and then again in 1981 during the Polish crisis.

Moreover, Soviet terms of trade with Eastern Europe have improved very rapidly since 1975 (Table 4), and in a manner consistent with the CMEA system of setting prices.[17] Although in real terms the East Europeans have not had to pay as much for oil as the rest of the world, they now ship almost 50 percent more goods to the Soviet Union for the same quantity of imports as in 1975. Bloc leaders may perceive transfers of wealth as having been from Eastern Europe to the Soviet Union, rather than in the reverse direction. However, the East Europeans have consistently pushed for increased deliveries of Soviet oil, even when reducing oil imports purchased for hard currency, indicating that they, and most probably the Soviets also, have been well aware of the differences between ruble and dollar prices for oil and the ensuing opportunity cost to the Soviets of oil exports to Eastern Europe.

The subsidy is, however, the result of the difference between relative prices for energy, especially oil, and machinery in CMEA trade and those on world markets, not differences in dollar/ruble prices for energy. Bloc leadership perceptions of high relative ruble prices for machinery are probably more mixed. Despite the acknowledgment by many East European manufacturers that the quality and servicing of their equipment are not at world market levels,[18] the extent of the difference is open to dispute. Naturally, East European exporters tend to believe their products are closer to Western quality and performance levels than would a more objective judge. Although the Soviet buyer may feel the gap is wider, in the absence of parallel production lines using Western machinery the Soviets cannot know what the difference is and have no way of measuring the subsidy. Even if a measure existed, the Soviets and the East Europeans would argue over its use. Thus the East Europeans probably do not perceive as large price differentials in machinery trade as M-V nor as large a subsidy.

The Polish, Hungarian and Romanian leaderships are aware that the cost of earning a ruble of foreign exchange is less than earning a dollar. In 1984, Hungarian exporters received 45 forints for each dollar of exports, and only 26 forints per ruble. In other words, the Hungarians valued the ruble at less than 60 percent of official Soviet rates; the ratio in Poland is similar.[19] These exchange rates, coupled with the oil price differential, indicate that although bloc leaders probably do not know the magnitude of Soviet opportunity costs in intra-CMEA trade, they are aware that such costs exist.

Price Differentials as a Payment for Sharing Risk

Another possible explanation for the differences between relative prices in the CMEA and world markets and the resulting opportunity costs is Soviet willingness to sign long-term contracts at fixed prices to offset price fluctuations. Long-term contracts are a standard feature of international trade. Exxon and Mobil have contracted with Saudi Arabia to purchase oil at fixed prices. The two parties trade potential short-run gains for long-run certainties. Thus when spot market prices fall below contract prices, Exxon is not subsidizing Saudi Arabia but is paying an opportunity cost for fixed prices and supplies.

In the CMEA, most trade is conducted under several such long-term contracts. In fact, the Soviet Union and its partners originally set up the CMEA pricing system during the Korean War commodity boom to safeguard against sudden changes in prices to spread this risk.

Soviet willingness to trade potential short-run gains from price fluctuations for stability is not surprising. Soviet planners prefer such a system because it provides them with the fixed quantities and commodity schedules they need to construct material balances. The Soviet government can also push for large joint projects in the CMEA more easily if it can assure East European governments that it will provide the needed raw materials in requisite quantities at a fixed price and will also purchase the output at a set price.

If this argument explains the subsidy, over the long run CMEA contract prices should fall somewhere in the middle of the range of spot prices, for if spot market prices are consistently above or below the contract price, one party always loses and therefore has no incentive to enter into the contract. I have attempted to test this hypothesis by comparing dollar/ruble price ratios as calculated by M-V with the dollar/ruble ratio that would prevail if intra-CMEA trade were conducted at spot market prices, i.e. the official exchange rate.[20] If the subsidy is really a price for risk-bearing, not a grant, the official exchange rate should bracket the M-V ratios over the long run.[21]

For the 1970-1983 period this hypothesis can be rejected for all commodity groups except raw materials and Soviet imports of energy.[22] Risk aversion could be used to explain trade prices in these commodity groups only; another rationale has to be sought to explain pricing for the other commodity groups.

Unconventional Gains From Trade

Marrese and Vanous argue that the Soviet Union provides *anticipated* (planned)[23] trade subsidies to Eastern Europe to secure the "allegiance" of the bloc. Furthermore, the Soviets set the level of per capita subsidies for each country in accordance with the level of allegiance the country provides. The Soviet and East European countries' leaderships have adopted this cumbersome way of transferring resources to disguise the transactions from their citizenry.[24] The Soviets wish to hide from their people transfers of wealth to the ungrateful East Europeans, and the East European elites want to cover the sale of national honor for a few barrels of oil.

Few would argue that one reason the Soviets set up and participate in the CMEA is to foster political control over Eastern Europe. Specialization programs, the construction of interlocking power grids and gas pipelines, and long-run trade agreements tie Eastern Europe to Soviet markets and Soviet sources of supply. The Soviets also use trade to favor selected countries. For example, Cuba receives very favorable prices for its sugar and pays concessionary prices for Soviet oil. Within the CMEA the Soviet Union appears to have rewarded Bulgaria by selling oil for rubles, some of which the Bulgarians then reexported to the West for dollars. Romania appears to have been penalized for its foreign policy independence, because it must pay world market prices in hard currency for Soviet oil.

This said, the M-V argument is unsatisfying. First, the magnitude of the subsidies is not an operational foreign policy instrument.[25] The Soviets can and do control the price and quantity of crude oil exports; political factors doubtless play a role in determining at least quantity levels.[26] The second side of the subsidy, the Soviet Union's willingness to purchase East European manufactures at prices that are higher than prices for Western goods, relative to the ruble price of oil, cannot be so easily ascribed to a conscious policy decision. Thousands of prices are set in machinery trade in sessions between Soviet and East European trade negotiators who use reference prices obtained from alternative Western suppliers, such as Siemens, the West German electrical and electronics concern, and MAN, the German truck manufacturer.[27] Unfortunately for the Soviets, these reference prices are for Western machinery, which tends to be more reliable, has better servicing, and often has higher operating rates than the East European products. Although Soviet negotiators may know this, it is extremely difficult to arrive at a "correct" quality discount, because they lack alternative base prices from which to bargain.

Although minor, cultural and systemic factors may also combine to increase machinery prices paid by the Soviets. Some East European negotiators reportedly take gifts of high-quality consumer items (wine, liquors, appliances, and clothes) with them to Moscow before negotiations begin. The Soviet negotiators are expected to reciprocate by accepting higher than warranted prices for East European exports.[28] Because Soviet trade negotiators work for the foreign trade organizations, not the factories that purchase the equipment, they suffer few, if any, repercussions if the purchased machinery is of lesser quality than promised. Given endemic excess demand for manufactured goods in the Soviet Union, Soviet factory managers would feel compelled to accept the imported goods rather than do without. The reverse situation, Soviet bribes to East European negotiators to pay higher prices for Soviet machinery, may also exist; but they would not be of such import, because machinery exports are proportionally smaller for the Soviets.

Why should the Soviet and East European leaderships go to such lengths to disguise the subsidy? Surely, the East European citizenry finds the Soviet military bases in Hungary, Czechoslovakia, the GDR, and Poland a far more blatant affront to sovereignty than the knowledge that they are receiving payments under the table for providing political support to the Soviets. Moreover, disguising the subsidy through concessionary pricing makes it nigh impossible for the Soviet and East European leaderships to know its size, especially as such a large share of the subsidy comes from machinery trade. How can a deal be made if neither side knows what it is getting in exchange?

Third, as Brada points out, M-V fail to define the supply curves and the composition of Soviet demand for "allegiance" in an operational manner.[29] They fail to explain how changes in Soviet perceptions of economic, political, and security concerns affect the size of the subsidy. Presumably the Soviets equalize the marginal benefits and marginal costs of "allegiance" across countries. A flatter supply curve for Bulgarian "allegiance" may explain why the Soviets purchase more from the Bulgarians than from the Romanians. It seems strange, however, that the Soviets failed to increase their expenditures on Polish allegiance more rapidly in 1980 and 1981 than in other, more stable countries such as the GDR or Czechoslovakia (Table 2), because the marginal cost of Polish unrest was doubtless very high. Without specifying the determinants of Soviet demand for "allegiance" in more detail, the model is not testable; we cannot predict how subsidy levels will respond to changes in the political and military environment.

Customs Union Effects

Holzman and Brada have argued that the differences in CMEA and world market terms of trade and the resulting subsidies are due to customs union effects.[30] They argue that the CMEA can be considered a customs union that promotes intragroup trade through administrative means (joint planning, a state monopoly on foreign trade, import permit schemes, etc.), rather than tariffs. Brada points out that according to the Hecksher-Ohlin theory of the determinants of international trade, relative prices within such a union may differ from those on the world market because of differences in factor endowments.[31] However, even countries that suffer from inferior terms of trade within the union may still find it economically advantageous to participate, because gains from trade due to increases in trade volume generated by the union may swamp the terms of trade losses.

This argument is buttressed by many of the characteristics of CMEA trade. Because energy has been fairly abundant within the CMEA and capital fairly scarce, the implicit prices Marrese and Vanous computed for machinery and oil are consistent with this theory. The union also appears to have generated substantial increases in intragroup trade. Trade with other members of the CMEA, especially Soviet trade, has expanded very rapidly since the union's formation in 1949. Moreover, countries that suffer the greatest terms of trade losses within the CMEA tend to trade most outside the union (Romania and the Soviet Union); those that benefit the most conduct the greatest share of their trade inside (Czechoslovakia, Bulgaria). These countries are behaving as predicted by the model.

If this hypothesis is true, the pattern of subsidies by country in the bloc should correspond to factor endowments. To test this hypothesis, I regressed per capita subsidies on capital/labor ratios, energy self-sufficiency, and the ratio of CMEA to world market oil prices.[32] I then used this equation to predict per capita subsidies for the CMEA Six.

Table 5 records the regression results. Based on the results of the regression, we may reject the hypothesis that the variation in subsidies is not due to customs union effects. The coefficients on the independent variables are of the right sign and are all significantly different from zero.

Table 5 also compares the sum of per capita subsidies by country between 1970 and 1982 with the sum of subsidies predicted by the model. Because of the poor quality of the capital data from these countries and the lack of confidence intervals for the M-V calculations, it is difficult to test whether these estimates are significantly different from the M-V calculations. Significant differences could stem from omitted variables (for example, a variable for endowments of agricultural land) or errors in measurement of the capital stock.

Of more import are the rank orderings. All the countries switch orderings, although none jumps rank. Tests indicated that the two series were at least correlated.[33]

The statistical evidence for this hypothesis is strong; leading to another question: Why do the Soviets participate in a trading system in which their terms of trade are so inferior to what they could get elsewhere? It is hard to believe that the gains to the Soviet Union from the increased volume of trade due to the creation of the CMEA surpass the opportunity costs of trading at CMEA relative prices, if the M-V subsidy estimates of 1/5 to 1/2 the value of Soviet exports to the region are to be believed. A much stronger argument is that the Soviets have a preference for trading with CMEA for security and political reasons. The next section examines this argument in detail.

East European Economic Problems
and the Soviet Union

Another Rationale for Subsidies

To answer why the Soviets are willing to incur these opportunity costs it is useful to analyze two separate Soviet policy decisions: (1) the decision to adopt the trading system used within the CMEA, and (2) specific decisions made by the Soviets and East Europeans on prices and quantities traded within this system.

Although the Soviet Union has suffered unfavorable terms of trade within the CMEA, it has important strategic, ideological, bureaucratic, and political stakes in the system. Soviet interest in using the CMEA to avoid both Soviet and East European economic dependence on the West is evident in both the 1984 CMEA summit conference communique "Statement on the Main Directions of Further Developing and Deepening the Economic, Scientific and Technical Cooperation of the CMEA Member-Countries" and in former Politburo member Grigorii Romanov's speech at the 1985 Hungarian Party Congress. The first document says:

> The planned development of the national economies of the CMEA member-countries and their mutual cooperation have made it possible in many fields...to counteract the aggressive course of the imperialist circles and the attempts of the U.S. and some of its allies to pursue a policy of economic pressure and discrimination.

Romanov's speech to the Hungarians contains the following warning:

> The strategic decisions it (the CMEA summit) took are of tremendous economic and political significance for each fraternal country and for the community as a whole...Political importance inasmuch as they lead to an improvement in the standard of collaboration and cooperation and to consolidation of our states' economic independence from the West.[34]

These statements show that the Soviets see the CMEA and the economic mechanisms used to integrate the community as strategically important because they prevent the West from dominating the bloc economically.

The Soviets also have an ideological stake in the CMEA. For example, the CMEA forms the socialist counterpart to the Common Market in Western Europe. The Soviets also point to the CMEA as proof of the superiority of planning over markets. Although the importance of ideology in

Soviet decisionmaking is open to question, it may be large enough to make the leadership willing to bear some costs to preserve the foreign trading system employed in the CMEA.

Csaba and Koeves both trace the pattern of intra-CMEA trade, which gives rise to the subsidies, to Soviet preferences, based on ideology, for the Stalinist development model.[35] Both the Soviet and East European leaderships interpreted economic development as the construction of heavy industry. In some cases, most notably Czechoslovakia, the Soviets pushed heavy industrial development harder than the local party leadership. Because the East Europeans lacked the raw material base on which to construct such industries, this strategy implied continuous large imports of Soviet raw materials and the present pattern of trade. In the 1950s and 1960s this ideological bias started a pattern of higher internal and external prices for manufactures, and shortages of raw materials through the neglect of investment in mining and agriculture. Koeves argues further that the present CMEA system has evolved in response to a bloc development policy based on growth through import substitution and central planning. Notwithstanding policy statements to the contrary, this policy has been pursued at the expense of "an active participation in the world economic division of labor,"[36] i.e., these countries have paid a high price in forgone efficiency because they were unable to exploit gains from trade.

Soviet planners also have a vested interest in the present trading system. Gosplan, the central Soviet economic control organ, has had a strong preference for material balancing. The present system of annual trade agreements negotiated under the auspices of the CMEA fits neatly into that system.

Finally, the Soviets use the CMEA to foster the integration of the East European economies with the Soviet Union. In other words, the CMEA is an economic tool for political control. Within the confines of the CMEA the Soviets are able to influence East European industrial development through long-term trading agreements. They also tie these countries to Soviet sources of supply through infrastructure investments and through trade and credit subsidies.

The Soviets have a great deal invested in the preservation of the CMEA trading system, and a great deal of the subsidies can be explained as a by-product of this system. Holzman's and Brada's argument that CMEA terms of trade differ from those on the world market because of different factor endowments is one logical outcome. So is the insistence on the use of world market prices as a base for intra-CMEA prices. These prices should minimize the costs of participating in the customs union. However, they also introduce a negotiating advantage for exporters of machinery, since West-East price comparisons are so much more difficult in this area.

Soviet preferences for the CMEA trading system do not, however, explain why the Soviets acquiesced to the continued use of the five-year moving average price system, which was so disadvantageous for them. Although the fall in world market prices of petroleum in the mid-1980s allowed the Soviets to partially recoup some of their previous losses, on balance the Soviets have lost from this arrangement. A plausible rationale for this policy decision is that the Soviets have tried to forestall domestic unrest in Eastern Europe, and the resulting military and economic costs of stamping it out, by gradually phasing in the costs to Eastern Europe of higher energy prices. Further, Soviet leaders found this cost tolerable because the rapid improvement in Soviet terms of trade with nonsocialist countries provided them with windfall gains, which lessened domestic economic pressures to increase oil prices to Eastern Europe to the same extent.

The Soviets are well aware that economic grievances have generally sparked political crises. The 1953 strikes in the GDR were set off by increases in work norms. The Hungarian revolution was spurred by the fall in living standards experienced under the Rakosi regime. The 1956, 1970, 1976, and 1980-1981 crises in Poland were set off by strikes in response to policies that workers feared would lead to a fall in the standard of living. The 1968 reforms in Czechoslovakia were in part a response to poor economic performance. The hypothesis that Soviet willingness to trade at disadvantageous terms with Eastern Europe stems from the desire to forestall political unrest is examined below.

East European Economies in the Early 1970s

The Soviet Union had little cause to subsidize Eastern Europe in the early 1970s. Economic growth in these countries was proceeding at a rapid rate; increases in national income surpassed those of the early 1960s in most of the bloc. Marer traces part of these increases to expanding trade within the CMEA.[37] For example, substantial increases in Soviet exports of petroleum contributed to the development of the petrochemical and motor vehicle industries, two of the most dynamic sectors in Eastern Europe at the time.

Marer also notes that Eastern Europe was given an economic boost in the 1970s through rapidly expanding trade with the West. Import-led growth was most noticeable in Poland and Romania; but even in orthodox Czechoslovakia, increases in the share of total trade conducted with the West coincided with accelerated economic growth.

Initially, expanded trade with the West helped to fuel large increases in investment in the region (Table 6). This investment drive not only expanded the capital stock but substantially improved its quality, because much of the new stock was composed of more productive Western machinery.[38]

Overt signs of Soviet economic assistance are minor in this period. All the countries of Eastern Europe recorded trade surpluses with the Soviets between 1970 and 1974. Moreover, in 1975 the Soviet Union broke the terms of the Bucharest accords[38] and raised the price of oil exports, indicating it thought the East Europeans could afford to pay higher prices for oil. Subsequently, the Soviets were able to reach an agreement with Eastern Europe to replace the old price setting system with a system whereby prices were adjusted annually according to a moving five-year average of the world market price. The new system, the Moscow formula, adopted in 1975, was much more favorable to the Soviets than the old Bucharest formula, although it continued to cushion the shock of the abrupt rise in the price of energy and raw materials in 1973-1974.

Economic Decline in the Late 1970s: The Road to Ruin

Eastern Europe continued to grow rapidly through 1977-1978, although some countries began to lose macroeconomic control. Trade accounts, both hard currency and ruble, were the first indicators of serious imbalances. The region had turned to international capital markets in a major way in the early 1970s, but initially loans had been designated for capital imports. Planners, especially in Poland and Romania, hoped that the new investments would generate high-quality manufactures that could be exported to pay off the debts. By 1975 the entire bloc had significant hard currency debts, but only Bulgaria showed signs of finding its debt burden becoming unmanageable.

Responding to deteriorating terms of trade with the Soviet Union and on world markets, borrowing accelerated following the 1974-1975 recession in the West. Initially, the Soviets were willing to forgo much of the increase in its terms of trade by advancing ruble trade credits. In the West, banks and governments were happy to fill hard currency current account gaps until 1980-1981.

Much of the new lending, dollar and ruble, was balance of payments loans[39] directed toward financing imports of agricultural goods and raw materials and components, not investments. For example, the large increases in Romanian debt in 1978-1980 stemmed from increasing imports of oil needed to fuel its newly constructed refineries.[40] Most new Polish loans went for agricultural products, raw materials, and debt service. Hungary and the GDR experienced similar patterns. As loans were redirected from investment to debt service and consumption, they provided less of a boost to growth.

Credit terms began to harden for the entire bloc in 1980, in part because of worries about Poland. Higher risk premiums on top of rapidly rising interest rates on international financial markets put great pressure on the hard currency balance of payments. When new credits began to dry up in 1981 and disappeared altogether in 1982, first Poland and then Romania requested a rescheduling. The GDR and Hungary reduced imports rapidly and frantically sought sources of funds to stave off a similar fate.

The hard currency credit squeeze coupled with an acceleration in the deterioration in terms of trade with the Soviet Union led to the 1981-1982 recession in Eastern Europe. With the exception of Poland, these countries had to rapidly increase the volume of exports to the Soviet Union to pay for diminishing imports of oil.[42] Simultaneously, hard currency imports were slashed to close the hard currency trade deficit; Poland and Romania cut them by half. Most of the countries adopted import curbs by default; banks and suppliers were no longer willing to provide import credits. Exports also declined in most countries (the GDR being the notable exception) but less rapidly than imports, so hard currency trade balances were forced into the black.

Stabilization

Import curbs worked. The credit crisis was over by 1984 for every country except Poland, although Hungary continues to be overborrowed.[43] Bulgarian and Hungarian hard currency export performance began to improve, but Polish and Romanian hard currency export levels in 1983 still lagged their previous peaks. The price for balance on the hard currency current account was a large fall in utilized national income, the goods and services consumed by a country. Declines in the standard of living in various years caused part of this reduction, but the brunt was borne by investment (Table 6). By and large, the East European governments traded future economic growth for external equilibrium and the preservation of the current standard of living.

Soviet Policies to Temper the Decline

The Soviets had good reason to be wary of the political consequences of economic decline in Eastern Europe. Throughout the bloc, dissident groups gained in strength after the signing of the Helsinki accords. More threatening was recurrent labor unrest. Major strikes broke out in Romania in the coal-mining region in the Jiu valley in 1977 and in Poland in Radom in 1976. The Romanians successfully quashed their strike. The Polish strike was followed by the rise of unofficial labor unions, which became the precursors of Solidarity. Strike demands concerning wages and working conditions were symptomatic of the widening differential between expectations and actual increases in living standards, as per capita consumption increases slowed to a crawl after the substantial rises in the first part of the decade.

Soviet foreign economic policies were structured to solve two difficult types of problems associated with Eastern Europe's economic decline: The first is to prevent the economic situation from deteriorating to where it would spark political challenges to local Communist rule; the second to manage crises when they develop.

Crisis Prevention

Many Soviet foreign economic policies during this period appear to have been designed to temper the costs of economic adjustment in Eastern Europe.[44] Soviet energy export policies are a case in point. The Soviets continued to adhere to the Moscow formula for setting oil prices despite the large price rises on the world market in 1979 and 1980.[45] Given the very favorable improvement in their terms of trade in Western markets, they seemed not to need to accelerate the improvement in terms of trade or CMEA markets. Apart from this passive policy, they also increased the quantity of oil exported to the bloc in the late 1970s, even as their extraction costs rose and world market prices were rising. The Soviets also used energy policies to support the hard currency balance of payments of favored countries. A large share of Bulgarian exports to the developed West have consisted of crude petroleum or refined oil products, over 60 percent in 1983.[46] In the late 1970s four-fifths of these exports were provided by the Soviet Union.[47] West German economists claim that East Germany was also able to use this device to generate hard currency;[48] over a quarter of East German hard currency exports have consisted of petroleum products in the 1980s. This is a very high ratio for a country that produces no oil of its own. Hungarian scholars also claim that Hungary reexported refined Soviet oil.[49] Other bloc members may have refined Soviet petroleum and exported these products in 1983 and 1984.[50] The Bulgarians were able to use this advantage to move from the position of the most heavily indebted member of the bloc in 1975 to a net hard currency creditor in 1984.[51]

Aside from small increases in oil exports in the late 1970s, the Soviets also encouraged the East Europeans to substitute gas for oil. The Orenberg gas pipeline, built under the auspices of the CMEA, has enabled the East Europeans to increase energy imports from the Soviets despite constraints on increased crude oil output in the Soviet Union.

Soviet acquiescence to large ruble trade deficits also appears to be a policy designed to soften the shock of deteriorating terms of trade. Between 1975 and 1982 Soviet terms of trade with Eastern Europe improved by 50 percent (Table 4). 1983 and 1984 saw further improvements. During the early 1980s, years when East European terms of trade deteriorated most rapidly and Eastern Europe suffered the greatest pressure on its hard currency balance of payments, the Soviets permitted the East Europeans to run up increasingly large ruble trade deficits (Table 7). In the late 1970s, Eastern Europe increased its borrowing from both the Soviet Union and the West; only in the early 1980s did Soviet lending rise as Western lending fell. The Soviet Union has also directly assisted East European countries with their hard currency balance of payments problems. Hungary has run hard currency trade surpluses with the Soviet Union since the early 1970s. Although this trade is mutually beneficial, the Soviets have simultaneously permitted Hungary to run deficits in bilateral ruble trade. The value to Bulgaria of reexports of Soviet oil for hard currency was noted above.

The Soviets have also not rushed to harden Eastern Europe's terms of trade. The Eastern Europeans have paid for the increasingly expensive Soviet oil primarily by expanding exports of machinery and other manufactured goods, not "hard" goods. The estimates of Marrese and Vanous indicate that these are precisely the goods on which the differential between world market and CMEA prices is now the greatest.

Crisis Management

The Soviet Union's most difficult problems with Eastern Europe have been periodic popular political challenges to the Communist regimes. The Soviets perceive these challenges as threatening Soviet security: militarily, because they could lead to the dismantling of the Warsaw Pact, the Soviets' Western security buffer; ideologically, because they challenge the thesis of the inevitability of the triumph of Marxist-Leninism; and politically, because they threaten Soviet domination of a bloc of countries.

The Soviets have resolved many of these conflicts through force, either through invasion or through the use of national police and troops. But the Soviets have also used economic policy instruments to stabilize the political situation.

Increased exports, especially of industrial inputs and consumer goods, and acceptance of lower return shipments have been important policy tools for stabilizing crises. For example, after the military takeover Polish leaders lauded the economic assistance the Soviets were providing to get the country back on its feet.[52] The Hungarians also made great mention of Soviet aid following the revolt in 1956.

Trade statistics buttress these assertions. Soviet trade surpluses with Hungary and Poland increased sharply in 1957, following the autumn upheavals in 1956. Surpluses also increased with Czechoslovakia in 1968, and

Poland in 1971, 1976, 1980, and 1981 (Table 8). In all these cases the Soviets increased exports to these countries and agreed to reduced imports. The Soviets have also provided infusions of hard currency to stabilize the economic situation. In 1981, although the umbrella did not go up, an edge was extended to Poland. Poland received substantial hard currency loans from CMEA banks and the Soviet Union, besides ruble trade credits.[53]

Trade subsidies as computed by Marrese and Vanous show no change between 1970 and 1971 or 1975 and 1976 for Poland. They did increase by $300 million between 1980 and 1981, but then declined rapidly, falling by $600 million in 1982, the year the Polish economy reached its nadir (Table 2). Subsidy calculations for Czechoslovakia also fell in real terms in 1969, following the 1968 crisis.[54] Thus implicit trade subsidies do not appear to have been used as economic policy instruments for defusing political crises.

Changes in the volume of Soviet oil exports appear to have been used in only a limited fashion for solving political crises in Eastern Europe. According to Teske, the Soviets agreed to boost crude oil shipments to Poland from 11 to 13 million tons annually in 1977-1980 after the Polish crisis of 1976.[55] However, in 1981 the volume of oil exports to Poland stagnated at the same level as 1980.[56] In 1982 Poland's oil imports were cut by only one percent rather than the 10 percent in Czechoslovakia, the GDR, and Hungary, but in 1983 they were cut an additional three percent.

The 10 percent reduction in oil exports to the other countries indicates limited Soviet willingness to use energy deliveries to bail out allies in crisis. Eastern Europe's hard currency balance of payment crisis peaked in 1982: Poland and Romania defaulted on their loans, and Hungary and East Germany escaped rescheduling by a whisker. Yet this is the year in which the Soviets reneged on their commitment to keep oil shipments level for the 1981-1985 five-year plan.

The Soviets also appear not to manipulate oil prices to bail out countries in distress. According to Vanous, prices paid by Poland for Soviet oil have not been reduced in years of unrest and have generally remained higher than those for Bulgaria, Czechoslovakia and the GDR.[57]

To sum up, the Soviet Union manipulates trade and credit flows to solve short-run crises in Eastern Europe. Its most important economic policy instrument for crisis management appears to be to allow the troubled country to let its trade balance deteriorate, both by increasing imports and decreasing exports. Implicit trade subsidies appear to have no role in solving short-run crises. Soviet willingness to accept less favorable terms of trade within the CMEA than in nonsocialist trade appears to stem from its desire to temper the effect of higher world market energy prices on the East European economies and thereby forestall unrest in the bloc. The differences in terms of trade within the CMEA and on the world market are not just a consequence of a Soviet decision to give Eastern Europe a break on energy prices. These differences also stem from a Soviet decision to adhere to the system of pricing and trade within the CMEA that the Soviets have preferred for political, military, and ideological reasons.

The Soviet Union and the Economic Future of Eastern Europe

Soviet Policy Goals in the 1980s

The Soviets' willingness to bear large opportunity costs in their economic relations with Eastern Europe appears to have worn thin. The conference communique of the 1984 CMEA summit meeting "Statement on the Main Directions of Further Developing and Deepening the Economic, Scientific and Technical Cooperation of the CMEA Member-Countries" listed several new goals for the CMEA. Of particular interest are those contained in the following paragraphs:

> In order to create economic conditions ensuring the carrying out and continuation of deliveries from the Soviet Union of a number of types of raw materials and energy sources to satisfy import requirements in amounts determined on the basis of coordination of plans and long-term accords, the interested CMEA member-countries, within the framework of agreed-upon economic policy, will gradually and consistently develop their structure of production and exports and carry out the necessary measures to this end in the field of capital investments, reconstruction and rationalization in their industries, with the aim of supplying the Soviet Union with products that it needs--in particular, foodstuffs, manufactured consumer goods, some types of building materials, and machinery and equipment that is of high quality and meets world technical standards. Mutually acceptable decisions on these questions will be worked out with consideration for the objective economic conditions of the USSR and the other CMEA member countries, as well as for the structure of these countries' production and mutual trade turnover.

This statement appears to have been written by Gosplan rather than the Soviet foreign policy establishment. The final document implicitly contains the following Soviet policy goals:

1. A reduction in East European trade deficits.[57]

2. Continued improvement in Soviet terms of trade, especially through deliveries of better quality goods for Soviet exports of raw materials.

3. Increased East European participation in the development of Soviet natural resources.[58]

4. Restructuring the East European economies so that they are better attuned to Soviet needs.

The Soviets have also put the East Europeans on notice that future supplies of raw materials and energy will depend on Soviet domestic demand and the availability of supplies.

Soviet Reasons for Wanting a Change

The Soviets' new emphasis on their own economic needs within the CMEA is probably a product of two factors. The first and most important is the Soviet economic slowdown that characterized the 1980s, caused in part by a decline in the rate of increase in capital and labor inputs, the primary sources of growth in the Soviet economy over the past several years. More worrisome from the Soviets' point of view has been a decline in factor productivity, which has been traced in part to transportation bottlenecks, especially problems with the railroads, the accelerated depletion of natural resources coupled with rapidly increasing costs of developing new deposits, and the concomitant shortages of raw materials.[59] These problems have been worsening and no easy solutions are in sight.

Changes in trade and credit policies toward Eastern Europe would mitigate these problems. Reductions in energy and raw materials deliveries, if coupled with unchanged deliveries to the West, would ease pressures on supplies in the Soviet Union and diminish demand for investment in the development of new deposits. Improvements in imported machinery from the bloc, which now account for a considerable share of Soviet machinery investment, could help reverse the decline in factor productivity.

The second potential factor is the lack of effectiveness of past Soviet policies. Eastern Europe has been a flawed asset in recent years.[60] Trade credits and favorable terms of trade have been rewarded with civil strife in Poland, greater foreign policy independence in Hungary and the GDR, and continued Romanian unwillingness to conform to the Soviet foreign policy line. Economic growth in the region has been slow, Poland has had to reschedule its debts with the Soviet Union as well as with the West, and the quality and technological levels of East European manufactured exports now lag those of the NICs. The Soviet Union may rightly be wondering what benefits past economic assistance have brought.

Soviet Potential for Achieving These Goals

The easiest Soviet goal to achieve will be closing transferable ruble trade deficits. With the exception of Poland and Hungary, the bloc has been running hard currency current account surpluses. Hard currency balance of payments problems are no longer a compelling argument for continued Soviet trade credits. The acquiescence of the East European citizenry to stagnating living standards has also weakened arguments for subsidies to forestall unrest. The Soviets may now believe that a crack of the whip does a far better job of controlling dissent than improvements in the standard of living. The slowdown in Soviet output growth, reductions in hard currency imports, and continued excess demand imply that Eastern Europe will continue to find Soviet markets for almost any goods they may export, so lack of demand will not be a constraint. Moreover, the Soviets appear to have no intention of increasing shipments to Eastern Europe, so balancing ruble trade appears feasible.

Further hardening of Soviet-East European terms of trade is unlikely, unless world market prices of oil rise. In 1985 at the official dollar/ruble exchange rate, Soviet oil export prices to Eastern Europe were roughly on a par with world market prices. In fact the recent decline in world market prices of oil lead to a period where Soviet prices were higher than world market prices at the official rate of exchange. As a result of declines in world market prices, Soviet prices have also been reduced, even if with a lag, which has lead to an improvement in East European terms of trade with the Soviets. Machinery prices continue to be relatively higher in CMEA trade than on the world market, but, as argued above, the way in which these prices are negotiated imparts an upward bias that will not be easy to eliminate. Moreover, at a time when the East Europeans are being pushed to balance their trade, it is difficult to imagine that Soviet trade negotiators would start to refuse East European export offers because of delivery or quality considerations.

The Soviets have also requested more food, building materials, and high quality manufactures than in the past. Increasing exports of these goods will be difficult, except possibly for food, because production is often costly and faces tight capacity constraints. This request could perhaps be fulfilled, but it would entail further cuts in domestic consumption or diversion of hard currency exports to the Soviet market.

The East Europeans have agreed to participate in the construction of a new natural gas pipeline, which will rival the Orenberg project in size. They are also involved in the construction of two nuclear power plants in the Ukraine, which will export electricity, and an iron ore processing plant at Krivoi Rog.[62] I am skeptical, however, that the East Europeans will agree to many more such investments in the Soviet Union. Domestic pressures for investment are far too strong. Over the past five years, as investment has fallen a backlog of investment needs has piled up. Machinery has become even more obsolete, and infrastructure bottlenecks in communications and transportation systems have tightened. Excess demand for housing remains endemic. Given the level of bureaucratic and popular pressures for domestic investment, as manifest in the increases in investment incorporated into the 1986-1990 five-year plans, and limited prospects for rapid growth, it is highly unlikely that Eastern Europe will invest much in the Soviet Union outside of projects to which the countries have already agreed.

The Soviet demand that Eastern Europe restructure its economy more in line with Soviet needs sounds like a bad joke. With the exception of Romania, Eastern European economic development has long been integrated with Soviet needs. Poland's shipbuilding industry, East Germany's oil equipment industry, the Hungarian bus industry, and Czechoslovakia's nuclear reactor industry are among the most important in these countries. They all export substantial percentages of their total output to the Soviet Union; in the case of Hungarian buses the share exceeds three quarters. They all face problems in marketing products produced in these industries in the West. The new Soviet demands really reflect dissatisfaction with the quality and variety of products produced from past East European attempts to satisfy Soviet demands.

The problem is then one of improving variety, quality, and delivery times rather than restructuring East European economies away from a hypothetical bent toward Western markets. Soviet prospects for succeeding in this endeavor are problematic. The same sluggish pace of technological change exists in such new industries as computers and robotics as plagued motor vehicles and machine tools in the past. The causes of Soviet dissatisfaction are systemic, not simply poor planning.

East European Policy Alternatives

Although the declines in ruble and hard currency terms of trade have moderated, energy shortages, hard currency debts, uncompleted investment projects, and low factor productivity continue to constrain economic growth in the region. As most of the economies emerge from recession, reductions in Soviet subsidies confront East European policymakers with some unpleasant choices. Three of the more important will be discussed below:

- Redirecting trade toward the Soviet Union.
- Reforming the economic system to improve factor productivity.
- Increasing investment to accelerate growth.

Redirecting Trade

One possible solution to declining levels of Soviet assistance is to redirect trade from the West to the Soviet Union and the rest of the CMEA. Theoretically, this could satisfy Soviet demands for better terms of trade and induce the Soviets to increase energy exports, thereby loosening this constraint on growth. It could also loosen the hard currency balance of payments constraint, if imports from the CMEA could substitute for hard currency imports.

This policy appears to be possible only in theory. Although the Poles and Czechs have stated that they are pursuing such a policy of redirecting trade from the West toward the CMEA, in practice the Eastern Europeans have tried to increase trade with the West as much as possible. Every country provides extra bonuses for managers of enterprises that increase hard currency exports or exceed hard currency export targets, and every country emphasizes increasing hard currency exports in annual plans.

Bloc trade patterns also fail to indicate a turn to the East. Exports to the Soviet Union have risen, but imports from the Soviet Union to the bloc have more or less stagnated. Bulgaria, the GDR, and Hungary have reduced their share of total trade conducted within the CMEA since 1979; the GDR has increased the share of its total exports going to the developed West by over nine percentage points during this period.[63] The share of Polish and Romanian imports originating in the CMEA has risen dramatically. But this change is primarily a consequence of balance of payments crises. Western suppliers simply stopped shipments and have yet to resume them on credit. Thus it appears the Poles have made a virtue of necessity by declaring that they want to rechannel trade toward the East; actual policies for reducing East European trade with the West have yet to be implemented.

These countries emphasize exporting to the West, because hard currency imports are vital for the operation of their economies. Agricultural products no longer take such a large share of hard currency imports. Raw materials, components, and semi-manufactures, necessary inputs for industrial production, now constitute the overwhelming share of these imports. As shown by the case of Poland and Romania, when these imports fall, output plummets. The GDR, Hungary, Poland, and Romania also have to export more to service their hard currency debts. The last three remain overborrowed in the sense that the pressure of servicing hard currency debt is a binding constraint on output growth.[64] The GDR's debt burden is somewhat more manageable, but it too faces balance of payments constraints. Hard currency debt service will necessitate increasing hard currency exports for the foreseeable future.

Another reason why the East Europeans are unlikely to deemphasize trade with the West is the realization that neither the Soviet Union nor the other members of the CMEA can provide the quality or level of sophistication of Western-made capital equipment, nor do they possess the requisite licenses or technical expertise. Without access to Western technologies, most of the technical elites believe that the productivity gap between East and West will widen. Although machinery imports have fallen, if investment is to rise once again, Western imports will play an important role, otherwise much of the new investment will be obsolescent upon installation.

Despite recent increases in Soviet oil production, long-term Soviet oil production appears to be headed down. Soviet exports of oil to Eastern Europe are likely to follow. The East Europeans have responded to past Soviet reductions in oil shipments by substituting Soviet gas, domestic sources of brown coal, and nuclear energy. As these alternatives are exhausted and world market prices have fallen, the East Europeans have made a few purchases of oil on the world market, indicating that imports of oil for hard currency may become a practical alternative for some countries, especially since hard currency balance of payments pressures have eased somewhat. This implies a greater, not lesser, emphasis on Western markets. For this reason, a turn to the East is unlikely.

A final reason for a continued emphasis on Western markets is the stimulus provided by Western competition. Hungary and the GDR especially see the ability to market in the West as a prerequisite for improving the competitiveness of their domestic industries. The very task of marketing in the West teaches their firms new management and production techniques that they hope will carry over into the domestic economy.

The Soviets may, however, apply pressure on Eastern Europe to reduce trade with the West. Soviet attitudes on trade between Eastern Europe and the West are ambiguous. On the one hand, the CMEA summit communique and the speech by Romanov cited above warn of the dangers of becoming overly dependent on the West. On the other hand, Soviet leaders continue to speak of the potential benefits from expanding East-West trade.[65] Even if the Soviets would prefer less trade, it is difficult to see how they would enforce such a policy when they are curbing exports of "hard" goods. Moreover, their emphasis on regional integration through plans rather than markets is unlikely to be any more successful in facilitating trade in intermediate goods, the most important East European imports from the West, than it has in the past.

Systemic Reform

Bornstein cautions that "reform" is used in two contexts in Eastern Europe.[66] The first he classifies as administrative decentralization: the devolution of decisionmaking power to lower levels of the economic hierarchy. The second is economic decentralization, which implies replacing administrative allocation of resources with allocation through markets in which independent enterprises respond to such indirect instruments as prices, tax rates, and subsidies. This definition is adopted in the discussion below.

Western scholars, probably more than the East Europeans, often tout economic reform as a solution to the low level of productivity and slow rate of adaptation seen in these countries. Observation of the Yugoslav and Hungarian reforms indicates that the process is more difficult and the economic side-effects more damaging than had generally been imagined by Western scholars. Nonetheless, half of the East European countries are currently attempting to reform their economic systems.

These countries see systemic reform as a means of accelerating factor productivity growth, improving hard currency export performance, and lowering energy consumption/output ratios. If Soviet subsidies are reduced, economic reform should also facilitate increasing ruble exports and adjusting to stagnating deliveries of energy and raw materials.

Past performance of reformed centrally planned economies gives some grounds for hope that economic decentralization will loosen the constraints on economic growth in these countries. Hungary has been the most efficient user of energy in the bloc. Poznanski argues that it has also been one of the most successful technological innovators. Hard currency export performance in Hungary and Yugoslavia has also been better than that of most other centrally planned economies, although hard currency debt problems have been as severe, or more so. Thus, successful reform could provide an answer to a decline in Soviet subsidies.

The Reformers

Bulgaria, Hungary, and Poland made considerable changes in their economic systems in the 1980s. They have concentrated on increasing the decisionmaking power of managers and providing incentives to increase profits, rather than concentrate on increasing output or sales. This new emphasis on lower level decisionmaking has necessitated revision of the price system. All three countries purport to link domestic prices of raw materials and other tradeables with world market prices. Interest rates are supposed to govern allocations of credit to some extent.

Another area of change has been the private sector. Some restrictions on private enterprise have been removed, and all three governments have stated their commitment to the continued existence of some private enterprise, which ostensibly provides entrepreneurs with a government commitment to regulatory stability.

Despite these changes, the prospects that reform will be successful are highly uncertain. Hungary and Poland have introduced far-reaching and fairly coherent changes. In Hungary the new measures, although sometimes inconsistent, are directed at the major flaws in the 1968 mechanism: the lack of competition on the domestic market and the "soft" budget constraint, ministerial willingness to finance poor investment decisions and loss-making operations. The Hungarians have tried to increase competition by breaking up large firms and trusts, encouraging firms to set up subsidiaries or subcontract out work to small cooperatives organized inside the firm. They have also encouraged private firms to enter markets by lessening tax burdens and permitting them to hire more employees than in the past. They have attempted to increase enterprise independence by replacing ministerial supervision of most firms with a workers' council, which elects the general manager. The banking system is also being decentralized, and the rudiments of a capital market are being constructed. These measures ought to "harden" the enterprise budget constraint and make managers more responsive to the world market.

The 1982 Polish reform outline contained some inconsistencies[67] but was far more coherent than the Bulgarian reform blueprint. Market forces were to have an important role in price formation, exports and imports were to be primarily regulated through the exchange rate, and enterprises were to make decisions on output and investments more or less independently from the center.

This reform provides the only plausible hope for Poland to resolve its hard currency balance of payments problems and improve living standards.[68] Proper implementation could lead to increased exports, more rational use of investment, and more efficient use of energy, thereby loosening many of the current constraints on economic growth. It would also permit Poland to weather the elimination of Soviet trade credits with little effect on the economy.

Unfortunately, the Poles have done a poor job of implementing the reform. Central allocation of resources has been preserved by "temporary" measures. Central control of enterprises continues through decisions on the allocation of inputs, special tax and subsidy dispensations, and the reemergence of associations, industrial organizations that allocated investments and inputs in the 1970s. Price controls have been reimposed in response to high rates of inflation, which can be traced to the creation of money to finance the national budget deficit. Budget deficits, in turn, are the result of the willingness of the authorities to provide open-ended subsidies to many industries and plants. Consequently, Polish enterprise managers operate in an environment of endemic excess demand, constantly shifting regulations, and inconsistent incentives. In this environment it is not surprising that the reform has shown such poor results.

In the fall of 1987 the Polish Parliament passed a new round of reform legislation including a reduction in the state bureaucracy and the creation of a two-tier banking system. These measures and official pronouncements indicate that the Polish leadership has made a renewed commitment to introducing the reform. However, given poor performance in implementing past reform measures, the successful introduction of the new measures remains highly uncertain. Poland's Western creditors and membership in the IMF may succeed in pushing the leadership toward more forceful implementation, but in its present guise, the economic reform will probably not loosen constraints on growth or soften the effect of the elimination of Soviet credits.

The outlook for the Bulgarian reform is bleak. The Bulgarians have introduced the most incoherent reform of the three countries. Compulsory plan targets continue to exist with incentives to maximize profits. This proviso was one of the crucial weaknesses in the Polish changes in the economic system introduced in the early 1970s, when managers were told to maximize value-added and fulfill plans. Because managers could not do both simultaneously, the hoped for improvements in efficiency did not materialize, especially as managers gave plan target fulfillment precedence over increases in value-added. Cost-plus pricing continues to be the favored mode for setting prices in Bulgaria; markets are explicitly rejected. Such a system provides the wrong signals to firms that produce exports or use imports and is unlikely to lead to improvements in factor productivity.

One plus for economic reform in Eastern Europe is the attitude of the new Soviet leadership. In the past the Soviets had an ambivalent position concerning economic reform in Eastern Europe. Romanov's speech at the Thirteenth Hungarian Party Congress contained the following statement:

> The Party performs all this work (intensification of production) making creative use of fundamental criteria of socialist economic activity like planned management, the consolidation of socialist ownership, and the priority of the social aims of economic development...

Although Romanov has since been relieved of his seat on the Politburo, these remarks probably reflect the preferences of others in the Soviet leadership who feel that central planning and state ownership are the hallmarks of a socialist system. An article in *Pravda* on June 21, 1985 took a hard line on economic reform, claiming that markets, private enterprise, and a smaller role for central planning destabilizes "the foundations of socialist economic management" and also leads to the "violation of social justice."[69]

However, now that the Soviet leadership has adopted its own reform package, the shoe is on the other foot. Hungarian and Polish leaders now have no fear that the Soviets will criticize or attempt to reverse proposals for systemic changes. In fact, leaders of countries which have abhorred reforms, Czechoslovakia and Romania, are now under pressure to improve their economic systems. Consequently, those East European leaders who wish to introduce more market-oriented measures no longer face external opposition to these moves, although internal resistance may still block major changes. Opposition to economic reform often appears to come more from domestic sources than from Moscow.[70]

Aside from the new support for economic reforms from the Soviet leadership, other Soviet policy concerns support the implementation of reforms. The Soviets are primarily concerned with stability in these countries, and, to a lesser degree, reducing the economic burden they impose on the Soviet Union. If the East European leaderships perceive systemic change as the only route to improved economic performance, and improved economic performance as the only safeguard of stability, the Soviets are likely to welcome reforms.

The Traditionalists

Romania and, to a lesser extent, Czechoslovakia have adhered to the Soviet model. In Romania none of the main features of the Soviet model have been tampered with. Enterprise managers continue to be evaluated according to output plan fulfillment. Investment and output decisions continue to be made at the association (centrala) or ministerial level. The exchange rate has little effect on export or import decisions. Relative prices differ from those on world markets. For example, energy prices remain far below world market levels despite IMF pressure for further increases.

Czechoslovakia has clung less tightly to the Soviet model. In 1980 a "Set of Measures," not an economic reform, was introduced to provide better signals and incentives for improving efficiency. These measures include closer links among domestic and foreign trade prices, bonuses for increasing hard currency exports, and enterprise profits. Wages were also to be more tightly linked to productivity. Plan targets continue to be set by the center and emphasize gross targets, although value-added has become a more important indicator. No move has been made toward market prices, and relative prices diverge from those on world markets.[71] However, after

Gorbachev's 1987 visit to Prague, Czech leaders have begun to speak of economic reform for the first time since 1968. The Czechs may join the reformers yet.

Given their adherence to the Soviet model, it is not surprising that neither country has been able to accelerate factor productivity growth. Increases in output in both countries appear to be predicated on increases in inputs. Surpluses in hard currency trade have been earned by reducing imports and curtailing domestic investment and consumption. Increases in hard currency exports have been won by reducing domestic consumption of raw materials, food, and energy, and exporting the surplus.

Past experience is probably a good guide to the future of these two countries. Improvements in the hard currency balance of payments, especially in Romania, imply that current account adjustment will probably not place a binding constraint on growth in the second half of the 1980s unless both governments persist in trying to repay their entire debt. Output increases will probably depend on increases in investment and the transfer of labor from agriculture to industry, not accelerated factor productivity growth. Because Czechoslovakia has reduced investment and can expect little growth in the industrial labor force, economic growth will be slow. Romania has been able to reduce consumption in the past to increase investment and has some reserves of labor in the countryside, so its prospects for growth are somewhat better. If, however, the Ceausescu government persists in attempting to liquidate Romania's hard currency debt without regard to the domestic costs of energy and food shortages, further declines in living standards and falls in output are likely. Neither country appears to be seeking a long-term solution to loosening past constraints on growth.

A reduction in Soviet subsidies and credits would have little effect on Romania, but could damage the Czech economy. Romania is not permitted to purchase Soviet oil except with hard goods, so it does not benefit from the preferential terms of trade granted to other members of the bloc. Czechoslovakia, however, has benefited handsomely from Soviet trade subsidies and has also received large ruble credits in recent years (Tables 2 and 7). Closing its ruble trade deficit has cost the country a tangible share of utilized national income.

The GDR--A CMEA Success Story?

In recent years the GDR has shown the best economic performance in the bloc. It has put its hard currency current account into surplus by rapidly increasing hard currency exports. It has also successfully reduced energy and input use per unit of output. Reported growth rates have been faster than those of the mid-1970s. It has not achieved these successes by adopting an economic reform along the lines of either the Hungarian or Yugoslav models. It has benefited from large hard currency payments by West Germany (approximately $1 billion annually) for transit privileges to West Berlin, payments for the release of political prisoners, and from an interest-free "swing" trade credit. But West German payments have been fairly constant over time; they fail to explain the dramatic turnaround on East Germany's hard currency trade balance.

East Germany's quick change from trade deficit to surplus in 1981-1982 was achieved by following Romanian policies. Imports were slashed and exports increased with little regard to cost. Some of the increases in exports in those years can be traced to destocking.[72] East European enterprises have far larger inventories of inputs than Western firms. Consequently, they can often continue production longer following a reduction in imports. In the case of the GDR some stocks of raw materials may actually have been reexported to raise cash. Dr. Jochen Bethkenhagen of the Deutsches Institut für Wirtschaftsforschung argues that reexports of Middle Eastern oil also played an important role in improving East German liquidity. In the early 1980s East Germany had the highest share (after Bulgaria and Romania) of raw materials and energy in its exports to the OECD in the bloc. Energy accounted for 30 percent of GDR exports to the OECD in the early 1980s.[73] To the extent that the GDR was able to purchase this oil with exports of manufactures, its trade performance improved, but some of these purchases may have been on credit.

Since the initial destocking, better inventory control, bonuses for reductions in materials and energy usage, and administrative curbs on consumption and investment probably account for the country's continued ability to run hard currency current account surpluses.

The GDR's improved hard currency balance of payments owes little to East German technology. East Germany's reputation for being the technological leader of the bloc is undeserved in terms of its hard currency export performance. The share of machinery (SITC 7) in East Germany's exports to the OECD actually declined from 15.7 percent in 1975 to 13.0 in 1981, while other members of the bloc succeeded in increasing the share in their exports.[74] Furthermore, the share of machinery in East Germany's exports to the OECD falls in the same range as other members of the bloc, except Romania's (which is lower), around 11 to 13.5 percent. East German unit values (a proxy for prices) of machinery exports (SITC 7) to the OECD have been the lowest in the bloc in recent years. Hungarian unit values are almost double; East German values even fail to exceed Bulgaria's.[75]

Dietz argues that some of East Germany's superior performance in economic growth can be traced to statistical changes. East German enterprises were merged into giant *kombinates* in the late 1970s and early

1980s. Simultaneously, net output replaced gross output as the most important plan target, and central planners stopped disaggregating plans below the *kombinate* level; the *kombinates* disaggregated plans themselves below this level. Central planners also gave the introduction of new products more emphasis. This combination of more new products, greater emphasis on net output, and the concentration of enterprises may have led to more hidden inflation in new product prices, as small modifications are made in products that are then released at higher prices, and enterprises are able to manipulate cost figures to increase reported value-added.

The extent to which these factors have inflated East German growth figures is an open question. Melzer argues that the changes mentioned above have led to more rapid real economic growth.[76] The emphasis on rewarding managers for reducing the use of materials and energy has led to reductions in per unit use. Melzer also argues that grouping enterprises in *kombinates* and giving *kombinates* the power to disaggregate plan targets among constituent enterprises improves allocative efficiency. *Kombinate* managers can reallocate inputs more efficiently than central planners because they have better access to information and shorter chains of command. Ministries also have better control because on the average they oversee 11 *kombinates* whereas previously they had to supervise tens of firms. These systemic features may permit the East Germans to continue to achieve improvements in efficiency, especially as hard currency balance of payments pressures have eased, permitting more imports of Western machinery and higher levels of investment.

East Germany appears to have weathered closing its trade deficit with the Soviet Union. Ruble trade surpluses may rise as the country pays off its ruble debt, but the resulting economic adjustments will probably be slight. More worrisome are long-term prospects for economic growth. As noted above, East Germany's hard currency export performance in machinery and other manufactures has been poor. The country does not have a comparative advantage in raw materials or energy. As long as it depends on raw materials and energy for much of its hard currency export earnings, it will probably be subject to recurring balance of payment crises, and economic growth will lie hostage to supplies of these goods for export.

Investment

Table 6 documents the severity of the investment cutbacks in Eastern Europe over the past several years. 1984 marked the first year in which Bulgaria, Czechoslovakia, Poland, and Romania increased investment. Declines in Hungary and the GDR moderated.

The East European leaderships may perceive increased investment, again, as a means of improving factor productivity and loosening energy supply constraints. After the reductions experienced in recent years, the number of projects with large potential returns has probably increased. Soviet demands for higher-quality manufactured goods and more competition in traditional hard currency export markets put pressure on these countries to increase investment by importing and installing new machinery that incorporates more efficient technologies.

Improvements in factor productivity and fuel consumption will have to be juxtaposed against a deterioration in the hard currency balance of payments. 1984 was the first year that the region, with the exception of Poland, felt hard currency balance of payments pressures ease significantly. Deterioration in the next few years would destroy much of the credibility on international financial markets that has been so painfully restored.

Increases in ruble exports will also curb the incipient investment boom. Countries that still run large ruble trade deficits with the Soviets are likely to face demands to pay off ruble debts before embarking on a full-scale investment boom.

Probably the tightest constraint on rapid increases in investment will be consumer demands for higher real incomes. Living standards have fallen or stagnated in most bloc countries during the past few years. In most cases the populace has peacefully, if complainingly, acquiesced to this state of affairs. If output begins to grow more rapidly, bloc leaderships, with the exception of Ceausescu, will probably feel compelled to increase incomes almost as fast as investment.

The worrying aspect of another investment boom is that with the possible exception of Hungary and Poland, none of the countries have implemented new methods by which to choose investment projects nor new instruments with which to keep the boom under control. Although neither Western nor Soviet bankers are likely to finance a boom of the duration of the last, Eastern Europe will probably soon find itself in the middle of another investment cycle.

Conclusions

Western scholars generally concur that Eastern Europe has benefited from large implicit trade subsidies, subsidized trade credits, and in at least one case hard currency loans from the Soviet Union during the past several years. Although the size of these subsidies is disputed, most scholars concur that they have totaled many billions of dollars. In that case, why have the Soviets acquiesced to such unfavorable terms of trade and why have they permitted CMEA countries to run persistent ruble trade deficits? And why have per capita subsidies differed from country to country?

After examining several hypotheses, I conclude that trade subsidies have been granted to ease the transition to higher relative energy prices in the CMEA. The incidence of these subsidies has been determined primarily by factor endowments within the CMEA and Soviet decisions on oil export volumes. Although the Soviets have included political factors in their calculus on oil export volumes, there is little evidence to indicate that the volume of implicit trade subsidies has been used as a policy instrument to extort political concessions. Trade credits appear to have been granted to soften the effect of higher energy prices as well, but the Soviets appear to have used them more often for immediate political objectives, especially to bolster states in political turmoil.

Slow economic growth in the Soviet Union, the very large opportunity costs currently incurred, and the limited effectiveness of these policies for curbing unrest may have contributed to a Soviet reassessment of its present economic relationship with Eastern Europe. Stagnating (and now declining) Soviet petroleum production coupled with falling world market prices of oil have also probably encouraged the Soviets to reassess past policies. A change in these policies appears to have been marked by the 1984 CMEA summit meeting, which concluded with a call for improved Soviet terms of trade, more East European investment in the Soviet Union, and a restructuring of East European economies to better serve the Soviet Union.

The probability that the Soviet Union will be able to achieve these goals is limited. Soviet statements at the CMEA summit may have been more a "wish list" than an operational policy change, for the political costs of forcing hard-pressed East European regimes to increase exports may exceed the economic benefits of reducing Soviet balance of payments loans. Moreover, although the Soviets can coerce the East Europeans into closing their ruble trade deficits and eventually repaying their ruble loans, they will face determined opposition to increasing investment in the Soviet Union. Improvements in Soviet terms of trade are also unlikely, unless the present system of determining prices in intra-CMEA trade is changed, an improbable eventuality.

If the Soviets force Eastern Europe to close the trade deficits, Eastern Europe will have to increase ruble exports, while economic growth continues to be constrained by declines or limits on imports of Soviet energy, hard currency debt service, small additions to present stocks of capital and labor, and low levels of factor productivity. Of the policy options available to the East European leaderships for accelerating economic growth in the face of Soviet reductions in subsidies, three stand out: (1) diverting trade from the West to the Soviet Union and the rest of the CMEA, (2) reforming the economic systems, and (3) embarking on another investment boom.

None of the three policies offers much promise. Difficulties in obtaining increased imports of intermediate goods from other countries in the CMEA coupled with continued large debt service payments on hard currency loans implies more, not less, East-West trade. Falling world market oil prices will also narrow the difference between the cost of imports of Soviet oil and Middle Eastern imports, making world markets more attractive to the East Europeans. Reform has great potential for improving productivity and export performance, but bloc leaderships have seemed incapable or unwilling to implement coherent reforms, except in the case of Hungary. This may be changing, however, with a renewed commitment on the part of the Polish leadership to implement its economic reform, and with Gorbachev's drive to reform the Soviet system itself. Present hard currency loans levels, the need to increase exports to the Soviet Union, and domestic demand for higher standards of living place sharp limits on Eastern Europe's ability to pursue growth through another investment boom. Slow growth and ad hoc measures to increase East-West trade appear to be the order of the day in the 1980s.

The long-run implications of this analysis are continued or increasing political unrest in the bloc. If living standards continue to stagnate or rise only slowly, popular discontent may increase. The probable response, at least as indicated by current practice in Czechoslovakia and Poland, will be greater reliance on the police. However, continued poor economic performance could provide a push to the Polish and Bulgarian reforms and an impetus for systemic change in Czechoslovakia after the replacement of the current leadership.[77] An expanded private sector and a more demand-oriented state and cooperative sector made possible by economic reforms could considerably improve the quality of life in these countries and provide a safety valve for popular discontent.

The Soviet dilemma is unlikely to go away. The Soviets may well succeed in reducing the economic costs of supporting Eastern Europe by pushing these countries to pay their ruble debts. Trade subsidies may also fall as the world market price of oil declines. But the Soviets show no signs of refusing to assist regimes with internal political problems. They will continue to incur large economic costs to preserve political control.

Present Soviet economic problems, its desire to reduce expenditures on Eastern Europe and Gorbachev's own reform program are providing a great deal of leeway in economic policymaking for East European leaders. The Soviets' own supply problems will prevent them from increasing exports to Eastern Europe or insisting on a decline in trade between Eastern Europe and the West. As long as they remain wedded to integration through plans, rather than markets, the increases in trade in intermediate goods needed to foster greater gains from trade in the CMEA are unlikely to be forthcoming, and the East Europeans will need to emphasize trade with the West if they wish to exploit these gains. Moreover, Gorbachev's own efforts at reform imply the Soviets are no longer likely to reimpose their own model on Eastern Europe. Thus the East European leaderships have some freedom to maneuver. Whether they take advantage of it is an open question.

APPENDIX

STATISTICAL TEST OF THE
CUSTOMS UNION HYPOTHESIS

To test the customs union hypothesis, I assumed that the CMEA is endowed with three primary factors: capital, labor, and energy. I then regressed per capita subsidies as calculated by Marrese and Vanous in 1984 dollars on measures of relative factor endowments: capital/labor ratios and the percentage of energy consumption produced domestically.[78] Because much of the increase in per capita "subsidies" in the 1970s was due to increases in differentials between CMEA and world market oil prices, the ratio between these two prices was also included in the equation. These measures were calculated for the CMEA Six (Bulgaria, Czechoslovakia, the German Democratic Republic, Hungary, Poland, and Romania). The results of the regression are given in Table 6.

Capital labor ratios were calculated by converting measures of productive capital[79] in constant prices[80] into dollars using purchasing power parity exchange rates constructed by Alton et al. These figures were then divided by total employment figures given in the statistical handbooks of the various countries. The capital stock figures for Romania and Bulgaria are probably biased upward; the exchange rates used are also questionable, but the resulting estimates are probably the best capital stock figures available.

CMEA and world market oil prices converted to rubles were taken from Dietz.[81] The percentages of energy consumption produced domestically were calculated from data in CIA and Vanous.[82]

Bibliography

Alton, Thad, Gregor Lazarcik, Elizabeth M. Bass, and Wassyl Znayenko, "East European Defense Expenditures, 1965-78," in Joint Economic Committee, *East European Economic Assessment*, Washington, D.C., 1981.

Bauer, Tamas, *Tervgazdasag, beruhazas, ciklusok,* Koezgaszdasagi es Jogi Koenykiado, Budapest, 1981.

Bauer, Tamas, and K. Attila Soos, "Inter-firm Relations and Technological Change in Eastern Europe--The Case of the Hungarian Motor Industry," *Acta Oeconomica*, 3-4, 1979, p. 285.

Bogomolov, Oleg, "Coordination of Economic Interests and Policy Under Socialism," *Kommunist*, No. 10, July 1985, pp. 82-93.

Boot, Pieter, "The German Democratic Republic Between East and West: The Margins of Socialist Dependencia," University of Amsterdam, Research Memorandum No. 8508, 1985.

Bornstein, Morris, *Plan and Market: Economic Reform in Eastern Europe*, Yale University Press, New Haven, 1973.

Brada, Josef, "Soviet Subsidization of Eastern Europe: The Primacy of Economics and Politics," *The Journal of Comparative Economics*, Vol. 9, No. 1, March 1985.

Brada, Josef, and John Michael Montias, "Industrial Policy in Eastern Europe: A Three Country Comparison," *The Journal of Comparative Economics*, Volume 8, No. 4, December, 1984, pp. 377-419.

Brown, Alan A., and Marton Tardos, "Transmission and Responses to Economic Disturbances in Hungary," in Egon Neuberger and Laura d'Andrea Tyson (eds.), *The Impact of International Economic Disturbances on the Soviet Union and Eastern Europe*, Pergamon Press, New York, 1980.

Brown, J. F., and A. Ross Johnson, *Challenges to Soviet Control in Eastern Europe*, The Rand Corporation, R-3189-AF, 1984.

Brus, Wlodimierz, "Economic Reforms as an Issue in Soviet-East European Relations," in Karen Dawisha and Philip Hanson (eds.), *Soviet-East European Dilemmas: Coercion, Competition, and Consent*, Holmes and Meier, London, 1981.

Bunce, Valerie, "The Empire Strikes Back: The Evolution of the Eastern bloc from a Soviet Asset to a Soviet Liability," *International Organization*, Winter 1985, p. 1.

Central Intelligence Agency, *Handbook of Economic Statistics*, Washington, D.C., various years.

Central Intelligence Agency, The Directorate of Intelligence, *The Cuban Economy: A Statistical Review*, June 1984.

Central Intelligence Agency, National Foreign Assessment Center, *Energy Supplies in Eastern Europe: A Statistical Compilation*, December 1979.

Childs, David, *The GDR: Moscow's German Ally*, George Allen and Unwin, London, 1983. bb Colitt, Leslie and David Buchan, "Oil Price Plunge Places East Europe in Economic Jeopardy", *Financial Times*, February 19, 1986.

Crane, Keith, *A Comparison of Foreign Trade Decision-Making in Poland and Hungary*, Ph.D. dissertation, Indiana University, 1983.

Crane, Keith, *The Creditworthiness of Eastern Europe in the 1980s*, The Rand Corporation, R-3201-USDP, January 1985.

Csaba, Laszlo, "Joint Investments and Mutual Advantages in the CMEA-- Retrospection and Prognosis," *Soviet Studies*, Vol. 37, No. 2, April 1985, pp. 227--247.

Dienes, Leslie, and Nikos Economou, "CMEA Energy Demand in the 1980s: A Sectoral Analysis," in *CMEA Energy 1980-1990*, NATO, Brussels, 1980, pp. 39-58.

Dietz, Raimund, "Advantages/Disadvantages in USSR Trade with Eastern Europe--The Aspect of Prices," The Vienna Institute of Comparative Economic Studies, Paper 97, August 1984.

Fallenbuchl, Zbigniew, "Poland's Economic Crisis," *Problems of Communism* (31) No. 2, March/April 1982, p. 1.

Fontenay, Patrick, *Hungary: An Economic Survey*, Occasional Paper No. 15, International Monetary Fund, Washington, D.C., December 1982.

Glowny Urzad Statystyczny, *Rocznik Statystyczny (RS)*, Glowny Urzad Statystyczny, Warsaw, various years.

-----, Rocznik Statystyczny Hardlu Zagranicznego (RSHZ), Glowny Urzad Statystyczny, Warsaw, various years.

Goldstein, Elizabeth, "Soviet Economic Assistance to Poland, 1981-82," in Joint Economic Committee of Congress, *Soviet Economy in the 1980s: Problems and Prospects, Part 2*, Washington, D.C., 1981, p. 567.

Gomulka, Stanislaw, and Jerzy Sylwestrowicz, "Import-Led Growth: Theory and Estimation," in Altman, Kyn and Wagner (eds.), *On the Measurement of Factor Productivity, Theoretical Problems and Empirical Results*, Gottinger Zurich, Vendenhoesch, Rupprecht, 1976.

Gustafson, Thane, "Soviet Oil Policy and Energy Politics, 1970-85," mimeo, 1985.

Hannigan, John B., and Carl H. McMillan, *East European Responses to the Energy Crisis*, Research Report 21, Institute of Soviet and East European Studies, Carleton University, Ottawa, October 1983.

Hannigan, John B., and Carl H. McMillan, "Joint Investment in Resource Development: Sectoral Approaches to Socialist Integration," Joint Economic Committee of Congress, *East European Economic*

Assessment, Part 2, Washington, D.C., 1981, p. 259.

Holzman, Franklyn D., *International Trade Under Communism*, Basic Books, New York, 1976.

Holzman, Franklyn D., "More on Soviet Bloc Discrimination," *Soviet Studies*, Vol. 17, No. 1, July 1965, pp. 44-65.

Holzman, Franklyn D., "Soviet Foreign Trade Pricing and the Question of Discrimination," *Review of Economics and Statistics*, Vol. 44, No. 2, May 1962, pp. 134-147.

Jackson, Marvin, "Romania's Foreign Debt Crisis: Its Causes and Consequences," Joint Economic Committee, U.S. Congress, *East European Economics in the 1980s*, Vol. 1, Washington, D.C., 1985.

Kemme, David, "Productivity Growth in Polish Industry," University of North Carolina-Greensboro, working paper, August 1984.

Kemme, David, and Keith Crane, "The Polish Economic Collapse: Contributing Factors and Economic Costs," *Journal of Comparative Economics*, No. 8, Spring 1984.

Koeves, Andras, "'Implicit Subsidies' and Some Issues of Economic Relations Within the CMEA," *Acta Oeconomica*, No. 31, 1983, pp. 125-136.

Kohler, Daniel, with Steve Salant, Don Henry, Keith Crane, and Mark Hopkins, *Economic Costs and Benefits of Subsidizing Western Credits to the East*, The Rand Corporation, R-3129-USDP, June 1984.

Lavigne, Marie, "The Evolution of CMEA Institutions and Policies and the Need for Structural Adjustment," October 1984, mimeo.

Levcik, Friedrich, "Czechoslovakia: Economic Performance in the Post-reform Period and Prospects for the 1980s," Joint Economic Committee of Congress, *East European Economic Assessment*, Part 1, Washington, D.C., 1980, p. 377.

Marer, Paul, "Economic Performance and Prospects in Eastern Europe: Analytic Summary and Interpretation of Findings," Joint Economic Committee of Congress, *East European Economic Assessment*, Part 2, Washington, D.C., 1981, p. 19.

Marer, Paul, "The Political Economy of Soviet Relations with Eastern Europe," in Sarah Meiklejohn Terry (ed.), *Soviet Policy in Eastern Europe*, Yale University Press, New Haven, 1984.

Marer, Paul, and John Michael Montias, *East European Integration and East-West Trade*, Indiana University Press, Bloomington, 1980.

Marrese, Michael, and Jan Vanous, *Soviet Subsidization of Trade with Eastern Europe*, Institute of International Studies, University of California, Berkeley, 1983.

Marrese, Michael, and Jan Vanous, "Soviet Trade Relations with Eastern Europe, 1970-1984," 1985, mimeo.

Melzer, Manfred, "The New Planning and Steering Mechanisms in the GDR-

-Between Pressure for Efficiency and Successes in Intensification Policy," The German Institute for Economic Research, Berlin, working paper, October 1985.

Mesa-Lago, Carmelo, *The Economy of Socialist Cuba: A Two-Decade Appraisal*, University of New Mexico Press, Albuquerque, 1981.

Ministerstvo Vneshnei Torgovli, *Vneshniaia Torgovlia SSSR: statisticheskii sbornik*, Finansy i Statistika, Moscow, various years.

National Bank of Hungary, *Quarterly Review*, Budapest, various issues.

Neuberger, Egon, and Laura d'Andrea Tyson (eds.), *The Impact of International Economic Disturbances on the Soviet Union and Eastern Europe*, Pergamon Press, New York, 1980.

Pecsi, Kalman, *The Future of Socialist Economic Integration*, M. E. Sharpe, Armonk, N.Y., 1981.

Poznanski, Kazimierz, *Technological Levels and World Trade: A Global View*, manuscript, n.d.

Reisch, Alfred, "Kàdàr Policies Get Seal of Approval from New Soviet Leadership," Radio Free Europe Background Reports, No. 195, 11 August 1983, p. 1.

Schroeder, Gertrude, "The Slowdown in Soviet Industry, 1976-1982," *Soviet Economy*, Vol. 1, January-March 1985, p. 42.

SEV, Sovet Ekonomicheskoi Vzaimopomoshchi, *Statisticheskii Ezgodnik Stran*, Finansi i Statistika, Moscow, various years.

Terry, Sarah Meiklejohn (ed.), *Soviet Policy in Eastern Europe*, Yale University Press, New Haven, 1984.

Teske, Gary R., "Poland's Trade with the Industrialized West," Joint Economic Committee of Congress, *East European Economic Assessment*, Part 1, Washington, D.C., 1980, p. 72.

Tyson, Laura, *Economic Adjustment in Eastern Europe*, The Rand Corporation, R-3146-AF, July 1984.

United Kingdom, *Soviet, East European and Western Development Aid 1976-82*, Foreign Policy Document No. 85, 1983.

Van Brabant, Jozef M., "The USSR and Socialist Economic Integration--A Comment," *Soviet Studies*, Vol. 36, No. 1, January 1984, p. 127.

Van Oudenaren, John, *The Soviet Union and Eastern Europe: Options for the 1980s and Beyond*, The Rand Corporation, R-3136-RF, March 1984.

Van Oudenaren, John, *The Urengoi Pipeline*, The Rand Corporation, R-3207-RC, December 1984, p. 8.

Vanous, Jan, "Bulgarian Economic Performance in 1984--Appreciable Upturn from Slow 1983," *Centrally Planned Economy Analysis*, Wharton Econometric Forecasting Associates, Vol. 5, No. 23-24, March 20, 1985a.

Vanous, Jan, "Bulgarian Foreign Trade Performance in 1984," *Centrally*

Planned Economy Analysis, Wharton Econometric Forecasting Associates, Vol. 5, No. 29-30, April 9, 1985b.

Vanous, Jan (ed.), "Developments in East European Energy Consumption, Production and Net Trade, 1979-1982," *Centrally Planned Economies Current Analysis*, Wharton Econometric Forecasting Associates, Vol. III, No. 40-41, June 3, 1983a.

Vanous, Jan, "Diverging Trends in CMEA Economies in 1984: Recovery in Eastern Europe and Downturn in the Soviet Union," *Centrally Planned Economy Analysis*, Wharton Econometric Forecasting Associates, Vol. 5, No. 25-26, March 27, 1985c.

Vanous, Jan, "East German Economic Performance in 1982 and During the First Half of 1983," *Centrally Planned Economy Analysis*, Wharton Econometric Forecasting Associates, Vol. 3, No. 62-63, August 12, 1983b.

Vanous, Jan, "Eastern European and Soviet Fuel Trade," Joint Economic Committee of Congress, *East European Economic Assessment*, Part 2, Washington, D.C., 1981, p. 541.

Vanous, Jan (ed.), "Recent Developments in Intra-CMEA Trade," *Centrally Planned Economies Current Analysis*, Wharton Econometric Forecasting Associates, Vol. III, No. 37, May 20, 1983c.

Vladimirov, O., "Questions of Theory: Leading Factor in the World to Revolutionary Process," *Pravda*, 21 June 1985, pp. 3, 4.

Whitesell, Robert, "The Influence of Central Planning on the Economic Slowdown in the Soviet Union and Eastern Europe: A Comparative Production Function Analysis," *Economica*, Vol. 52, No. 206, May 1985, pp. 235-244.

Wolf, Thomas A., "An Empirical Analysis of Stability, Price Discrimination, Bilateral Clearing and Aid in Soviet Trade with Developing Countries," *Soviet Economy*, Vol. 2, No. 4, December 1985.

Wolf, Thomas A., "On the Economic Costs and Benefits of the Soviet 'Extended Empire'," 14 December 1983, mimeo.

Wolf, Thomas A., "Soviet Trade with the Third World: A Quantitative Assessment," *Osteuropa Wirtschaft*, Vol. 30, No. 4, December 1985.

Zoeter, Joan, "Eastern Europe: The Hard Currency Debt," Joint Economic Committee, U.S. Congress, *East European Economic Assessment*, Vol. II, Washington, D.C., 1981.

Zwass, Adam, *Money, Banking, and Credit in the Soviet Union and Eastern Europe*, M.E. Sharpe, White Plains, N.Y., 1979.

Table 1

OUTSTANDING SOVIET RUBLE LOANS TO EASTERN EUROPE

(Millions of rubles)

Year	Bulgaria	Czecho-slovakia	GDR	Hungary	Poland	Romania	Total
1970	109.9	-385.2	1156.3	NA	585.1	NA	NA
1971	9.2	-371.8	1144.7	NA	517.6	NA	NA
1972	-93.2	-490.3	780.8	NA	427.5	NA	NA
1973	-186.4	-541.9	528.3	NA	247.5	NA	NA
1974	-133.5	-549.2	542.2	NA	112.5	NA	NA
1975	-5.1	-421.4	879.4	41.7	427.5	NA	NA
1976	82.8	-323.7	1318	222.7	495.0	NA	NA
1977	246.9	-80.2	1912.9	603.1	540.1	138.7	3361.5
1978	393.9	-136.8	2183.7	806.4	652.6	141.1	4040.8
1979	532.9	42.7	2483.2	993.6	832.6	258.6	5143.5
1980	754.2	154.9	3030	1397.5	1575.2	389.6	7301.3
1981	1431.8	432.4	3401.5	1641.7	3125.0	536.5	10569.0
1982	2028.3	748	4044.9	1909.3	3747.1	282.2	12759.7
1983	2485.8	1199.2	4247	2376.1	3850.0	266.0	14424.1
1984	3002.2	1773.5	4361.2	2481.2	4800.0	NA	NA
1985	3401.7	1971.3	4439.4	2239.0	5600.0	NA	NA
1986	3998.2	2361.9	5195.5	1959.0	6500.0	NA	NA

Sources: Bulgarian, Czechoslovakian and East German Debt--Cumulative trade deficits with the Soviet Union (*Vneshniaia Torgovlia SSSR: statisticheskii sbornik*, various years).

Hungary--Fontenay, 1982, p. 57, and *Quarterly Review*, National Bank of Hungary, various issues.

Poland--"Bilans platniczy Polski w latach 1971-1981," *Finanse*, June 1982, p. 57; and *Rocznik Statystyczny*, 1984.

Romania--*Economic Memorandum*, Romanian government

Notes: (a)First three quarters of 1984 only.

Table 2

MARRESE-VANOUS ESTIMATES OF SOVIET TRADE SUBSIDIES TO EASTERN EUROPE
(millions of 1984 dollars)

	Bulgaria	Czecho-slovakia	GDR	Hungary	Poland	Romania	CMEA Six
1970	-9	541	1165	264	454	176	2589
1971	-26	606	1108	261	448	102	2499
1972	-110	380	959	114	367	70	1780
1973	250	592	1284	351	566	28	3071
1974	1352	1669	2673	1090	1340	59	8183
1975	1030	1361	1820	649	1341	12	6213
1976	1008	1605	2223	672	1350	82	6941
1977	1022	1634	2300	542	1307	96	6901
1978	1185	1494	2099	598	946	154	6475
1979	1655	1915	2605	989	1705	169	9037
1980	2700	3399	3958	1654	2974	303	14987
1981	2782	3534	4059	1653	3234	289	15552
1982	2324	2917	3455	1524	2611	277	13107
1983	1658	2374	2677	1115	2019	322	10165
1984	1744	2425	2758	1246	2148	379	10700

Source: Marrese, Michael, and Jan Vanous, "Soviet Trade Relations with Eastern Europe, 1970-1984," 1985, mimeo.

Table 3

SOVIET SUBSIDIES ON EAST
EUROPEAN RUBLE DEBTS[*]

(Millions of 1984 dollars)

Year	Total Subsidy	Bulgaria	Czecho- slovakia	GDR	Hungary	Poland	Romania
1975	970	140	130	350	40	310	0
1976	1000	110	120	500	190	90	0
1977	1370	190	260	670	180	70	0
1978	980	170	0	380	220	130	2
1979	1410	190	210	460	230	210	110
1980	2280	340	210	880	550	750	160
1981	2990	750	350	650	360	1710	160
1982	2940	690	380	880	380	800	-180
1983	1790	450	380	420	420	310	0
Total	17420	3020	2020	5270	2570	4380	260

[*]Discount rate--10%, Interest rate--3%, Loan length--10 years, no grace period, deflator--implicit Soviet trade deflators from *Vneshniaia Torgovlia SSSR*, various years.

Table 4

SOVIET OIL EXPORT PRICES AND TERMS OF TRADE

(per metric ton)

Year	Soviet Oil Prices		Soviet Terms of Trade		Ratio of (3) to (4)
	CMEA (Transferable Rubles)	World Market	with the CMEA	with the West	
	(1)	(2)	(3)	(4)	
1970	15.3	11.9	100.0	100.0	1.00
1971	15.4	15.5	100.6	112.5	.89
1972	15.7	17.7	100.1	83.7	1.20
1973	16.0	21.1	100.8	96.4	1.05
1974	18.1	60.7	101.0	120.1	.84
1975	33.8	63.5	106.6	129.9	.82
1976	37.1	70.2	110.2	145.2	.76
1977	46.9	73.7	114.9	154.6	.74
1978	55.9	68.9	118.0	159.8	.74
1979	63.6	93.4	120.5	209.0	.58
1980	74.7	159.7	122.2	244.6	.50
1981	95.0	192.5	133.5	250.2	.53
1982	117.4	179.4	148.3	NA	NA
1983	138.8	159.5	NA	NA	NA

Source: CMEA Oil Price 1970-1971--Calculated from *Vneshniaia Torgovlia SSSR: statisticheskii sbornik*, 1971. World Market Price 1970-1971--Vanous, 1981, p.554. All other data--Dietz, 1984, Tables 1 and 6.

Table 5
FACTOR ENDOWMENTS AS A PREDICTOR OF TRADE SUBSIDIES

	Bulgaria	Czecho-slovakia	GDR	Hungary	Poland	Romania
Per Capita Ranking						
Actual	2	3	1	4	5	6
Predicted	1	4	2	3	6	5
Cumulative Per Capita Amounts--1970-1982						
M-V Estimates	1710	1440	1770	980	530	80
Predicted	1570	1300	1550	1340	220	530

Regression Equation

$$\text{Per Capita Subsidy} = -92.21 + 68.1 \times KL - 138.23 \times E + 40.2 \times OP$$
$$(-2.85) \quad (2.78) \quad (-5.0) \quad (3.63)$$

where KL is the capital/labor ratio, E is the percentage of energy consumed produced domestically, and OP is the ratio between CMEA and world market oil prices in rubles. Figures in parentheses are T statistics. The number of observations was 78. The F statistic was 16.7 which was significant with a probability of over one in 10,000. Source information is in the Appendix (p. 112).

Table 6
INCREASES IN INVESTMENT, NMP AND UNI
IN EASTERN EUROPE
(In percent)

Year	Bulgaria	Czecho-slovakia	GDR	Hungary	Poland	Romania
Net Material Product						
1971-75[a]	7.8	5.7	5.4	6.2	9.8	11.2
1976-80[a]	6.1	3.7	4.1	3.2	1.2	7.3
1981	5.0	-0.1	4.8	2.5	-12.0	2.2
1982	4.2	0.2	2.6	2.6	-5.5	2.7
1983	3.0	2.4	4.4	0.3	6.0	3.4
1984	4.6	3.6	5.5	2.5	5.6	5.9
1985	1.8	3.0	5.0	-1.4	3.4	7.7
Utilized National Income						
1971-75[a]	8.6	6.1	4.7	5.6	11.6	n.a.
1976-80[a]	2.8	2.2	3.6	1.9	-0.2	6.9
1981	7.7	-3.4	1.3	0.7	-10.5	-5.7
1982	1.9	-1.6	-3.4	-1.1	-10.5	2.2
1983	1.2	0.7	0.3	-2.7	5.4	0.7
1984	5.2	1.2	3.0	-0.6	5.0	3.4
1985	2.3	3.2	4.0	-0.6	3.8	n.a.
Net Investment						
(Accumulation Fund)						
1971-75[a]	12.9	8.4	2.9	8.1	18.1	n.a
1976-80[a]	0.1	1.4	3.0	-2.0	-11.8	6.6
1981	14.8	21.7	-3.4	-8.6	-27.6	-22.1
1982	-3.3	-3.6	-19.9	-12.4	-6.6	-4.3
1983	-3.6	-7.2	-1.9	-20.4	4.9	2.0
1984	0.3	-6.6	-4.9	11.3	6.1	11.4
1985	8.6	5.8	3.7	-15.0	1.6	6.0

SOURCES: 1971-83: National Statistical Yearbooks (for all countries except Romania) and unpublished official Romanian statistics as reported in *WEFA*, Vol. 5, No. 25-26, March 27, 1985.
1984-85--National Statistical Yearbooks
[a]Average annual rate of growth.

Table 7
SOVIET TRADE SURPLUSES
WITH EASTERN EUROPE
(Millions of rubles)

Year	Bulgaria	Czecho-slovakia	GDR	Hungary	Poland	Romania
1970	-128.5	-27.8	181.2	36.7	80.0	-29.4
1971	-100.7	13.4	-11.6	101.0	54.9	-82.5
1972	-102.4	-118.5	-363.9	-74.5	-188.9	-112.1
1973	-93.2	-51.6	-252.5	-112.3	-110.3	-92.1
1974	52.9	-7.3	13.9	-13.3	92.8	-33.8
1975	128.4	127.8	37.2	41.7	41.1	-121.6
1976	87.9	97.7	438.6	181.0	265.2	-59.5
1977	164.1	243.5	594.9	156.0	323.8	-18.4
1978	147.0	-56.6	270.8	331.0	-150.4	-18.0
1979	139.0	179.5	299.5	576.0	2.0	34.0
1980	221.3	112.2	546.8	696.0	809.7	5.0
1981	677.6	277.5	371.5	519.0	1117.0	13.0
1982	596.5	315.6	643.4	594.0	651.0	-23.0
1983	457.5	451.2	202.1	424.0	490.0	-91.0
1984	516.4	574.3	114.2	400.0	772.4	52.0
1985	399.5	197.8	78.2		931.4	-346.1
1986	596.5	390.6	756.1		686.6	408.1

Hungary--Calculated from the difference between Soviet trade, socialist trade, trade with Yugoslavia, China and North Korea, and ruble trade in the *Hungarian Foreign Trade Yearbook (Kuelkereskedelmi Statisztikai Evkoenyv)*, various years.

All other countries--Trade deficits recorded in *Vneshniaia Torgovlia SSSR: statisticheskii sbornik*, various years.

Table 8
SOVIET TRADE SURPLUSES WITH EAST EUROPEAN COUNTRIES IN CRISIS
(millions of rubles)

Year	Czechoslovakia	GDR	Hungary	Poland
1951		-26.3		
1952		60.9		
1953		19.6		
1954		-121.5		
1956			5.5	66.5
1957			128.6	157.5
1958			34.8	100.5
1967	-13.3			
1968	43.3			
1969	-4.5			
1970	-27.8			
1970				80.0
1971				134.9
1792				-54.0
1975				-30.4
1976				234.8
1977				558.6
1978				408.2
1979				2.0
1980				809.7
1981				1117.0
1982				651.0
1983				490.0

Source: *Vneshniaia Torgovlia SSSR: statisticheskii sbornik*, various years

Notes

The author wishes to express his appreciation for the insightful comments and criticisms provided by Abraham Becker, Harry Gelman, A. Ross Johnson, and Benjamin Zycher of the Rand Corporation, Paul Marer of Indiana University, John Van Oudenaren of the Wilson Center, and Gur Ofer of the Hebrew University of Jerusalem.

1. For a more detailed explication of the benefits the Soviets desire from control of Eastern Europe, see J. F. Brown and A. Ross Johnson, *Challenges to Soviet Control in Eastern Europe* (Santa Monica, CA: The Rand Corporation, R-3189-AF, 1984); Sarah Meiklejohn Terry ed., *Soviet Policy in Eastern Europe* (New Haven: Yale University Press, 1984).

2. Michael Marrese and Jan Vanous, "Soviet Trade Relations with Eastern Europe, 1970-1984," 1985, mimeo.

3. Ibid.

4. An example should make this procedure clearer. Suppose Bulgaria imports 1 billion rubles of fuel and 1 billion rubles of machinery from the Soviet Union and exports 1.5 billion rubles of machinery in return. M-V obtain a dollar equivalent for Soviet fuel exports by multiplying 1 billion rubles worth of fuel by the dollar/ruble exchange rate for fuel, say 2. They do the same for machinery, this time using the dollar/ruble exchange rate for machinery, say 0.5. The dollar value of Soviet exports would then be 2 billion dollars for energy plus 500 million dollars for machinery, for a total of 2.5 billion dollars. The same procedure is used to calculate the value of imports from Bulgaria. Assuming the same exchange rates, these imports would be worth 750 million dollars. Something must be done about the ruble deficit, however, because supposedly this credit will eventually be repaid. M-V convert this into dollars and then subtract it from the subsidy. The deficit is converted to dollars using the dollar value of a ruble of a market basket of imports from the country. In the example, this equals 0.5, the dollar value of a ruble of Bulgarian exports to the Soviet Union. Thus the total subsidy in this case is 2.5 billion dollars (Soviet exports) minus 750 million dollars (Soviet imports) minus 250 million dollars (the dollar value of the deficit) for a total of 1.5 billion dollars.

5. Paul Marer and John Michael Montias, *East European Integration and East-West Trade* (Bloomington: Indiana University Press, 1980); Raimund Dietz, "Advantages/Disadvantages in USSR Trade with

Eastern Europe--The Aspect of Prices," The Vienna Institute of Comparative Economic Studies, Paper 97, August 1984; Jozef M. Van Brabant, "The USSR and Socialist Economic Integration--A Comment," *Soviet Studies*, vol. 36, no. 1, January 1984, p. 127; Andras Koeves, "'Implicit Subsidies' and Some Issues of Economic Relations Within the CMEA," *Acta Oeconomica*, no. 31, 1983, pp. 125-136.

6. Paul Marer, "The Political Economy of Soviet Relations with Eastern Europe," in Sarah Meiklejohn Terry ed., *Soviet Policy in Eastern Europe* (New Haven: Yale University Press, 1984).

7. Patrick Fontenay, *Hungary: An Economic Survey*, Occasional Paper No. 15, International Monetary Fund, Washington, D.C., December 1982, p. 58; and Rocznik Statystyczny Hardlu Zagranicznego (RSHZ), (Warsaw: Glowny Urzad Statystyczny, 1983), p. 73.

8. *Ekonomika*, 1977; Ministerstvo Vneshnei Torgovli, *Vneshniaia Torgovlia SSSR: statisticheskii sbornik*, Finansy i Statistika, Moscow, 1981, 1984.

9. Marrese and Vanous, "Soviet Trade Relations," op. cit.

10. These are rough averages for interest rates on Polish and Hungarian ruble loans. Fontenay, *Hungary: An Economic Survey*, p. 58; and Glowny Urzad Statystyczny, *Rocznik Statystyczny (RS)*, (Warsaw: Glowny Urzad Statystyczny, 1983), p. 73.

11. Marrese and Vanous, "Soviet Trade Relation," op. cit.

12. This equals average real return on U.S. 10 year bonds during the period when the loans were granted.

13. Kalman Pecsi, *The Future of Socialist Economic Integration*, M. E. Sharpe, Armonk, N.Y., 1981, p. 13.

14. Tamas Bauer and K. Attila Soos, "Inter-firm Relations and Technological Change in Eastern Europe--The Case of the Hungarian Motor Industry," *Acta Oeconomica*, 3-4, 1979, p. 285.

15. John B. Hannigan and Carl H. McMillan, "Joint Investment in Resource Development: Sectoral Approaches to Socialist Integration," Joint Economic Committee of Congress, *East European Economic Assessment, Part 2*, Washington, D.C., 1981, p. 259.

16. Laszlo Csaba, "Joint Investments and Mutual Advantages in the CMEA--Retrospection and Prognosis," *Soviet Studies*, vol. 37, no. 2, April 1985, p. 238.

17. Raimund Dietz, "Advantages/Disadvantages in USSR Trade with Eastern Europe," p. iii.

18. Keith Crane, *A Comparison of Foreign Trade Decision-Making in Poland and Hungary*, Ph.D. dissertation, Indiana University, 1983.

19. Raimund Dietz, "Advantages/Disadvantages in USSR Trade with Eastern Europe," op. cit.

20. If CMEA trade was conducted at world market prices and these prices were converted at the official rate, the dollar/ruble ratio for each commodity group would be identical to the official rate. Therefore, the extent to which the M-V ratios differ from the official rate reflects the difference in CMEA and world market prices.

21. One problem with this approach is that CMEA prices are supposed to be moving averages of world market prices. During a period of large changes in relative prices, such as the 1970s, windfall gains or losses may accrue to one party over a substantial period of time, which would make the system appear one-sided.

22. A binomial test was used with a one percent region of rejection. When the official exchange rate exceeded the M-V rate it was assigned a value of one; when below, a value of zero.

23. M-V differentiate between the total subsidy, (which is partially determined by changes in the world market price of oil, and the anticipated subsidy, equivalent to the amount the Soviets would presumably have planned to transfer if relative world market prices had been stable. Marrese and Vanous, "Soviet Trade Relations,"op. cit. p. 4.

24. Michael Marrese and Jan Vanous, *Soviet Subsidization of Trade with Eastern Europe*, Institute of International Studies, University of California, Berkeley, 1983, p. 11.

25. Raimund Dietz, "Advantages/Disadvantages in USSR Trade with Eastern Europe," op. cit. p. 54.

26. Evidence that ruble prices are varied from country to country on political grounds is not as clear. Ruble prices for planned deliveries of oil may be the same for each member of the bloc. Differences noted in average prices may be due to above plan purchases or other commercial arrangements.

27. The domestic cost of manufacturing the products is also taken into consideration.

28. Conversations with East European economists.

29. Josef Brada and John Michael Montias, "Industrial Policy in Eastern Europe: A Three Country Comparison," *The Journal of Comparative*

Economics, vol. 8, no. 4, December 1984, pp. 377-419.

30. Franklyn D. Holzman, "Soviet Foreign Trade Pricing and the Question of Discrimination," *Review of Economics and Statistics*, vol. 44, no. 2, May 1962, pp. 134-147; and Brada and Montias, "Industrial Policy in Eastern Europe," op. cit.

31. Brada and Montias, "Industrial Policy in Eastern Europe," op. cit.

32. The data and rationale for the form of the regression are given in the appendix.

33. To judge whether the shift in ranks was highly significant, I conducted a Spearman rank order test of the hypothesis that the two orders were uncorrelated. Although this hypothesis was rejected at the 10 percent level of significance, this test merely indicates that there is a positive correlation between the two patterns, not that they are the same.

34. *Pravda*, 27 March 1985, p. 4.

35. Csaba, "Joint Investments and Mutual Advantages in the CMEA," op. cit; Andras Koeves, "'Implicit Subsidies' and Some Issues of Economic Relations Within the CMEA," *Acta Oeconomica*, No. 31, 1983, pp. 125-136.

36. Andras Koeves, "'Implicit Subsidies,'" op. cit.

37. Paul Marer, "The Political Economy of Soviet Relations with Eastern Europe," op. cit.

38. Stanislaw Gomulka and Jerzy Sylwestrowicz, "Import-Led Growth: Theory and Estimation," Altman, Kyn, and Wagner, eds., *On the Measurement of Factor Productivity, Theoretical Problems and Empirical Results*, Gottinger Zurich, Vendenhoesch, Rupprecht, 1976.

39. The Bucharest accords, adopted in 1958, stipulated that prices in intra-CMEA trade were to be fixed for the entire five-year plan period on the basis of average world market prices during the preceding five-year period.

40. Joan Zoeter, "Eastern Europe: The Hard Currency Debt," Joint Economic Committee, U.S. Congress, *East European Economic Assessment*, vol. II, (Washington, D.C.: U.S. Government Printing Office, 1981).

41. Marvin Jackson, "Romania's Foreign Debt Crisis: Its Causes and Consequences," Joint Economic Committee, U.S. Congress, *East European Economics in the 1980s*, vol. 1, (Washington, D.C.: U.S. Government Printing Office, 1985).

42. Jan Vanous, "Diverging Trends in CMEA Economies in 1984: Recovery in Eastern Europe and Downturn in the Soviet Union," *Centrally Planned Economy Analysis*, Wharton Econometric Forecasting Associates, vol. 5, no. 25-26, March 27, 1985c.

43. Keith Crane, *The Creditworthiness of Eastern Europe in the 1980s*, (Santa Monica, CA: The Rand Corporation, R-3201-USDP, January 1985).

44. This is not to argue that economic policy instruments have not been used to pursue other Soviet foreign policy goals. Aside from the differences in Soviet treatment of Bulgaria and Romania noted above, the Soviets reportedly express their unhappiness with East European domestic and foreign policies by reducing export supplies or by delays in signing import contracts for goods from major East European industries.

45. Raimund Dietz, "Advantages/Disadvantages in USSR Trade with Eastern Europe," op. cit.

46. Jan Vanous, "Bulgarian Economic Performance in 1984--Appreciable Upturn from Slow 1983," *Centrally Planned Economy Analysis*, Wharton Econometric Forecasting Associates, vol. 5, no. 23-24, March 20, 1985a.

47. Jan Vanous, "Bulgarian Foreign Trade Performance in 1984," *Centrally Planned Economy Analysis*, Wharton Econometric Forecasting Associates, vol. 5, no. 29-30, April 9, 1985b.

48. Leslie Colitt and David Buchan, "Oil Price Plunge Places East Europe in Economic Jeopardy," *Financial Times*, February 19, 1986.

49. *Fordulat es Reform*, Version I, as translated in Joint Publications Research Service, JPRS Report: East Europe, JPRS-EER-87-013, August 19, 1987, p. 8.

50. Comments by Soviet economists.

51. Jan Vanous, "Bulgarian Economic Performance in 1984--Appreciable Upturn from Slow 1983," op. cit.

52. *l'Humanit'e'*, June 3, 1985, p. 8.

53. Elizabeth Goldstein, "Soviet Economic Assistance to Poland, 1981-82," in Joint Economic Committee of Congress, *Soviet Economy in the 1980s: Problems and Prospects*, Part 2, (Washington, D.C.: U.S. Government Printing Office, 1981) p. 567.

54. Marrese and Vanous, *Soviet Subsidization of Trade with Eastern Europe*, op. cit.

55. Gary R. Teske, "Poland's Trade with the Industrialized West," Joint

Economic Committee of Congress, *East European Economic Assessment*, Part 1, Washington, D.C., 1980, p. 72.

56. Rocznik Statystyczny Hardlu Zagranicznego (RSHZ), (Warsaw: Glowny Urzad Statystyczny, 1981, 1982).

57. Jan Vanous, "Eastern European and Soviet Fuel Trade," Joint Economic Committee of Congress, *East European Economic Assessment, Part 2*, Washington, D.C., 1981, p. 554.

58. The document contains the passage, "planning and foreign-trade agencies...should coordinate...measures to increase mutual deliveries of goods, the main proportions and structures of reciprocal trade turnover," which I interpret as calling for balanced trade.

59. The "Statement" goes on to say, "They [the member countries] will carry out appropriate measures, including the participation of interested countries in capital investments and in providing exporter countries with other economic incentives on a bilateral or multilateral basis by the interested countries." Policy goal three seems implicit in this passage.

60. Gertrude Schroeder, "The Slowdown in Soviet Industry, 1976-1982," Soviet Economy, vol. 1, January-March 1985, p. 42; and Thane Gustafson, "Soviet Oil Policy and Energy Politics, 1970-85," mimeo, 1985.

61. J. F. Brown and A. Ross Johnson, *Challenges to Soviet Control in Eastern Europe*, (Santa Monica, CA: The Rand Corporation, R-3189-AF, 1984); Sarah Meiklejohn Terry, ed., *Soviet Policy in Eastern Europe* (New Haven: Yale University Press, 1984).

62. Marie Lavigne, "The Evolution of CMEA Institutions and Policies and the Need for Structural Adjustment," October 1984, mimeo, p. 23.

63. SEV, Sovet Ekonomicheskoi Vzaimopomoshchi, *Statisticheskii Ezgodnik Stran*, Finansi i Statistika, Moscow, 1980, 1984.

64. Keith Crane, *The Creditworthiness of Eastern Europe in the 1980s*, op. cit.

65. "USSR's Tikhonov Cited," *Foreign Broadcast Information Service*, 26 June 1985.

66. Morris Bornstein, *Plan and Market: Economic Reform in Eastern Europe*, Yale University Press, New Haven, 1973.

67. Price controls were to remain in many industries, and fixed prices were to be set for many inputs. This ruling sharply limits the effectiveness of prices as a guide to what to produce and in what to invest.

68. Keith Crane, *The Creditworthiness of Eastern Europe in the 1980s*, op. cit.

69. *Pravda*, 21 June 1985, pp. 3, 4.

70. Wlodimierz Brus, "Economic Reforms as an Issue in Soviet-East European Relations," in Karen Dawisha and Philip Hanson eds., *Soviet-East European Dilemmas: Coercion, Competition, and Consent*, (London: Holmes and Meier, 1981).

71. Friedrich Levcik, "Czechoslovakia: Economic Performance in the Post-reform Period and Prospects for the 1980s," Joint Economic Committee of Congress, *East European Economic Assessment, Part 1*, Washington, D.C., 1980, p. 420.

72. Jan Vanous, "Bulgarian Foreign Trade Performance in 1984," op. cit.

73. Pieter Boot, "The German Democratic Republic Between East and West: The Margins of Socialist Dependencia," University of Amsterdam, Research Memorandum No. 8508, 1985.

74. Ibid.

75. Kazimierz Poznanski, *Technological Levels and World Trade: A Global View*, manuscript, n.d., p. 52.

76. Manfred Melzer, "The New Planning and Steering Mechanisms in the GDR--Between Pressure for Efficiency and Successes in Intensification Policy," The German Institute for Economic Research, Berlin, working paper, October 1985.

77. It is hard to imagine economic reform in the GDR. Comparative economic performance has been good, and the *raison d' e'tre* of a socialist Germany disappears if central planning is replaced with markets. Ceausescu's highly personal rule in Romania makes political predictions for that country very difficult.

78. Marrese and Vanous, "Soviet Trade Relation," op. cit.

79. Total capital in the cases of Romania and Bulgaria.

80. Both Romania and Bulgaria appear to calculate capital stock figures by summing net investment (Thad Alton, Gregor Lazarcik, Elizabeth M. Bass, and Wassyl Znayenko, "East European Defense Expenditures, 1965-78," in Joint Economic Committee, *East European Economic Assessment*, Washington, D.C., 1981, p. 405). The resulting sum is a muddle, but in periods of low inflation it may be a reasonable approximation of the capital stock.

81. Dietz, "Advantages/Disadvantages in USSR Trade with Eastern

Europe," op. cit.

82. Central Intelligence Agency, National Foreign Assessment Center, *Energy Supplies in Eastern Europe: A Statistical Compilation*, December 1979; and Vanous, Jan, "East German Economic Performance in 1982 and During the First Half of 1983," *Centrally Planned Economy Analysis*, Wharton Econometric Forecasting Associates, vol. 3, no. 62-63, August 12, 1983b.

6

WESTERN INTERESTS IN AND LEVERAGE ON THE SOVIET AND EAST EUROPEAN ECONOMIES[1]

Donato Di Gaetano

Introduction

A number of structural economic changes took place in East-West trade in the 1965-1980 period. During this period, exports of the EEC to CMEA European countries grew 12 times from 2 to 23.5 billion dollars. By way of comparison, in the same period exports of the EEC to the United States grew only 7 times, that is, from 5 to 36 billion dollars. This trend of improving economic relations between East and West Europe reflects the basic economic complementarity of the two regions and is why Europeans consider East-West trade important to their future development. Moreover, this is not a matter of economic dependence of Western Europe on the East. This is evident from the fact that the proportion of the Community's external trade with the CMEA countries, while by no means negligible, is not much greater than the percentage represented by Switzerland. "When two great economic entities live next to each other, and when their economies are to a considerable extent complementary, one would expect higher trade figures."[2]

In 1984 the EEC exported about 26 billion ECU to Switzerland and 21 billion to Eastern Europe. As a percentage, EEC exports to Eastern Europe represent seven percent of the total extra-EEC exports (to the United States fifteen percent, Switzerland eight percent, and Sweden five percent). The most surprising fact is that the Eastern market is less relevant for the EEC countries than the Swiss market! It is useful to add that the EEC trade turnover (seven percent in 1984) with Eastern Europe is larger than the quota of trade for the United States (1.5 percent) and Japan (two percent).

At the present time we look forward to a new phase in the development of economic relations between socialist and capitalist countries. Today the prospects for change in those relations are greater than they were only a few years ago. In the following pages I shall concentrate on the present state of East-West economic and financial relations and will sketch a feasible though slippery path of East-West commercial and financial cooperation.

The Present State of East-West Economic and Financial Relations: Some Critical Remarks

Following the high expectations for East-West trade at the end of the 1960s and first half of the 1970s, as well as the "guilty uncertainties" of the second half of the 1970s, the first half of the 1980s was characterized by retrenchment. Changes took place at the governmental, banking and firm levels with respect to overall strategy, goals, and leverage.

The high level of imports of CMEA European countries (mainly of industrial equipment but also of consumer goods) during the 1970s and the modest East European exports to the West produced a build-up of hard-currency indebtedness which reached a maximum of $89 billion in 1981. The imbalance was financed mostly by Western credits until 1979-1980. After that date, the heavy repayment burden made it difficult for many Eastern countries to obtain new credits. In this context it is interesting to underline that U.S. bank credits to Eastern countries reached a peak of $9 billion in 1978. At present the total amount is not more than $2.2 billion.[3]

The solution the six smaller countries of Eastern Europe pursued to reduce their indebtedness was to curtail their hard-currency imports from the West, especially from the EEC countries. For some of them (Romania, Poland and East Germany) this decision was part of a drastic change in their growth policy. In fact, a deflationary policy was adopted in order to balance the growing external deficits and many investment projects were canceled.

Western exports to Eastern Europe substantially decreased in the period 1980-1982. The percentage changes in trade volume were -2, -5, and -16 respectively in 1980, 1981 and 1982. Exports to the Soviet Union, on the contrary, registered increases in the same period of +9, +15 and +5 (see Table 1).

Concerning Western imports from Eastern Europe, the percentage changes were -2, -8 and -4 in the period 1980-82. For the Soviet Union negative percentage changes were registered for 1980 (-5) and 1981 (-8), but a positive one in 1982 (+10). By the end of 1982, the first East European convertible currency account surplus since the 1960s appeared. This has been one of the most important structural changes that took place in East-

West trade in the 1980s. In 1983-84, East-West trade continued to expand and East European countries increased their convertible currency account surplus and, consequently, reduced their gross debt. At this point it is useful to concentrate on the economic relations between EEC countries and CMEA European countries (Soviet Union included). More than 80 percent of East-West trade comes from economic agreements with Western Europe.

For the 1980-1984 period, one can discern very different trends in trade between the EEC and the six smaller countries of Eastern Europe and trade with the Soviet Union. Prior to 1982, the EEC trade balance with Soviet Union was characterized by a persistent deficit, while that with the smaller CMEA countries had a substantial surplus. The EEC imports from the Soviet Union doubled in five years: from 11,214 in 1980 to 22,430 billion ECU in 1984. During the same period imports from the six CMEA European countries first declined in 1981, then increased moderately in 1982 and, they experienced substantial growth in 1984 (see Tables 3 and 4).

One also has to distinguish the Soviet Union from Eastern Europe with respect to EEC exports. EEC exports to the Soviet Union reached a peak of 12,022 billion ECU in 1983, but in 1984 had a negative rate of growth (-0.2 percent). Eastern Europe, on the other hand, curtailed imports from the EEC. For some countries, such as Poland, East Germany and Romania, imports from the Community were reduced dramatically (see Table 4). As a result, by 1982 the Community's overall trade surplus with the six smaller CMEA European countries had been turned into a deficit: from 988 million to 3.3 billion ECU in 1982 and 1984, respectively. Poland's trade deficit with EEC countries (118 and 245 million ECU in 1980 and 1981) became a surplus in 1982 (+205 million ECU), 1983 and 1984 (+905 million ECU). Hungary's trade deficit was reduced from 428 (in 1982) to 295 (in 1983) million ECU. Only Bulgaria increased its imports and the trade deficit to the EEC increased from 408 to 675 million ECU respectively in 1981 and 1984 (see Table 4). At the end of 1984 the overall EEC trade deficit with the CMEA seven member countries was 13,745 billion ECU.[4]

The foreign economic strategy of the six CMEA countries towards the EEC succeeded. They reduced their hard-currency imports and managed to keep their exports stable. As a result, East European net debt to Western banks in 1983 shrank by $12 billion (although parts of this reduction was due to exchange rate effects).[5]

I previously noted that the six Eastern European countries adopted rigorous policies of adjustment to keep under control their trade balances with the West. At the end of 1979 the authorities of the six Eastern European countries started a restrictive policy of domestic demand and imports. By 1982 one can observe a strengthening of the Eastern countries' financial position (reflected in larger current account surpluses), a rising accumulation of assets to BIS with a subsequent declining net debt. In fact, the total net debt of Eastern Europe declined in the 1981-1984 period by $12 billion, from $58.3 to $47.0 billion In 1984, because of the dollar appreciation, even Poland's net debt decreased by $0.5 billion (-1.5 percent).[6]

The new situation at the end of 1984 could be summarized as follows:

> ... Supported by the growing eastern trade surplus in East-West trade, there was a further increase in the convertible currency surplus in the aggregate current account of the East European countries and the Soviet Union in 1984. The East European surplus rose from $3 billion in 1983 to $4 billion in 1984 and that of the Soviet Union from $6 billion to $8 billion. Though interest rates were rising during the year, the impact on the current account was largely offset by the continuing decline in the stock of debt outstanding. It is estimated that the total net debt of Eastern Europe and the Soviet Union fell from $70 billion at the end of 1983 to some $62 billion at the end of 1984. The appreciation of the United States dollar played a significant role in this change.[7]

The new attitude of international banks towards Eastern Europe in the 1980s strongly influenced the firmness of the adjustment process carried out by these countries. Western banks in 1980 and particularly in 1981 reduced credit flows to CMEA European countries. In 1982 new bank credits disappeared. The slowing-down of the supply of external financial resources compelled the East European countries to strengthen central control over their economic activity.

After the economic crisis of 1981 and 1982, East European economies recovered in 1983 and 1984. This made access to commercial credits easier, especially for the Soviet Union. The terms and conditions obtained by many Eastern countries are the best they have obtained since 1979 (see Table 5). It is useful to emphasize that through 1985 the success of the Soviet Union, Hungary and East Germany has been achieved without the involvement of the major U.S. banks. Moreover, the number of banks willing to participate in lending to Eastern countries has also grown. In 1984 more than $3 billion in medium and long-term funds was raised by Eastern countries. In contrast to previous years, in 1984 the request of official and guaranteed loans by Eastern borrowers appears to have decreased.

In the first half of 1985 this adjusting process encountered some difficulties. Because of the extremely cold winter weather, the drought in the spring and summer, the reduction of arm exports to the Third World (Middle East), and the decline in Soviet oil exports, the forecasts of the CMEA European countries convertible current account surplus were revised downward. In the case of the Soviet Union, exports to the developed West declined 27 percent. East European exports to the same area went down by six percent. Consequently, the trade surplus of Eastern Europe with the West contracted from $1.4 billion to $400 million. The change for the Soviet Union is especially sharp: from a surplus of $770 million to a deficit of $2.8 billion (see Table 2).

It is relevant to consider that during the second quarter of 1985 the Soviet Union increased its borrowing from Western banks and certain offshore centers by $2.7 billion and added $700 million to its deposits with the Western banking system. The Soviet Union suddenly became the biggest single borrower of international banking funds outside the Western industrialized world.

This change will slacken a further increase in the convertible currency surplus in the aggregate current account of East European countries and of the Soviet Union in 1985. This, of course, will affect the possibility of reducing the CMEA European countries' net debt.

The Future of East-West Relations: Some Doubts in a Changing Scenario

The scenario of East-West trade and financial relations described above is characterized by both a growing dynamism and uncertainties.

East-West relations have a global character, and many variables (political and economic) are interlinked. They include the volume of indebtedness and the burden of interest payments of the Eastern socialist countries, the state of the world economy, the import policy of Western countries, technology transfer, etc. To this list can be added the actions of policymakers in governments, international institutions, and the banking community.

The decisive role played by politics for the outlook of East-West trade was stressed during the 1985 Geneva summit between President Reagan and General Secretary Gorbachev. This meeting and subsequent ones between the two leaders created a better climate for mutual understanding, though many issues remained unresolved. Nevertheless, some doubts about the future of East-West relations remain, in part because of discrepancies between U.S. and EEC policies toward East European countries. These discrepancies have their roots in the different economic interest of the United States and Western Europe.

At the beginning of the chapter I indicated the relative importance of East European markets for the EEC and for the United States and Japan. It is important to emphasize that European industry in particular paid the cost of balancing the financial external exposure of the Eastern countries. In fact, from 1980 to 1983 many contracts failed. The impact of the adjustment policy carried out by the Eastern governments on U.S. exports to the CMEA area was negligible. This was not the case with respect to Western Europe. Moreover, if there is an objective interest on the part of the United States to improve the economy of Latin America (which is one of the most important foreign markets for U.S. industrial and consumer production), there is also an objective interest on the part of the European Economic Community to create better conditions for East-West trade.

The Reagan Administration gave great weight to security considerations in its economic relations with the Soviet Union. The current debate in Washington on East-West economic relations is also characterized by a very large concern over the political implications of trade policy towards Eastern socialist countries. The concern

> ... is rooted in an awareness that two successive Presidents have been unsuccessful in their attempts to use a strategy of selective trade denial in order to achieve political objectives. Both acted from high moral purposes in response to Soviet behavior that was widely condemned here [in the U.S.] and abroad. Yet, both engendered domestic political difficulties, dissension from within their own parties and disagreements within the Western alliance. Both are perceived to have harmed U.S. economic interests.[8]

A large segment of the American business community is not sympathetic to the use of controls based strictly on foreign policy considerations. The controls are damaging U.S. firms' foreign trade and have caused a sharp reduction of their U.S. share of Eastern markets.

Two recent pieces of legislation illustrate the discrepancies of U.S. and European thinking. The first piece of legislation is a bill to amend the Export Administration Act of 1979 to authorize controls on the export of capital from the United States.[9] One section of the amendment by Senator Jake Garn states that "Loans and other transfers of capital to the Soviet Union and its allies from public and commercial sources significantly increase the ability of those countries to obtain sensitive goods and technology, thereby damaging the security interests of the United States and its allies."

A second example is the testimony on September 25, 1985 by Richard Allen, former assistant to the President for National Security Affairs. In a statement presented to the Senate Committee on Banking, Housing and Urban Affairs, Allen said that "... I support this bill not only because I consider it a very valuable addition to the arsenal of the President to guide and keep close control of our relations with communists and other adversary nations, but also because it makes good strategic sense for the United States." The intent is clear. It would give the United States leverage over the Soviet

Union's international financial behavior.

During the same time period, the Political Affairs Committee of the European Parliament discussed a report drawn up by Mr. V. Bettiza.[10] The report dealt with relations between the European Community and the countries of Central and Eastern Europe. It states that:

> ... Although trade links between the two blocks are made practically impossible by the structural differences between EEC and Comecon, *there is no reason why we should renounce* (emphasis added) the attempt to establish, within a more general framework, contacts aimed at promoting dialogue and the exchange of ideas and information with Comecon as a whole.

Later the document affirms:

> ... these critical and cautious remarks of an economic nature should not constitute a barrier to the development of our overall relations with the countries of Central and Eastern Europe. Even if trade and politics should be kept separate, the development of reciprocal economic relations cannot but help take account of other considerations of a political, cultural and human nature, with a view to strengthening the solidarity and civil unity of our continent.

The "Slippery Path" of Economic and Financial Cooperation Between Eastern and Western Countries

I wish to emphasize the economic complementarity of EEC and CMEA European countries. With this in mind, one can anticipate a definite, though slippery, path of development of East-West economic relations.

The financial condition of most of the Eastern countries has improved. The real constraint to the further development of East-West trade is in the strategic decision made by the CMEA countries to balance, in the future, their commercial and financial relations with the West. "Only if the East Europeans are enabled to expand their exports in the West will they be able to earn enough convertible currencies to guarantee their debt service and also be able to import more from the West."[11]

This constraint could be overcome by a change in the commercial relations between the EEC and CMEA European countries. At present, the community trade policy vis-à-vis CMEA countries is based on a strictly bilateral agreement of member states with CMEA countries and on regulations concerning trade of specific products (see Table 6 for more details). The protectionism of the EEC trade policy does not help in the search for new approaches to East-West trade.[12]

The future course of East-West trade and technology transfer is difficult to predict. Much will depend on the political climate generated in Moscow and Washington during the coming years. Political uncertainties, mutual concern over Western Europe's trade dependence (energy), changes in the Eastern policy of importing advanced technology, export controls, and the external constraint of hard-currency debt are factors which could influence the future trend of East-West trade. Nevertheless, today there is a better understanding of the process of technology transfer and financial export controls. It is generally acknowledged that the flow of technology and financial credit to the East cannot be halted, it can only be delayed. On this assumption one can only hope that dissension and acrimony over East-West commercial and financial relations during the past years will serve as a lesson for more coherent and productive policies in the future.

Conclusions

Given the high degree of interaction in the world economy, the economic interests of Western and Eastern countries coincide in numerous fields (e.g., industry, ecology, and space). For the developed West, the CMEA European socialist countries are potential buying markets.

The technological level of some Eastern economies is higher than originally thought, and this could help to develop scientific-technological cooperation. In this sphere, a question is posed by the role of the COCOM list which gives rise to a whole series of delicate political decisions among Western countries.

A further result of improved East-West political relations, such as we are witnessing in early 1988, might be the acceleration of inter-enterprise cooperation by the promotion of more joint ventures. This could create suitable conditions to overcome the one-way technology transfer concept and to expand real East-West industrial cooperation (e.g., non-waste technology, energy sector, R & D, etc.).

The growing difficulties of depletion of energy sources, the world demographic situation, and environmental pollution are problems for economic systems both in the West and in the East and will require the more cautious exploitation of natural and human resources. Trade and technological-scientific cooperation in numerous fields, from the energy sector to the biochemical, nuclear, and electronic sectors, may help in finding optimal solutions.

The structural imbalances of Eastern economies cannot be overcome by only deflationary policies. The solution must be found in a framework of expansion rather than of restriction of East-West trade. This conclusion suggests the desirability of more flexibility and rigor during negotiations in order to find acceptable forms of economic and financial cooperation. This is valid both at the intergovernmental and at the microeconomic level.

Bibliography*

B.S. Baganov, *Vneshzhnyaya torgovliya SSSR v poslevoennyi period*.

N.I. Berdennikov, "Nauchno-tekhnicheskoe sotrudnichestvo: vashnaya baza dlya razvitiya torgovliya mezhdu vostokom i zapadom" Draft, 1985.

O.T. Bogomolov, *Mirovoe sotsialisticheskoe khozyaistvo. Voprosy politicheskoi ekonomii*. Moscow: Ekonomika, 1982.

Bastida B., T.V. Bonet, "Technology and Crisis: the USSR." Paper presented to the Third World Congress on Soviet and East European Studies. Washington, 1985.

S.A. Chapman, "The Economic Relations Between the EEC and the CMEA: a Survey of Problems and Prospects." Rome, November 1985.

S. Demcsak, "On the financing of East-West trade." VARNA II, 1985.

D. Di Gaetano, *L'economia sovietica: uno sguardo dall'interno*, Franco Angeli Ed. Milano, 1984.

D. Di Gaetano, "Rapporti economici East-Ovest e alcuni aspetti dell'interscambio dell'Italia con i paesi europei del Comecon," in *Rivista di Diritto valutario e di economia internazionale*, Vol. XVII-IV (1983).

R. Di Leo, "The Role of Europe in the Making of a New East-West Relationship," Naples, June 1985.

G. Fink (Editor), *East-West Economic Relations Now and in the Future*, Springer-Verlag, Wien 1985.

G. Graziani, *Comecon, domination et dependances*, F. Maspero, Paris 1982.

European Parliament Working Document 425/74 of 9 January 1975, Klepsch Report, *Report on the European Community's Relations with East European State-Trading Countries and Comecon*.

European Parliament Working Document 89/78 of 11 May 1978, Schmidt Report, *Report on the State of Relations Between the EEC and East European State-Trading Countries and Comecon*.

European Parliament Working Document 1-846/81 of 8 January 1982, Aigner Report, *Report on Exports of Community Agricultural Products to the USSR and the State-Trading Countries*.

European Parliament Working Document 1-424/81 of 28 August 1975, De

---

* The bibliography reported here is selective and does not include all the sources I consulted. I benefited from participating in the VARNA II FORUM on "East-West trade: Status and Prospects" (Varna, Bulgaria, September 1985) and the Third World Congress for Soviet and East European Studies (Washington, 1985).

Cle *Report on Relations Between the European Community's and the East European State-Trading Countries and the Comecon*.

European Parliament Working Document 1-531/82 of 28 July 1982, Irmer Report, *Report on Relations Between the European Community's and the East European State-Trading Countries and the Comecon*.

European Parliament Working Document A 2-III/85 7 October 1985, V. Bettiza, *Report on Relations Between the European Community and the Countries of Central and Eastern Europe*.

E. A. Hewett, "Foreign Economic Relations" in *The Soviet Economy: Toward the Year 2000*, George Allen & Unwin, 1983.

J.E.C. *East-West Technological Transfer: A Congressional Dialogue with the Reagan Administration*. Washington, 1981.

J.E.C. *Transfer of United States High Technology to the Soviet Union and Soviet Bloc Nations*. Washington, 1982.

R. Rode and H.O. Jacobsen, *Economic Warfare or Détente. An Assessment of East-West Relations in the 1980s*. Westview Press, London 1985.

A. Nove, "The Contribution of Imported Technology to Soviet Union Growth," Paper presented to the Third World Congress on Soviet and East European Studies, Washington 1985.

M. Nuti and W. Maciejewski, "Economic Integration Between CMEA Countries and Prospects for East-West Trade." E.U.I., Florence, June 1985.

M. Lavigne, *Economie internationale des pays socialistes*, Armand Colin, Paris, 1985.

K.A. Sahlgren, "Status and Prospects of East-West Economic and Industrial Cooperation," Varna II, 1985.

G.B. Smith (Editor), *The Politics of East-West Trade*, Westview Press, 1984.

G. Schiavone (Editor), "East-West Relations: Prospects for the 1980s," MacMillan, 1982.

E.A. Stent (Editor), *Economic Relations with the Soviet Union. American and West German Perspectives*. Westview Press, London 1985.

C.T. Saunders (Editor), *East-West Trade and Finance in the World Economy. A New Look for the 1980s*. MacMillan, 1985.

Ya. Sita, *Perspektivy obzheevropeiskogo ekonomicheskogo sotrudnichestva*. Budapest, 1979.

U.N. Economic Commission for Europe, *Economic Bulletin for Europe*, November 1985.

M.G. Watts (Editor), *Economic Relations Between East and West*, MacMillan, N.Y. 1978.

TABLE 1

EAST-WEST TRADE: CHANGES IN TRADE VOLUME, TRADE BALANCES

(percentage change and billions of U.S. dollars)

	1980	1981	1982	1983	1984
Western exports to:					
Eastern Europe	-2	-5	-16	-	6
Soviet Union	9	15	5	2	1
Western imports from:					
Eastern Europe	-2	-8	-4	9	19
Soviet Union	-5	-8	10	7	3
Western trade balances					
(U.S. billions) with:					
Eastern Europe	3.2	2.3	-0.3	-1.3	-3.7
Soviet Union	-2.9	-0.2	-0.7	-1.0	-1.6

Source: *Economic Survey of Europe in 1984-1985*. U.N., Geneva.

TABLE 2

SOVIET AND EAST EUROPEAN NON-SOCIALIST TRADE DURING JANUARY-JUNE 1985

(in millions of current dollars)

	Exports (fob)			Imports (fob)			Trade Balance	
	1-6 1984	1-6 1985	Percent Growth	1-6 1984	1-6 1985	Percent Growth	1-6 1984	1-6 1985
Non-Socialist Trade								
CMEA Seven	33715	28160	-16.5	29108	29061	-30.2	4607	-901
-Soviet Union	18910	14472	-23.5	16923	16720	-1.2	1987	-2248
-Eastern Europe	14805	13688	-7.5	12185	12341	1.3	2620	1347
-Bulgaria	1483	1298	-12.5	1153	1342	16.4	330	-44
-Czechoslovakia	2149	1838	-14.5	1533	1329	-13.3	616	509
-East Germany	3760*	3690*	3.5*	3736*	3951*	5.8*	-66*	-261*
-Hungary	1736	1376	-20.7	1658**	1618**	-2.4	78	-242
-Poland	2605	2461*	-5.5	1798	1832*	1.9	807	629*
-Romania	3162*	3025*	-4.3	2307*	2269*	-1.7	855*	756*
Developed West								
CMEA Seven	23335	19150	-17.9	21144	21467	1.5	2191	-2317
-Soviet Union	13009	9456	-27.3	1232	12246	0.1	777	-2790
-Eastern Europe	10326	9694	-6.1	8912	9221	3.5	1414	473
-Bulgaria	519	444	-14.5	781	819	4.9	-262	-375
-Czechoslovakia	1450	1277*	-11.9	1144	1009*	-11.8	306	268*
-East Germany	3030*	3082*	1.7	3326*	3521*	5.9	-296*	439*
-Hungary	1322	1046	-20.9	1200**	1380**	15.0	122	-33*
-Poland	1953	1874*	-4.0	1471	1502	2.1	482	372*
-Romania	2052*	1971*	-3.9	990*	990*	0.0	1062*	981*

Source: Plan Ec Report, October 1985, National Statistics.

*Estimate

**Hungarian Imports are reported on a cif basis

TABLE 3

IMPORTS, EXPORTS AND TRADE BALANCE OF THE EEC WITH CMEA EUROPEAN COUNTRIES*

	1980	1981	1982	1983	1984	84/83%
Imports	20068	22257	26330	28416	34860	23.1
Soviet Union	11214	13541	17045	18615	22430	20.5
Exports	16773	17321	17298	20376	21115	+3.6
Soviet Union	7583	7886	8984	12011	11985	-0.4
Trade Balance	-3295	-4936	-9032	-8040	-13745	+70.9
Soviet Union	-3631	-5655	-8061	-6593	-10445	+58.5

Source: *Eurostat*, various years

* The group includes Soviet Union, East Germany, Poland, Czechoslovakia, Hungary, Romania, Bulgaria.

TABLE 4

ECONOMIC RELATIONS OF THE EEC
WITH SINGLE CMEA EUROPEAN COUNTRIES

(millions of ECU)

	Imports					Exports					Trade Balance				
	1980	1981	1982	1983	1984	1980	1981	1982	1983	1984	1980	1981	1982	1983	1984
SOVIET UNION[a]	11214	13541	17045	18615	22430	7583	7886	8984	12022	11985	-3631	-5655	-8061	-6593	-10445
EASTERN EUROPE[b]	8799	8629	9193	9712	12430	9125	9361	8205	8254	9130	+326	+732	-988	-1458	-3300
East Germany*	911	1158	1293	1414	1636	842	1048	710	792	856	-69	-110	-583	-622	-780
Poland	2723	2062	2256	2415	3291	2841	2307	2051	2074	2381	+118	+245	-205	-341	-910
Czechoslovakia	1505	1564	1751	1873	2117	1368	1385	1399	1451	1626	-137	-179	-352	-422	-491
Hungary	1415	1461	1534	1662	1868	1592	1959	1962	1957	2159	+177	+498	+428	+295	+291
Romania	1767	1829	1170	1819	3003	1708	1699	1060	885	918	-59	-130	-710	-934	-2085
Bulgaria	478	555	589	529	515	774	963	1023	1095	1190	+296	+408	+434	+566	+675
CMEA Seven (a+b)	20013	22170	26238	28327	34860	16708	17247	17189	20276	21115	-3305	-4923	-9049	-8051	-13745

Source: *Eurostat*, Various years
*Inter-German trade not included.

TABLE 5

LOANS, TERMS AND CONDITIONS ON OFFER TO THE SOVIET UNION AND EASTERN EUROPE

	1976–1984		1976		1977		1978		1979		1980		1981		1982		1983		1984	
	Number of loans	Amount ($ billion)	(A)	(B)	(A)	(B)	(A)	(B)	(A)	(B)	(A)	(B)	(A)	(B)	(A)	(B)	(A)	(B)	(A)	(B)
USSR*	39	9.5	1.03	5.00	1.09	6.75	0.73	8.50	0.57	7.85	-	-	0.56	4.75	0.62	5.25	0.92	5.38	0.63	6.50
Hungary	41	5.6	1.25	5.00	1.08	6.00	0.76	7.75	0.58	8.30	0.56	5.50	0.62	5.73	1.22	2.33	1.21	2.30	1.02	5.00
East Germany	51	3.8	1.30	5.00	1.17	6.00	0.84	6.80	0.65	5.57	0.66	5.29	0.64	4.50	0.71	7.33	1.00	5.00	0.96	4.00
Poland	45	3.4	1.50	5.60	1.50	6.00	1.37	4.38	1.28	3.63	1.49	5.25	-	-	0.75	2.58	-	-	-	-
Rumania	12	2.4	-	-	1.25	5.00	0.76	6.00	0.76	10.00	0.69	7.00	0.72	4.67	-	-	-	-	-	-
Czechoslovakia	18	1.4	1.25	5.00	-	-	0.75	7.00	0.59	10.00	0.74	7.33	-	-	-	-	1.13	4.00	-	-
Bulgaria	17	1.0	1.40	1.10	5.67	0.85	5.67	0.69	8.00	-	-	-	-	-	-	-	-	-	-	-

(A) Average weighted margin above labor (%)
(B) Average maturity (years)

* includes international investment Bank financings

Source: Euromoney, Nov. 1984, BIS (various years)

TABLE 6

CONVENTIONAL RELATIONS OF THE EEC WITH THE FOLLOWING CMEA COUNTRIES

COUNTRIES	GATT	GENERAL TRADE AGREEMENT	TEXTILE AGREEMENT	SPECIFIC AGREEMENT IRON AND STEEL PRODUCTS	OTHER INDUSTRIAL PRODUCTS AGREEMENTS	SPECIFIC AGREEMENT SOME AGRICULTURAL PRODUCTS	JOINT COMMITTEE
BULGARIA			+	+		+	
HUNGARY	+		+	+		+	
POLAND	+		+	+		+	
ROMANIA	+		+	+	+	+	+
CZECHOSLOVAKIA	+		+	+		+	

Notes

1. This paper summarizes some parts of a larger research project in progress on the status and prospects of East-West economic relations. The author is grateful to many people for comments and for helpful suggestions on various points of the paper. The usual disclaimer applies.

2. J. Maslen, "The European Community's relations with the State-Trading countries 1981-1983," *Yearbook of European Law*, no. 3, 1983.

3. *Federal Reserve Bulletin*, November 1985.

4. More than 25 percent of this deficit is due to the Italian trade deficit with the CMEA seven (about $3.2 billion in 1984).

5. See *The maturity distribution of international bank lending*, first half 1983, BIS December 1983.

6. According to estimates of Vienna Institute for Comparative Economic Studies, *Mitgliederinformation* 1985/3.

7. K.A. Sahlgren, "Status and Prospects of East-West Economic and Industrial Cooperation," Varna II, 1985.

8. R.F. Kaufman, "Changing US attitudes towards East-West economic relations," *External economic relations of CMEA countries: their significance and impact in a global perspective*, Nato Colloquium, 1983.

9. *Document 99th congress, first session S. 812*, March 28, 1985.

10. European Parliament Working Documents Series A Document A2 - 111/85, 7 October 1985.

11. F. Levcik and J. Stankovsky, "East-West economic relations in the 1970s and 1980s," C.T. Saunders,(ed.) *East-West Trade and Finance in the World Economy. A New Look for the 1980s*, MacMillan, 1985.

12. Recently, a number of high-level expert meetings have been held between officials from the EEC and the Comecon Secretariat. Discussions have focused on the text of a Joint Declaration which would provide a framework for future cooperation between the two organizations.

7

THE WARSAW PACT AT THIRTY: SOVIET AND EAST EUROPEAN SUCCESSES AND FAILURES

Marco Carnovale

Introduction

T he focus of this chapter is on the developments of the Warsaw Pact, officially the Warsaw Treaty Organization (WTO), with respect to both its original goals and those which arose during its thirty-year life. After briefly outlining the background of relevant political and economic components of Soviet-East European relations, I will discuss the goals which were at the roots of the Pact's formation in 1955, note how they evolved, and how new goals subsequently arose; and assess the degree to which both sets of goals have been achieved. I will then draw some conclusions with respect to Soviet-East European politico-military relations in the Pact. Finally, I will discuss some implications of these developments for the West.

My main theses are the following. (1) While the WTO was initially mainly an outgrowth of Soviet military considerations, over time it developed into an increasingly political organization with a distinct and decisive East European component. (2) The Soviet Union successfully achieved its initial military objectives but subsequently failed to achieve the new political objectives which arose (the East Europeans, on the other hand, failed to achieve their initial military objectives, but succeeded in achieving many of their new political ones). (3) The success of the Soviets in consolidating the alliance on the military plane made it possible for the East Europeans to diverge on the political plane, as became evident during the process of renewal of the treaty itself during late 1984 and early 1985.

The Background:
The USSR and the Integration of Eastern Europe

It cannot be overemphasized that, for historical, military, politico-ideological and economic reasons, from the Soviet point of view, Eastern Europe remains the most important and sensitive region of the world. The Soviet Union, and Russia before it, has periodically tried to integrate it into a greater Russian-dominated political entity, and it has to a large extent been successful.

The historical and military reasons are closely connected and well known: the Soviets, and especially the Russians, will not easily forget that most major threats to the integrity or even the survival of Russia as a political entity came either from or through Eastern Europe. The post-World War II era is the first one in which the Soviets wield virtually complete control of the region and hence are assured that no military threats to their homeland will originate from it. This is the oldest and most deeply felt Soviet security concern with the region, and the one which will likely be the most difficult to eradicate.

From the politico-ideological point of view, Eastern Europe became particularly important only after the defeat of Nazi Germany and the establishment of communist regimes in the various countries of the region. These countries are now part of what the Soviets see as the kernel of the world communist system-to-be, and have therefore acquired paramount importance for Soviet domestic politics: the loss of all or part of Eastern Europe would put tremendous pressure on the ideological legitimacy of the Soviet regime vis-à-vis both its own people and other communists around the world. This concern is much newer, but hardly less important, than the previous one, and there is no reason to think it will become any less important for the foreseeable future.

Economically, Eastern Europe has recently become to a large extent complementary to the colossus to the East: it can absorb raw materials and provide manufactured goods in exchange. From the Soviet point of view, the economic convenience of this trade has recently become questionable, but Eastern Europe still provides several imports which the Soviets could not acquire elsewhere--e.g., in high technology. This is the newest and probably the least important of all Soviet concerns in the region, as well as the most volatile and subject to change even in the short term.

For these three broad reasons, the Soviet Union strives toward the integration of East European countries with itself and among each other. This process of integration, which has been particularly noticeable after Stalin's death, has extended over the economic, the political and the military fields, albeit in different forms and with different degrees of success. Parts of the region, of course, have been absorbed in the USSR altogether--the Baltic states, Moldavia, Ruthenia and parts of Galitia and Eastern Prussia. On the contrary, Finland, Yugoslavia, Albania and Turkey, at the extreme fringes of the region, have managed to resist all Soviet pressure. But the core of Central-Eastern Europe falls somewhere in between these two extremes.

Economically, after the war Stalin did little more than exploit Eastern Europe. The various means and procedures used to this end are well known and need not be repeated here; the bottom line was simply that resources flowed eastward much more than westward, and integration was a zero-sum game in which Eastern Europe played the role of an oil well rapidly being driven toward exhaustion. This process of outright exploitation ceased in the mid-1950s, when Khrushchev put economic relations on a more equitable basis. The trend continued until the 1970s when the Soviet Union began actually to subsidize both exports to and imports from Eastern Europe. This phenomenon is dealt with in Keith Crane's chapter in this volume and will not be expanded upon here. Suffice it to say that in the course of 20 to 25 years the net flow of resources had reversed its direction and has become increasingly costly for the Soviet Union: Economic integration has moved from exploitation to subsidization and is now a Soviet net economic liability.

Politically, Soviet-East European relations were originally based on straightforward subordination. After Stalin's death, it became apparent that the prevailing view among his successors was that East European regimes should be enticed to cooperate rather than just obliged to obey unquestioningly. This was due in great measure to Khrushchev's belief that fraternal parties in Eastern Europe could be trusted and did not need constant Soviet whipping. Even though he was burned by events in Hungary and Poland in 1956, the pattern of Soviet-East European political relations did not revert to the Stalinist scheme. Inevitably, however, the dilution of subordination brought along a measure of divergence in the initially monolithic political scenario of Soviet-East European relations, with Albania leaving the bloc altogether.

For the most part, the existing divergences within the bloc are not dangerous for the USSR because they have developed within a consolidated alliance framework in which the leaderships of all members still share fundamental interests and perspectives. The differences are on matters which are not vital for the political cohesion of the alliance itself. Such political cohesion is facilitated by East European economic dependence on the USSR and by the military interdependence. In sum, political relations still constitute an asset for the Soviets, even if they contain the potential for deterioration should either East European perceptions further diverge from those of the USSR or Soviet subsidies become too expensive for Moscow to sustain.

Military integration is the best asset which the Soviet Union has been able to build within the framework of its relations with the junior members of the alliance. Such integration has been gradually developing within the framework of the Warsaw Pact. 1985 marked the thirtieth anniversary of the Pact's foundation as well as the expiration of the initial thirty-year term. The formal treaty was renewed in April 1985 in Warsaw, in the very same hall where it had been signed in 1955, for another thirty-year period. It is appropriate to evaluate the performance of the military alliance from the point of view of its members in light of its initial objectives, new objectives which developed over time and events which punctuated its history.

The Origins of the Warsaw Pact

The Treaty of Friendship, Cooperation and Mutual Assistance was signed in Warsaw on 14 May 1955, in the wake of the ratification of the Paris agreements which sanctioned West Germany's entry into NATO and one day before the signing of the Austrian Treaty which reinstated sovereignty to a nonaligned government in Vienna. While both of these events certainly contributed to the Soviet decision to create a military alliance among the socialist countries of Eastern Europe[1], other considerations played a role as well. The object of this section is to outline some of these other factors.

It is important to emphasize that the creation of the WTO was essentially a Soviet decision, to which the East Europeans did not object in the least. Four factors operated simultaneously to give the Soviets virtually unopposed power over the formation of the military alliance. These four factors were: a) Soviet military domination of and actual presence in Eastern Europe; b) the then-still close loyalty of all of the national communist parties to the CPSU; c) the prostrated state of the economies of Eastern Europe; and d) the fact that no credible sign of support for East European resistance against the USSR came from the West.

Yet, Soviet preponderance notwithstanding, the leadership of the East European countries had reasons of their own to welcome the institutionalization of their military pact with the USSR. It would be erroneous to think that the WTO was merely a Soviet imposition upon the smaller socialist countries, even if the USSR possessed the wherewithal to force such a decision upon them. As one observer notes, "in retrospect, as it was set up, the Warsaw Treaty served multiple Soviet and to a less extent East European purposes."[2]

There is no agreement among Western analysts as to which objectives were more or less important in the minds of the Soviet and East European leaders. Moreover, Soviet leaders differed among themselves as to the the emphasis that each of them attached to the treaty. Molotov, the then-Foreign Minister, saw the Pact mostly as a useful tool for "socialist consolidation," i.e., as a mechanism for internally oriented bloc politics. Khrushchev, on the other hand, wanted the new socialist alliance to become one more asset in the struggle against the West, and thus expected it to play more of an externally-oriented foreign policy role.[3]

East Europeans surely differed among each other at least in the emphasis that each placed on any particular aspect of the treaty. However, for analytical purposes, it is useful to group together the common denominators of East European motives and compare them with those of the Soviets.

In general, two considerations are in order. First, the Soviets were much more successful that the East Europeans in achieving their ends. Second, both Soviet and East European objectives were predominantly, even if not solely, of a military nature.

Soviet Initial Objectives in the WTO

Initial Soviet military objectives, in the formation of the Warsaw Pact can be summarized as follows:

a) Improve the military effectiveness of the East European military establishments.
b) Counter the then on-going build-up of NATO, and particularly of the Federal Republic of Germany.
c) Gain a legal justification for the continuing presence of their troops in Hungary and Romania.
d) Shift some of the military burden for the defense of "socialist gains" to the East Europeans.

There was also one political goal which the Soviet leaders probably also had in mind: create the image of a genuine alliance for their East European satellites.

Improve East European military effectiveness. As Malcom Mackintosh aptly pointed out, one major military problem for the Soviets was that East European forces were very poorly organized to fight effectively against NATO forces.[4] In 1955 there was a need for both organizational and hardware improvement in these forces.

Organizationally, one should bear in mind that, during Stalin's time, these forces were controlled through non-institutional personal links--the example of Soviet Marshal Rokossovski serving as Minister of Defense of Poland being only the most glamorous case of a long list of high and middle-rank officers whom the Soviets employed to maintain strict control of East European forces. After Stalin's death, however, this system was no longer considered either desirable or viable in the long run. It was not viable because Khrushchev could see the disruptive effect of such direct Soviet interference on the pride and morale of the East Europeans. It was not desirable, because Khrushchev believed that the East European fraternal parties could be trusted more than did Stalin.

Therefore, the old system began to be dismantled. In its place there arose a need for an alternative system of control which could ensure the continuing effective coordination of the East European military establishments with the Red Army should their contribution be required in a conflict.[5] Hence the need for a multinational institutionalized organization that could achieve this end without the blatant breaches of sovereignty of previous years.

East European forces needed also more and more modern arms and equipment. Much of what they had was World War II vintage and fairly obsolete by 1955.[6] The Soviets did provide additional weaponry as well as military education for the East European officer corps. The USSR thus contributed somewhat to the modernization of those forces,[7] and thereby naturally became more interested in increasing military cooperation and coordination with them. The Soviets also dropped their previous insistence on very high manpower levels and allowed a rationalization of the force structure which entailed force cuts.[8]

However, it should be emphasized that, until 1961, this was coordination and not integration. It was only in 1961, one year after Marshal Grechko had replaced Marshal Konev at the helm of the Pact,[9] that real steps toward integration were initiated by the Soviets. Meetings of the Political Consultative Committee became more frequent, more and better equipment was provided to the junior allies, the training of East European officers in Soviet academies was intensified and, perhaps most importantly, joint maneuvers began to be held. This shift from coordination to integration was dictated by military consideration, but carried with it the beginning of the erosion of Soviet absolute preponderance within the alliance. The junior partners began to have more and more opportunities to raise their individual national concerns at multilateral meetings where they would not have to face the Soviets alone as was previously the case.

In sum, the Soviet Union has been fundamentally successful with respect to the first military goal. It is true that the effectiveness of the East European military contribution to the Warsaw Pact is still doubtful because the Soviets are reluctant to share the use of the most advanced weaponry and because of the shaky political reliability of most junior partners in the alliance.[10] Nevertheless, the overall military potential of the bloc in the event of a confrontation with NATO has certainly benefited from the collective modernization, coordination and integration which has developed through the years within the context of the Warsaw Pact.[11]

However, in recent times the combat value of East European troops has fallen from the top priority list of the Soviet Union.[12] Probably as a consequence of both economic constraints and, more importantly, of political second thoughts after the events in Czechoslovakia and in Poland in the late 1960s and through the 1970s and early 1980s, the Soviets have slowed down their transfers of advanced weapons to their East European allies. The one exception to this trend seems to be the highly modernized National People's Army of the German Democratic Republic, which, however, does not command front level units, is closely integrated with the Group of Soviet Forces in Germany, and would not operate in any strategically significant independent way in case of war.

Counter NATO and particularly FRG build-up. It has been persuasively argued that, because of the formation of NATO, Stalin's successors at the helm of the USSR felt a need for the involvement of the East Europeans in the defense of their own territory so as to strengthen the Soviet buffer zone facing NATO.[13] Stalin himself was of course much too suspicious of the satellites to delegate any major responsibility of the defense of their own homelands, but by the mid-1950s Soviet-East European relations had changed. Khrushchev had much more faith than his predecessor in the potential of the people's democracies for achieving political legitimacy and economic viability. He thought he could entrust them with military responsibilities as well.

The admission of the Federal Republic of Germany into NATO surely strengthened Khrushchev's confidence that the East Europeans would prove reliable allies against NATO. The war was then less than ten years past, Nazi horrors had hardly been forgotten and Bonn's revanchism was quite unequivocable. The nightmare of a new rebirth of Prussianism and German militarism loomed large in Eastern Europe,[14] and was only made worse by the prospect of West Germany acquiring nuclear weapons at some time in the future. With the benefit of hindsight, we can argue today that entry into NATO actually worked to temper German revanchism and that the continuing presence of U.S. forces and nuclear weapons contributed significantly to the West Germans' decision to forego their own nuclear force.

But this could not have been so clear to the East Europeans in 1955.

Robin Remington takes this argument to the extreme and argues that the formation of the Warsaw Pact can be interpreted as one aspect of the Soviet Union's German policy.[15] Her thesis is reinforced by the fact that the East Germans--whose value in fighting West Germans must have seemed highly questionable in 1955--were initially kept out the the Treaty altogether and later gained only a partial capability to conduct autonomous military operations.

The Soviets have not been as successful with respect to this second goal as they were with the first. The WTO did not deter or reverse either West Germany's integration into NATO or its development of the Bundeswehr into a formidable conventional deterrent. But they were successful in a more general military sense in that the greater effectiveness of Soviet and allied forces which resulted from the formation of the Pact was achieved partly thanks to the political steam provided by the FRG's integration in NATO.

Acquire a permanent legal right to station troops in Eastern Europe. With the signing of the Austrian Treaty in 1955, the Soviet Union lost the official justification for the continuing presence of its troops in Hungary and Romania. The treaty provided for a complete withdrawal within forty days of the signing. It was hardly a coincidence that the WTO document was signed within twenty-four hours of the Austrian Treaty.

While it can be argued that the USSR did not necessarily need the WTO to keep its troops in Hungary and Romania, there are several reasons to contend that the treaty made things easier for Moscow. First, as of 1955 there were still no status-of-force agreements with the individual East European countries, and those agreements were only finally signed--with the exceptions of Albania and Czechoslovakia--in the 24 months which followed the WTO founding. There is reason to believe that their smooth conclusion was made easier by the previous existence of the multilateral WTO. Second, the WTO substituted for bilateral agreements in one strategically important country with which no agreement was signed, Albania. No Soviet troops were permanently stationed in Czechoslovakia until 1968.

The creation of the WTO contributed, from the Soviet point of view, to the military stabilization of Eastern Europe by facilitating and reinforcing an international legal framework by which the USSR legitimized its right to a perpetual military presence in the region. This framework was further strengthened by the lack of any treaty provision for the withdrawal of a member state before twenty years, and then only after a notification of one full year, during which the Soviets would have time to exert pressure to reverse the decision.[16]

Shift military burden to East Europeans. Several authors have emphasized that one reason the Soviets wanted to involve the East Europeans more directly in a collective defense mechanism was to better exploit their resources. The three main ways in which this could be done were: 1) to tap their manpower reservoir; 2) to push them to increase their financial contributions; and 3) to force them to restructure their armaments industry so as to exploit the comparative advantages that each country had to offer.

The manpower motive is a convincing one.[17] The East European armed forces had large but underutilized conscript armies, which included considerable skilled manpower. As mentioned above, however, the integration of combat forces in the Pact did not begin until the early 1960s; in the first several years East European skilled manpower was utilized mostly for non-combat roles.[18] This represented an economic burden on the East Europeans in that it drained skilled labor from their civilian economies.

The financial motive is less clear, because the prostrated state of the East European economies could hardly have appeared to be a promising source of financial contribution to the Soviets. In any case, the well-known pattern of economic exploitation which the USSR already had in place did not require the additional infrastructure of the WTO. The USSR continued to contribute the overwhelming share of WTO expenses. One author estimates that share to be roughly equal to 80 percent of all Pact expenditures.[19] Moreover, the WTO burden sharing is closely intertwined with the broader web of Soviet-East European economic relations, which in turn is heavily influenced by political considerations. Suffice it to point out that, for political reasons, the Soviet Union has in recent years subsidized other CMEA member states, and that such subsidies have been guided by non-military considerations. There appears to be a correlation between the common defense and Soviet subsidies. Subsidies have increased for the GDR, which also increased its military contribution to the WTO. They decreased for Romania, which not only reduced its military effort but also made public its disagreement with the other allies on this matter. Subsidies remained stable for Hungary, Czechoslovakia and Bulgaria, whose military efforts also remained fairly constant. The only exception to this pattern is Poland, which because of the particularly shaky state of its economy was awarded increased subsidies while its defense expenditures were reduced.[20]

The final burden-sharing motive derived from straightforward military considerations. The division of labor in the military industries produced several desirable effects from the Soviet point of view. First, it exploited more effectively the comparative advantages of individual countries through larger economies of scale. Second, it made each East European country dependent on the others, and most of all on the USSR for the supply of many military hardware items, while only the USSR remained fully self-sufficient. Third, it helped the penetration of Soviet design and technologies throughout the arms industries of the alliance, thus making these industries increasingly dependent on Soviet input of know-how and increasing Soviet political as well as military leverage.[21]

In sum, the Soviets were quite successful in shifting the national resources of East European countries toward the pursuit of WTO objectives. Apart from the fuzzy question of defense expenditures, the East Europeans did incur opportunity costs in terms of skilled manpower and in terms of independent military technology development. The fact that they, too, somewhat benefited from the increased economies of scale does not take away from the fundamental conclusion that the USSR succeeded in its effort to increase the collective effort in a defense establishment in which it commands a preponderant position.

Create an alliance image for the bloc. One of the undesirable products of Stalin's handling of Soviet-East European relations was the creation of an image problem for the bloc, both within the member states and vis-à-vis the West. The creation of a formal multilateral alliance among nominally sovereign states was intended to boost the image of the East European socialist regimes both at home and abroad.

This was particularly needed in light of the existence of NATO[22] on the Western side and of the upcoming Geneva negotiations, which at that time were seen by some to be possible precursors to long-term pan-European talks.[23]

In contrast to their successful achievement of military objectives, the Soviets on the whole were unsuccessful in pursuit of this political goal. The image of the USSR in Eastern Europe did not benefit a great deal from the new organization, and the West was never convinced that the creation of the WTO marked the birth of a new Soviet-East European military and foreign policy consensus or the end of Soviet interference.

Some Western analysts contend that the Soviets felt the need to increase their control over the military establishments of Eastern Europe by decreasing that of the national command authorities over their own respective armies.[24] Others argue that the WTO served to maintain Soviet control in the wake of the withdrawal in 1955 of thousands of Soviet officers who had served in East European services since the end of the war.[25] These analysts further argue that Romania, Yugoslavia and Albania were able to maintain their national sovereignty precisely because they maintained national control over their national armies.

On the contrary, the Khrushchev leadership appears to have intended to restore national control over the East European national armies by 1955. It is also the case that until the early 1960s there was hardly any Soviet effort toward the effective integration of the WTO armed forces. Confirmation for this can also be found in authoritative Soviet sources such as the 1962 edition of Marshal Sokoloviski's *Military Strategy*.[26]

The WTO played no role in the suppression of the Hungarian revolution of 1956. No meeting of the Political Consultative Committee was held after January 1956 and there was never any mention of Soviet-East European consultation after the invasion. Nor was there any East European endorsement of the Soviet action.[27] In the Czechoslovak action of 1968, the WTO played only a marginally greater role than in 1956. It did put political pressure on Dubcek by issuing declarations of disapproval for his policies and it did ask for maneuvers on Czechoslovak soil. But the actual military contribution to the invasion was small. Romania did not participate, Albania used it as a pretext to formally abandon the Pact altogether; Bulgaria sent only token representatives; and Poland and the GDR sent four divisions but pulled them out almost immediately. Moreover, all operations were conducted under direct Soviet, not WTO, command.[28]

East European Initial Objectives in the WTO

The East European did not have the leverage in 1955 to alter Soviet policies in their region in any meaningful sense. Nonetheless they did not just give in to Soviet pressure when they agreed to sign the treaty. On the contrary, they had at least three military reasons of their own to do so.

Soviet nuclear protection. In 1955, it was far from clear which countries would gain access to their own nuclear arsenals in the next few years. Prediction varied, but the consensus was that the number would be much higher than turned out to be the case. Given the economic and technological superiority of the West European countries and the general cold war political climate, it was not irrational on the part of the East European regimes to assume that it was in their best interest to try and find a way to tie their defense and survival to that of the USSR.[29] It is unlikely that they expected to be attacked by the West, and it is also unlikely that they expected that the Soviet Union would risk nuclear war with the United States for their sake. But it nonetheless probably seemed reasonable to them that a formal alliance with the USSR would help restrain the West Europeans, and particularly the West Germans, from any action that did not have the full and unconditional backing of the United States.

In retrospect the East Europeans did not clearly accomplish their objective. Nuclear weapons did not proliferate to the extent expected and West Germany agreed to give up the pursuit of a nuclear weapons capability. These developments, however, could not be attributed to the Soviet nuclear umbrella. Moreover, the Soviet Union seemed no more ready than before to accept the risk of its own nuclear destruction for the sake of Eastern Europe.

In many ways the WTO non-nuclear states face the same dilemma that confronts the non-nuclear NATO states: how to achieve extended deterrence by their nuclear superpower.

Counter German revanchism. With or without nuclear weapons, in 1955 Germany must have looked like a long-term threat to the East European regimes. One need only remember that the Munich agreement of 1938 had not yet been repudiated--and would not be until 1966. The East Europeans also remembered that the USSR did not resist German expansionism in the region in the late 1930s, at least in part because it did not have the military wherewithal to do so. Joining forces with the Soviets and allowing them to be based closer to the West German border was a way to assist the USSR to defend Eastern Europe.

The effect of the WTO in containing the perceived West German threat is also doubtful. A good case can be made that NATO and Willy Brandt did more to moderate West German territorial ambitions that did creation of the Warsaw Pact.

Maintain power at home. When discussing Soviet-East European relations, it must be remembered that the leadership of all states in the WTO, including Romania, share an important long-term strategic interest: to remain in power. This requires not only fending off external threats but also repressing internal ones. Hence, membership in the alliance under the patronage of the Soviet Union was probably considered by the East European leaders to be a good insurance policy against internal as well as external turmoil.[30]

Here too, the East European regimes were unsuccessful. Their restless populations have not been deterred by the USSR. When the discontent over domestic conditions built up, they rose against their leaders in defiance of the Soviets. Soviet intervention (or threat thereof) did of course contribute to the repression of internal upheavals, but it would have done so also without the WTO. In short, the formal alliance with the Soviets did very little to prevent such upheavals.

Transformations in the Warsaw Pact

The late 1960s witnessed a gradual increase in the political significance of the WTO. This increase manifested itself formally though an upgrading of the institutional framework. It also was reflected in the overall higher emphasis accorded to intra-alliance political debate. The institutional framework of the Pact was developed and expanded in 1969 with the creation of the Military Council, which greatly increased the access of the East Europeans to the decision-making process. Meetings of the Pact's policy-making bodies became more frequent and regularized. This transformation was made easier by the fact that the WTO had always been a basically peacetime organization, structured around peacetime rather than wartime requirements. Malcom Mackintosh is right when he states that the WTO already looked in many ways like a traditional European War Office, with a largely administrative role.[31]

At a more general noninstitutional level, there were at least two domestic and two international reasons why the WTO acquired a greater political and a lesser military face in the late 1960s and early 1970s. First, the Czechoslovak crisis convinced the Soviets and the loyalists in Eastern Europe to place more emphasis on collective political as opposed to military action.

Second, political debate within the alliance increased with respect to East-West issues. This process began in the mid-1960s, when U.S. intervention in Vietnam provided the Soviets convenient ammunition for the collective political mobilization of their junior allies. The dawn of detente called for increased coordination of the foreign policies of the WTO, and the East Europeans--with the notable exception of Ulbricht--were eager to pursue the new opportunities afforded by the Soviet-German and Soviet-American dialogue.[32]

A domestic explanation for the transformation is also linked to the Czechoslovak crisis. In its aftermath, the Soviets feared the destructive effect that the breach of Czechoslovak sovereignty could have in the struggle for East European regime legitimacy. Giving the junior allies a greater visibility in collective security arrangements was intended to aid that struggle.

Some analysts also point to a second domestic reason behind the increased political character of the WTO. They argue that the organization had over the years become a consolidated bureaucracy, and therefore displayed a natural tendency to expand and widen its scope.[33]

Without trying to rank the priority of these factors, it is important to note that the transformation affected the nature of the objectives and expectations of all the members of the alliance. Both Soviet and East European objectives in the WTO acquired an increasingly political character.

New Soviet Objectives in the Warsaw Pact

During the second decade of the Warsaw Pact's existence, there arose two new broad Soviet objectives which either did not exist or were largely dormant before. They involved creation of instrument for the coordination of the foreign policies of the various East European governments, and coordination of the military establishments of the alliance's member states.

Integrate the foreign policies of Eastern Europe. While Khrushchev did want to involve the East Europeans more directly in bloc affairs, he certainly did not wish to allow the foreign policies of the individual countries to diverge from that of the Soviet Union. In light of the declining relevance of the Cominform--which was dissolved in 1956--the WTO was seen as the logical alternative to ensure political cohesion in the bloc. Shifting the emphasis from inter-party to inter-state relations was considered more in tune with the new image that the Soviets were trying to create for the East Europeans. Not everyone in the Kremlin, however, was happy with the arrangement. The hardliners complained in the late 1950s that the Pact was not as effective as the Comintern and Cominform had been and advocated the rebirth of an inter-party organization.[34] On the whole they were probably right; the political role of the WTO was negligible in the early years, But it is not clear that a new Cominform would have been more effective.

Until the Czechoslovak crisis of 1968, Moscow did not make extensive use of the WTO as an instrument to channel foreign policies directives to its junior partners.[35] Foreign policy coordination was very often pushed informally, and the official declarations of the WTO never ceased to stress the sovereign rights of each member state. The one formal aspect of the treaty which was useful in this respect was the provision which forbade member states to join conflicting alliances. This kind of constraint would clearly have been more difficult to build into the bilateral treaties.[36]

After the events of 1968, the political bodies of the WTO witnessed increasingly frequent and intense activity. Vietnam, detente, China, defense expenditures and Afghanistan have all been discussed among the allies, and the USSR has often had to compromise over the text of collective declarations. Without going into the details of the many meetings that took place in the last fifteen years or so, one need only recall the bland criticism of China in 1978 and 1983, the bland approval of the Soviet intervention in Afghanistan in 1980, and the bland endorsement of Soviet policies in the Middle East to conclude that, while the Soviets certainly remained the most influential voice in the alliance, they have had to repeatedly accommodate and compromise with the East Europeans.[37]

In recent years, the Soviet Union has added another dimension to the political debate within the WTO over the policy toward the Third World. Wolfgang Berner deals with the economic side of this issue in his chapter in this book. On the military side, the USSR has reportedly tried to expand the scope of the WTO in terms of both its membership and its defense responsibilities.[38] Such attempts however, have consistently and successfully been resisted by the East Europeans--and particularly by the Romanians--on the basis of a narrow interpretation of the letter of the treaty, which confines the responsibilities of the signatories to the European continent.[39] It is no accident that, with the exception of some East German military advisers who have served in various countries of the Third World, the Soviets have sought the cooperation of Cuba, rather than that of WTO allies, when they did not want to intervene directly but needed military proxies.

Military integration. Military integration was only pursued in the WTO after 1961, when a new commander, Soviet Marshal Grechko, began to hold regular joint maneuvers. Such a decision was taken, at least in part, in order to break away from the military structure of the WTO 1958 and 1961.[40] The Soviets pushed for the adoption of a "coalition defense" strategy, which certainly makes good military sense for defense planning against NATO, but also has the collateral advantage of restricting the East European ability to opt out of a conflict.[41]

These exercises also served as a catalyst for a whole series of other measures directed toward the amalgamation of the fighting forces of Eastern Europe and the USSR. They included the activation of the Joint Command, standardization of the arsenals of the various countries, adoption of common fighting doctrines, further integration of administrative structures, and increased requirements for joint officer training, most of which takes place at Soviet schools and academies. The intent was to build an *esprit de corps* among officers around the region and thus confer a further element of homogeneity to the various national forces.[42]

New East European Objectives in the WTO

The East Europeans, for their part, also developed distinctively new objectives in the WTO. These included using the WTO as a collective political forum against both the Soviet preponderance and possible national deviation, and increasing bloc cooperation but resisting integration.

WTO as a political forum. There are indications that the East Europeans successfully tried to increase their political leverage against the USSR by making use of the collective WTO bodies, particularly those which were created in the last fifteen years or so when the political role of the WTO was ascendant.[43] Such new bodies include the Council of Defense Ministers, the Military Council and the Committee on Coordination of Military Technology--created in 1969--and the Council of Foreign Ministers and the Joint Secretariat--created in 1976.

Instances of resistance to Soviet foreign policy positions have already been mentioned above; suffice it here to reiterate that this resistance was in all likelihood made easier, maybe possible, by the opportunity that the various WTO organisms provided for collective--as opposed to bilateral--Soviet-East European debate. While Romania has been the most vociferous to resist Soviet policies--e.g. with its public rejection of the Soviet request for an increased defense budget in 1978--several other countries have been able to articulate their separate voices at various times.

In other words, when issues of disagreement arise, the East Europeans find it easier to confront the Soviets in multilateral gatherings than to face the Soviets alone.[44] Comparing the present situation with that of some twenty years ago, it appears that the East Europeans have achieved a good measure of success in their effort to increase their political input into the WTO. The extent of this success is, of course, subject to some uncertainty, but the negotiations leading to the renewal of the Pact during 1984-85 seem to indicate that it was not negligible, and that it is likely to continue.

Promote cooperation but resist integration. The regimes of Eastern Europe share common long-term political goals with the USSR. Both they and the Kremlin desire to perpetuate their rule indefinitely. This commonality of goals constitutes the basis for a mutual search for cooperation between the Soviet Union and its allies. None of the regimes of Eastern Europe, no matter what their particular disagreements with the Soviets, would feel more secure without the presence of the Soviet military might on the continent.

However, the East Europeans do not have as much of an objective interest in integration with the USSR or among themselves. They have, in fact, resisted Soviet attempts at integration. Even on the military plane they have been at least partially successful: witness the Political Consultative Committee's communique after the 1976 Bucharest meeting which talked of cooperation but not of integration. This does not, of course, mean that no military integration has taken place; much has indeed. But it does mean that international security considerations do not detract from the nationalistic desire of all East European governments to avoid any outside interference in their internal affairs and in their diverse relations with the West.

Prospects for Soviet-European Relations in the WTO

There are strong reasons to expect both continuity and some change in Soviet-East European relations in the WTO. On the one hand, there continues to be a fundamental identity of security interests among the various leaderships of the WTO. These interests include both the preservation of a strong military posture vis-à-vis NATO and the prevention of destabilizing national deviations within the region. All current WTO members agree on this, and even the defiant Romanians alternate expression of dissent on specific issues with reiterations of solidarity and support for the alliance. Bucharest resists the perfecting of the WTO but remains firmly committed to its existence in its present form.[45]

On the other hand, several factors might cause a fundamental change in intra-alliance relations. First, the evolution of the WTO indicates that the

East Europeans are increasing their input, especially at the political level. Although the Soviets have had their own reasons to allow this to happen, in the long run East European leverage may develop beyond what the Soviets intended.

The case of Romania is particularly relevant here. The military problem posed by Bucharest's defiant attitude is not an insurmountable one. While the WTO might need Romanian help against either the Southern flank of NATO or Yugoslavia--or both--neither of these poses a major military threat for the USSR. However, given the increasing political importance of the WTO, Ceaucescu's policy of autonomy is harmful because it very often prevents the Soviets from reaching consensus. It also might eventually open the Pandora's box of East European nationalism, with consequences for bloc unity which are difficult to forecast but which might well become unmanageable for the Soviets.

Second, East European nationalism is on the rise. The conflict between nationalists and "Muscovites" is not new among the ranks of the communist parties of the region, but in recent times the former seem to be gaining strength, particularly in Hungary and East Germany. Nationalist feelings have always been high in Poland and Romania, and remain so. There are some symptoms of nationalism also in Bulgaria, while Czechoslovakia seems to be the only country where the Muscovites are basically unchallenged.

Finally, economic problems might also work to increase East European leverage vis-à-vis the USSR, in the WTO as well as in other bloc bodies. The USSR cannot allow its junior allies to risk political destabilization because of popular discontent. Therefore, it may find itself obliged either to provide economic aid or to allow national reforms in order to let each country achieve economic viability on its own.[46] If the economic performance of both the USSR and of its allies deteriorates further, the former might very well be unable to continue to provide sufficient economic support to the latter, and might then be forced to allow for more domestic reforms than would otherwise be deemed desirable. While Gorbachev is clearly intent on promoting East European economic efficiency, he cannot but be as wary as his predecessors about reforms acquiring diversified political overtones and thus working to the detriment of overall bloc cohesion.

In sum, while the probability of sudden and dramatic change in Soviet-East European security relations is low, there are political and economic reasons to expect that the current trend toward increasingly high East European input in bloc affairs is likely to continue. The Soviets will likely experience greater difficulty in the realization of their main current objectives in the WTO, both in the coordination of bloc foreign policies and in the further integration of Pact military forces.

Implications for the West

The WTO had only minimal impact on East-West relations during the first decade of its existence. It was not taken very seriously in the West, where it was seen as little more than a transmission belt for Soviet military policies and interests. This Western perception has changed since the mid-1950s, particularly after the Romanian declaration of autonomy of 1964. Bucharest's new stance convinced many in the West that something was changing in intra-Pact politics and that the East Europeans were trying with some success to play a more active role in it.

In a very concrete sense, then, Romanian defiance has helped to improve the image and the respectability of the Pact in the West and elsewhere, and thereby served one of the Soviet's objectives.[47] The less glamorous but no less important recent attitudes of Hungary and East Germany also enhance the image of the Pact as a collective body.

At the same time, to the extent that it has contributed to diluting Soviet power in the region, Romania--and more recently Hungary and East Germany--also served Western interests. West Europeans can now deal directly with East Europeans to a much larger extent than had been the case prior to the late 1960s. Other factors have contributed to the improvement of direct contacts between Eastern Europe and the West, but the political emancipation of several East European countries in the WTO has been an important one.

The main implication of Soviet-East European relations for the West is that a continuation of current trends is in the latter's interest, and should be encouraged to the extent that it is feasible to do so. By current trends I mean both the politicization of the WTO--which has been taking place for the last twenty years--and the increasing role of the East Europeans in it. There are three reasons why both should be seen favorably in the West. First, a higher political stature for the East Europeans makes it possible to continue the process of European detente even if relations with the USSR deteriorate. In other words, greater East European political leverage vis-à-vis the USSR decreases the latter's influence in Western Europe.

Second, the declining emphasis on the military aspects of the WTO decreases the reliability of the Pact as a military instrument--especially for offensive purposes[48]--and puts a greater burden on the Soviet forces. This should translate into greater Soviet caution, and therefore greater insurance against war in case of a serious crisis.

Third, the continuing fundamental commitment of the East European governments to the WTO is a source of stability as it provides continuing reassurance to the USSR that its basic security interests are not jeopardized. The East Europeans will remain committed to the WTO--and, implicitly, to the status quo in Europe--as long as they perceive it to be worthwhile for them to do so. West Europeans are in a similar situation in NATO. To the extent that West Europeans wish to maintain the status quo in Europe, or to change it only very gradually and only by peaceful means, it is in their interests that the WTO not undergo destabilizing changes which might provoke political and military deterioration on the continent.

In conclusion, both the politicization of the WTO and the increasing political voice of the East Europeans should be seen as favorable developments. The West should encourage their continuation.

A more difficult question is how to do so. This brings up issues that are intertwined with the enormous web of East-West political, economic, social, and other relations, and range beyond the scope of the WTO. Therefore, only general criteria can be outlined here. With this caveat in mind, I suggest the following:

a) Western countries should develop closer bilateral political ties with the East Europeans, so as to increase the leverage of the latter vis-à-vis the USSR.

b) At the same time, the West should discourage attempts on the part of East European countries to break away from their alliance system--WTO, CMEA, etc.,--because that would risk destabilizing the region and because even if it did not, it would deprive the West of an indirect means to influence the USSR. In other words, Romanian, East German or Hungarian disagreements with the Soviets would be more beneficial to the West if those countries remain in the WTO. Moreover, should the USSR be pushed toward new military interventions in Eastern Europe, this would result in decreased political diversity in the bloc and this, too, runs against Western interests.

In sum, the West's interests require that a finely-tuned policy between overtures and restraint be followed in order to both maintain stability and cultivate diversity in Eastern Europe. Overtures to Eastern Europe are needed because they can increase its leverage with the Soviets and thereby also our own. Restraint is mandatory because change must be peaceful and gradual if it is to take place in a direction that is favorable to the West. As was clear in 1956, in 1968, and again in 1981, the West cannot and will not risk confrontation with the USSR in order to prevent the repression of rapid or violent change in Eastern Europe.

Notes

1. The German Democratic Republic was fully integrated in the WTO in 1956, while Albania pulled out of all Pact activities in 1961 and formally withdrew in 1968, after the invasion of Czechoslovakia.

2. Robin A. Remington, *The Warsaw Pact* (Cambridge: M.I.T. Press, 1971), p. 165.

3. Ibid, p. 26.

4. Malcom Mackintosh, "Military Considerations in Soviet-East European Relations," Karen Dawisha and Philip Janson, eds., *Soviet-East European Dilemmas: Coercion, Competition and Consent* (London and New York: Holmes & Meier Publishers, 1981), p. 138.

5. Thomas Cason, "The Warsaw Pact," Michael J. Sodaro and Sharon L. Wolchik, *Foreign and Domestic Policy in Eastern Europe in the '80s: Trends and Prospects* (New York: St. Martin Press, 1981), p. 215.

6. Malcom Mackintosh, "The Warsaw Treaty Organization: A History," Jane Sharp and David Holloway, eds., *The Warsaw Pact; Alliance in Transition* (Ithaca: Cornell University Press, 1984), p. 42.

7. Dale R. Herspring, "The Warsaw Pact at 25," *Problems of Communism*, September/October 1980, pp. 5-6.

8. Lawrence T. Caldwell, "The Warsaw Pact: Directions of Change," *Problems of Communism*, September/October 1975, p. 17.

9. Thomas Cason, "The Warsaw Pact," *op.cit.*, p. 227.

10. There is no simple answer to the question of to what degree WTO armies are "reliable" allies of the Soviet Union. To a good extent, the answer depends on the purpose towards which the small allies' reliability would be tested against Soviet demands and potentially diverging East European interests. For example, East European reliability would probably be higher in a defensive war against a NATO attack than in an unprovoked offensive against Western Europe or the neutral countries in central Europe. The issue of reliability is thoroughly discussed in Daniel N. Nelson, ed., *Soviet Allies: The Warsaw Pact and the Issue of Reliability* (Boulder: Westview Press, 1984).

11. Lawrence T. Caldwell, "The Warsaw Pact," *op.cit.*, p. 17.

12. Richard C. Martin, "Warsaw Pact Force Modernization: A Closer Look," *Parameters*, Summer 1985, p. 9.

13. Malcom Mackintosh, "Military Considerations," *op.cit.*, passim.

14. Thomas Cason, "The Warsaw Pact," *op.cit.*, p. 215.

15. Robin A. Remington, *The Warsaw Pact, op.cit.*, p. 165.

16. Ibid.

17. John Erickson, "The Warsaw Pact--The Shape of Things to Come?," Dawisha and Hanson eds. *op.cit.*, p. 161.

18. Malcom Mackintosh, quoted in Thomas Cason, "The Warsaw Pact," *op.cit.*, pp. 218-220.

19. John Erickson, "Stability in the Warsaw Pact?" *Current History*, #478, November 1982, p. 394.

20. William M. Reisinger, "East European Military Expenditures in the 1970s: Collective Good or Bargaining Offer?" *International Organization*, Winter 1983, p. 154.

21. Condoleezza Rice, "Defense Burden Sharing," Jane Sharp and David Holloway, eds., *op.cit.*, pp. 65ff.

22. Robin A. Remington, *The Warsaw Pact, op.cit.*, p. 165.

23. Thomas Cason, "The Warsaw Pact," *op.cit.*, p. 215.

24. Christopher D. Jones, "National Armies and National Sovereignty," Jane Sharp and David Holloway, eds., *op.cit.*, passim.

25. Mark N. Kramer, "Civil-Military Relations in the Warsaw Pact: the East European Component," *International Affairs* (London), Winter 1984, p. 55.

26. Malcom Mackintosh, "The Evolution of the Warsaw Pact," Adelphi Papers Number 58, the International Institute for Strategic Studies, June 1968, p. 6.

27. Robin A. Remington, *The Warsaw Pact, op.cit.*, pp. 66-67.

28. Ibid, p. 169; Thomas Cason, "The Warsaw Pact," *op.cit.*, p. 218; Richard C. Martin, "Warsaw Pact Force Modernization," *op.cit.*, p. 10.

29. John Erickson, "The Warsaw Pact--the Shape of Things to Come?," Dawisha and Hanson eds. *op.cit.*, p. 169.

30. Robert L. Hutchings, *Soviet-East European Relations: Consolidation and Conflict, 1969-1980* (Madison: University of Wisconsin Press), p. 168.

31. Malcom Mackintosh, "The Evolution of the Warsaw Pact," *op.cit.*, passim.

32.   Lawrence Caldwell, "The Warsaw Pact," *op.cit.*, pp. 16-19.

33.   Ibid, p. 18.

34.   Robin A. Remington, *The Warsaw Pact, op.cit.*, p. 41.

35.   Thomas Cason, "The Warsaw Pact," *op.cit.*, p. 215; Moreton, "Security, Change and Instability in Eastern Europe," Derek Leebaert ed., *European Security: Prospects for the '80s* (Lexington, MA: Lexington Books) p. 168.

36.   Robin A. Remington, *The Warsaw Pact, op.cit.*, p. 165.

37.   Robert L. Hutchings, *Soviet-East European Relations, op.cit.*, pp. 104-108.

38.   Dale R. Herspring, "The Warsaw Pact at 25," *op.cit.*, p. 13.

39.   Robert L. Hutchings, *Soviet-East European Relations, op.cit.*, p. 166.

40.   Christopher D. Jones, *Soviet Influence in Eastern Europe: Political Autonomy and the Warsaw Pact* (New York: Praeger, 1981), p. 229.

41.   Mark N. Kramer, "Civil-Military Relations," *op.cit.*, pp. 57-58.

42.   Christopher D. Jones, *Soviet Influence in Eastern Europe: Political Autonomy and the Warsaw Pact* (New York: Praeger, 1981), p. 231.

43.   Robert L. Hutchings, *Anatomy of the Warsaw Pact*, Unpublished paper, 1983, passim.

44.   John Erickson, The Warsaw Pact--The Shape of Things to Come?" Dawisha and Hanson eds., *op.cit.*, p. 169.

45.   Robin A. Remington, *The Warsaw Pact, op.cit.*, p. 7.

46.   J.F. Brown, "The Future of Political Relations in the Warsaw Pact," Jane Sharp and David Holloway, eds., *op.cit.*, pp. 205ff.

47.   Thomas Cason, "The Warsaw Pact," *op.cit.*, p. 226.

48.   See note 10 above.

8

SOVIET-EAST EUROPEAN COOPERATION IN THE FIELD OF MILITARY AID TOWARDS THE THIRD WORLD

Joachim Krause

Introduction

S ince the mid-1970s, a new pattern of collaboration among the member states of the Warsaw Pact has emerged: the division of labor in the field of military assistance for Third World states and liberation movements. Although these activities attracted considerable attention during the second half of the 1970s (i.e., the events in Angola and Ethiopia), few scientific works were written on the subject.[1] Moreover, most information is from "U.S. government sources," a phrase that assures that the data were issued by intelligence agencies. Independent sources in the open literature, like SIPRI and IISS, provide only limited information. One has to live with conjecture and data which are difficult to verify. Consequently, the findings presented in this chapter can only be of a tentative kind. On the other hand, there is some merit in pulling together information which seems to be serious.

Whenever mention is made of this division of labor in Soviet and East European military aid, two aspects are emphasized: first, the role the smaller Warsaw Pact members have assumed within the context of Soviet global strategy, and second, the question of whether the East Europeans and the GDR, by participating in collective military aid efforts, were pursuing interests which were not fully identical with those of the Soviet Union. The first section of this chapter focuses on the role the smaller Warsaw Pact countries play in the eyes of the Kremlin, or, in other words, on their contribution to a Soviet military aid diplomacy in the Third World that aims in the long run at changing the worldwide "correlation of forces" in favor of the "forces of peace and socialism." The second section deals with the special national interests of the GDR, Poland, Czechoslovakia, Hungary, Bulgaria and Romania; do their interests fit into the Soviet strategy? What has changed within the last 20 years in this regard? The third section addresses the implications for Western security, i.e., is there reason to assume that by doing their "internationalist duty" the smaller Warsaw Pact states gain leeway for their own foreign policy?

The Global Dimension of Warsaw Pact Military Aid

When mention is made of "military aid" towards Third World countries, all kinds of military assistance are meant, ranging from the supply of weapons, ammunition, and spare parts to the training of Third World military men, officers, and technicians, the delivery of arms production facilities or the dispatch of the donor's own military personnel as advisors, instructors or even in a--mostly limited--combat role (as for pilots etc.). For the Soviet Union, within the last 25 years military aid has become the most important instrument in dealing with Third World countries. By means of military aid policy, Moscow repeatedly succeeded in bringing in its influence to bear on major political events outside Europe, thus helping the Kremlin to establish itself as a real global power. By delivering weapons, training soldiers and granting other kinds of military services, the Soviet Union helped Hanoi, for example, to win its more-than-decade-long war against South Vietnam and the United States. The Soviet Union backed the Arab side in its fight with Israel and brought itself into a position as a veto-power in the Middle East. Moscow also had a strong impact on political developments in the former Portuguese colonies in Africa after they became independent after 1974, and the Soviet Union was able to build strong and enduring relationships with some rather important Third World nations, such as India, Algeria, and Iraq. Although Soviet military aid diplomacy towards the Third World has not been a success story at all times (Indonesia, Egypt, China, and Somalia are former arms clients which now lead the "anti-Soviet front") and although it has not met all expectations, it turned out to be the most important instrument to deal with the "liberated countries" and to have a bearing upon the worldwide "correlations of forces" between the Soviet bloc and the western alliance.[2]

Since the mid-1950s--that is, from the beginning of Moscow's arms aid diplomacy towards the non-aligned countries--the Kremlin has made use of individual Warsaw Pact allies. Beginning in the late 1960s, these endeavors became more and more coordinated and showed that the Soviet Union has tried to integrate its allies into an overall strategy. There were, and still are, several reasons which rendered it reasonable in the Soviet point of view to resort to their Warsaw Pact partners.

Historically, the first reason for this was that the Kremlin wanted to avoid risks. Especially in the 1950s, when the Soviet Union was militarily inferior to the U.S. and lacked experience in the arms sales business, the Kremlin was anxious to avoid too strong a direct engagement in Third World crises or military affairs. The Soviet leadership feared unforeseeable consequences-- such as strong internal opposition within the arms recipient country, or hostile reactions by neighbors, countermeasures by Western powers or combinations of all these developments--which could force the Soviet Union either to retreat or to overshoot itself. By first sending aid from Czechoslovakia, Poland or other East European states, Moscow often kept open the option of silent and face-saving retreat, in case things developed in an unfavorable manner. Due to the growth in the overall military strength of the Soviet Union and to its growing experience with arms aid, the importance of the people's democracies' role as an opener for Soviet influence in Third World regions has diminished. But the East Europeans or the GDR are still asked to assume responsibilities in the military aid field when Moscow is reluctant to establish direct military ties--as for instance in the case of Iraq from 1981 to 1983, when the Soviet Union still held open its Teheran option in the Gulf War.

The second reason for the Kremlin to seek the cooperation of its Warsaw Pact allies was the hope of enhancing the effectiveness of its military aid policy. Czechoslovakia and Poland have impressive arms production capacities. In some central categories of ground equipment (tanks, artillery, armored vehicles) their industrial output is larger than--or at least equal to-- that of all West European NATO states taken together (Table I). They either deliver weapons and ammunition directly to Third World clients or they send them to the Soviet Union from which they are re-exported to arms customers in Asia, Africa, the Middle East or Latin America. By this means, more than 50 percent of Polish and Czechoslovakian arms exports go either directly or indirectly into the Third World. Czechoslovakia exported weapons worth nearly $4 billion between 1979-1983, Poland slightly more than $3 billion in the same period. How strongly their arms exports are integrated into and subordinated to Soviet military aid diplomacy can be inferred from the fact that more than two-thirds of these arms shipments are of indirect kind--i.e., they are first transferred to the Soviet Union and are afterwards sold by Moscow.[3] The Soviet Union's ability to deliver large amounts of arms within a short time--much shorter than the United States--is in part a consequence of this use of its East European allies. The same is true with respect to military training and education: today, of all non-communist Third World soldiers who go to East bloc countries for training, 30 percent are moving to the GDR or other smaller Warsaw Pact countries. Thousands of East German and East European military advisers, teachers and instructors are currently doing their job in Third World countries, most of them coming from the GDR.[4]

A further reason to integrate smaller Warsaw Pact countries into the Kremlin's arms aid policy was to share the burden of military aid. A big part of Soviet arms deliveries (today about 40 percent, until 1973 more than 70 percent) are either on concessional terms (whereby repayment often is deferred or even canceled) or free of charge. Thus, Moscow was keen to convince its Warsaw Pact partners to assume at least a portion of that military aid burden. Interestingly enough, the Soviet Union never was very successful in this respect. In 1966, for instance, the smaller Warsaw Pact countries consented to a Soviet proposal to provide 20 percent of all arms deliveries of the East bloc for North Vietnam. Although they all sent fact-finding missions to Hanoi and dispatched a few ships with weaponry, their respective share never came close to the agreed amount.[5] The same is true today. Those Third World countries which are getting weapons on favorable terms from the communist world are almost exclusively Soviet arms customers. Cuba, Vietnam, Laos, Cambodia, and Afghanistan get virtually no weaponry from Czechoslovakia, the GDR, Poland, Romania, or Bulgaria.

Beyond that, the Soviet leadership expects that participation by other countries of the Warsaw Pact or even by non-aligned states could result in a legitimizing effect for its military aid policy. Moscow wants to eschew the impression that its arms aid diplomacy serves the selfish interests of a superpower. Organizing collective military aid endeavors--especially when non-Warsaw-Pact members also participate--gives the Soviet leadership a chance to pretend that these activities are something other than a superpower game.

In order to organize the division of labor in the most appropriate way, the Soviet leadership undertook various approaches. In the first phase--in the 1950s--the Kremlin built upon its bilateral relationships with Poland and Czechoslovakia. Both countries proved to be helpful in the early years of Soviet military aid diplomacy as arms exporters and in granting military training programs. In the second phase--in the 1960s--the Soviet Union tried to make use of the Warsaw Pact machinery in order to integrate all people's democracies and to have a clear division of labor among them. This endeavor failed mainly due to a combination of political and practical reasons. Some of the East European governments found themselves unable to make more than a slight contribution (like Bulgaria and Hungary), while Romania flatly refused any participation in Warsaw Pact military aid operations outside Europe.[6] Moreover, even from the Soviet point of view there was not much sense in extending the responsibilities of the Warsaw Pact to areas outside Europe. This could have backfired or had a detrimental effect on the credibility of Moscow's propagandistic rhetoric against NATO. Thus, only a limited kind of division of labor was decided upon in 1972: the Soviet Union, Czechoslovakia, the GDR, Poland and Hungary came to an understanding of how to coordinate their activities in the field of military training and education for Third World arms customers. The success of that step is evident if one looks upon the respective figures provided by the U.S. government: until the mid-1970s, less than 10 percent of the military training activities of the Warsaw Pact for Third World states were done by the smaller Pact countries. By the beginning of the 1980s their respective share had climbed up to about 30 percent (Table II).

Not surprisingly, in the 1970s the Soviet Union began to organize the division of labor in the field of military aid in a more flexible way. The Kremlin forbore to refer to all Warsaw Pact members in order to get assistance but included also formally non-committed states like Cuba and sometimes even Vietnam, South Yemen or North Korea. The division of labor was largely agreed upon on a case-by-case basis. This gave Moscow the chance to make full use of the capabilities of its allies without involving the Warsaw Treaty Organization. On the other hand, it offered the smaller Warsaw Pact states and Cuba a chance to play a more important and independent role in international politics.[7]

The Role of the Smaller Warsaw Pact Countries

The Soviet quest for participation in cooperative military aid efforts met with different expectations and interests in the smaller Warsaw Pact countries. In order to understand the complex ways that they conceive their role, it is the best to carry out a country-by-country survey.

First is Czechoslovakia, which has the longest experience in arms exports and military assistance. The CSSR has since the late 1940s wanted to attain and to maintain a special status within the East bloc due to its rather high level of industrialization and degree of modernization. Participating in the Third World arms business provided Prague with an early chance not only to become Moscow's most important partner in a central foreign policy area but also to win some kind of leeway and independent profile in international politics. By making available weapons for the Soviet Union to re-export to

Third World countries, Prague had a strong argument against any efforts by the Soviet Union to further curtail both quantity and quality of Czechoslovakian armaments production. Besides that, Prague was able to offset the rather high bill for arms imports from the Soviet Union. Selling arms to Moscow even contributed to the adjustment of the big deficit in trade with the Soviet Union. According to U.S. government sources, between 1979 and 1983 Czechoslovakia exported nearly twice as much weaponry to the Soviet Union as it imported from there (Table III). These data are corroborated by calculations based on official CMEA data.[8]

During the "Prague Spring" and shortly after its suppression by the invading Warsaw Pact forces, the importance of Czechoslovakia in the military aid sector declined. But starting in the early 1970s, the government in Prague tried everything to assure the Kremlin of its allegiance and to win back its political influence by becoming a strong advocate of Soviet foreign policy and by assisting Moscow in Third World areas. Beyond these intra-Pact aspects, Czechoslovakia also managed to draw profits from selling weapons directly to Middle East customers for cash. More than two percent of its export income and up to 10 percent of its hard currency revenues in the last ten years resulted from such arms exports. Prague has also tried to establish bilateral economic relations with arms customers in order to diversify its exports and to gain some freedom of action in the economic field.

The GDR today is strongly engaged in the military aid field, with more than 2360 military advisers and security instructors in the Third World.[9] In contrast to Czechoslovakia or Poland, the GDR has no significant arms industries. Thus, East Germany is not an important arms exporter (Table IV), but it has time and again delivered more or less sophisticated non-lethal items for military use in Third World armies, such as trucks, medical equipment, and communications electronics. The GDR's principal emphasis is on training of technical, administrative and medical personnel as well as the training of military cadres, security services and members of national liberation movements. The main interest of East Berlin in doing this is to gain an independent political profile and latitude within Warsaw Pact by giving as much assistance as possible to every Soviet military endeavor in the Third World. The rationale behind this is that the more strongly the GDR supports the Soviet Union, the more independent it will become in both internal and external affairs. Economic considerations do not play an important role. The main inducement for the GDR leadership is the desire to overcome the rather exclusive dependency on the Soviet Union and to have an independent impact on international politics. It is the hope of the ruling SED that activities of that kind may contribute to the development of an independent political identity of the GDR.

Poland, like Czechoslovakia, is mainly interested in the economic benefits of arms sales, both from within the Warsaw Pact and from outside. Due to the relatively small importance of armaments production for its industry and its technological development, Poland's arms exports range behind that of Czechoslovakia (Tables III and IV). There is no Polish strategy of reassuring the Kremlin of its allegiance by over-readiness or even officiousness in the military aid field, as for instance in the case of the GDR. As in Czechoslovakia, Polish arms exports mainly are going into the Soviet Union, thus helping Moscow to fulfill its military aid obligations towards Third World countries. Weapons exports to the Soviet Union also are an instrument to mitigate Warsaw's enduring trade deficit with Moscow. There are only a few contingents of Polish military advisers or instructors in the Third World. It seems that the current Polish government is mainly concerned with its internal problems, but it is still looking to acquire an independent international economical and political profile by having direct links with various Third World nations.

Hungary and Bulgaria do not play an important role. Both have sold arms to Third World countries only on a small scale. They have sometimes figured as intermediaries in cases where the Soviet Union did not want to be directly involved. Bulgaria has often played a role in arms smuggling and some other dubious business which, inter alia, resulted in Bulgarian arms deliveries to South Africa.

Romania is an exceptional case, since it has sometimes flatly refused to participate in a military aid diplomacy that only supports the strategic designs of the Soviet Union in the Third World. That does not imply that Romania refrains from military aid activities in the Third World or that Romania is not prepared to cooperate with the Soviet Union. In any case, the leadership in Bucharest is anxious to decide on its own whether and under which circumstances it will give military aid. Thus, there were incidents where Romania granted military assistance to state governments or liberation movements which were hostile to Soviet-supported powers. In other cases, Romania participated in concerted Pact efforts to help militarily Third World countries. Romania also exports weapons into the Soviet Union from where they may be re-transferred. The main interest of Romania is to keep its own rather independent foreign policy profile. The slowdown of the Romanian economy within the last decade has calmed the rhetoric of independence from Soviet supremacy and Bucharest has avoided any individual step which could have further alienated its relationship with Moscow. On the other hand, due to its urgent need for hard currency income, Romania has increased its arms sales to the Middle East within recent years, especially to Iraq.

As Table V shows, the smaller Warsaw Pact states have a respectable share of the overall arms exports of the Eastern bloc into the Third World, although these figures do not cover communist arms deliveries to Cuba, Vietnam or Laos.[10] One should not forget that the Soviet arms deliveries to Third World nations in part consist of items which were imported earlier from Poland, Czechoslovakia or Romania. Thus, the actual share of these countries is larger than the figures may suggest. It is noteworthy that their arms export share has increased since 1980. This is mainly due to the war between Iraq and Iran where Romania, Poland and Czechoslovakia delivered huge amounts of weaponry to Iraq, as long as Moscow refrained from being involved there directly.

Besides that, some political differences remain. In the field of military aid policy, the main interest of the Soviet Union in having a division of labor within the Pact is of a global and strategic kind. The main interest of the smaller Warsaw Pact members is more or less oriented towards enhancing their political and economic position within the East bloc, to win some kind of international political influence and to strengthen the internal position of the regimes. This does not mean that the Soviet Union is not concerned about intra-Pact relations or that the political leaders of the GDR and East Europe are indifferent to the goal of the global expansion of communism. But the emphasis they put on these aims do differ substantially.

Impact on Western Security

In other words, the intentions the smaller Warsaw Pact members associate with their contributions in the military aid field are aimed at gaining some foreign policy and economic leeway vis-à-vis the Soviet Union. This search for at least a small portion of independence is not confined to military aid policy. In recent years, western observers repeatedly have pointed out developments of that kind in the Eastern bloc. Especially after the worsening of U.S.-Soviet relations in 1983/84, some of the people's democracies-- mainly the GDR--played an important role in calming down the situation and limiting the damage. Most observers agreed that this new role of the GDR could open some chances for securing détente or even for some further progress in that direction.[11] While the East German policy of "damage limitation" is in fact an example of a search for a new political role for East Berlin that the West should encourage, things look different with respect to the GDR's (or the other smaller Warsaw Pact members') role in the military aid area. Their participation is clearly aimed at restraining and driving back Western influence in Asia, Africa, the Middle East or Latin America in order to weaken the world-wide strategic position of the West as a whole. This implies that the Western world should not be delighted with the emancipation of Warsaw Pact states if this goes at the expense of Western security and welfare.

Although one should not be too alarmist about communist military aid activities in the Third World, since they do not constitute the main focus of Soviet world policy and have been less successful than Soviet leaders may have expected, it should be kept in mind that not all divergences within the Warsaw Pact automatically lead to a more benign policy towards the West. Western policymakers should be very careful in separating between those two different outcomes of intra-Pact developments. They should also be aware of the fact that, from the point of view of the smaller Warsaw Pact members, it is always easier to look for more political leeway in an area where the Kremlin estimates that this would promote its global ambitions than somewhere the Soviet leadership could feel uneasy about its allies. Besides that, chances for Western governments to influence the behavior of political leaders in East Berlin, Prague, Warsaw, Budapest or Bucharest in that respect seem to be dim. At most, one could try to establish some system of incentives and disincentives, consisting of a set of various measures on different levels. In this respect, the West could try to make use of some contradictions in the policy of East European governments, thus urging them to show their hands. The GDR, for example, by assisting the Soviet Union in various military aid endeavors in Africa and elsewhere in the mid-70s, strongly contributed to the worsening of U.S.-Soviet relationship as a whole. The SED policy of damage-limitation in the 1980s is in fact a political maneuver to contain a deterioration in East-West relations the GDR once had helped to engender. There would be some positive impact on East-West political relationships if Western political leaders could find a way to strengthen the sensibleness of the smaller Warsaw Pact states towards these implications of their foreign policy.

Table I

Annual Average Production Output of Major Weapons Systems in NATO and Warsaw Pact 1974-1983

arms systems	USSR	other WTO	USA	other NATO
tanks	2370	415	625	420
armored fighting vehicles	4550	990	600	1150
field artillery, mortars and rocket launchers	2600	350	160	200
tactical aircraft	840	160	350	380
large naval craft	9	2	8	9
attack submarines	7	-	3	3

Note: Calculations based on figures provided by U.S. Department of Defense, Report of Secretary of Defense, C.W. Weinberger, FY 1985, Washington 1984, p. 23.

Table II

Military Personnel From the Less Developed Countries Trained in East Bloc Countries

	USSR	Non-Soviet WTO
1955-1976	39,950	4,375
1977-1984	20,645	9,415

Sources: CIA, *Communist Aid Activities in Non-Communist Less-Developed Countries, 1979* and 1954-79, Washington 1980; CIA, *Handbook of Economic Statistics, 1984 and 1985*, Washington D.C. 1984 and 1985.

Table III

Arms Transfers Within the Warsaw Pact 1979-1983 in Million U.S. Dollars

arms importing countries:	arms exporters				
	USSR	Czechosl.	Poland	Romania	others
USSR	-	2,200	1 800	190	440
Czechosl.	1,200	-	5	-	5
Poland	1,200	260	-	-	130
Romania	655	40	30	-	10
GDR	1,600	20	70	290	-
Hungary	650	90	5	-	20
Bulgaria	1,100	-	-	-	5
Total	6,170	2,610	1,910	480	610

Source: U.S. ACDA, *World Military Expenditures and Arms Transfers, 1985,* Washington 1985, p. 133.

Table IV

Arms Exports of the Warsaw Pact States 1979-1983
(in Million U.S. Dollars)

USSR:	56,400
Czechoslovakia:	3,950
Poland:	3,100
GDR:	560
Hungary:	560
Romania:	1,980
Bulgaria	840

Source: U.S. ACDA, *World Military Expenditures and Arms Transfers, 1985*, Washington, D.C. 1985, Table II.

Table V

East-Bloc Military Aid Deliveries to
Non-Communist Third World Countries 1975-1984
(in Millon U.S. Dollars)

	USSR	Other Warsaw Pact
1975	2,035	275
1976	3,110	350
1977	4,815	355
1978	6,075	550
1979	8,340	645
1980	8,125	635
1981	8,105	1,315
1982	8,065	1,970
1983	7,130	1,845
Total	62,935	9,000

Source: CIA, *Handbook of Economics Data, 1985*, Washington D.C. 1985, p. 109.

Notes

1. Cf. Trond Gilberg, "East European Arms Transfers to the Third World," in John F. Copper and Daniel S. Papp eds., *Communist Military Assistance* (Boulder, CO: 1983); Condolezza Rice, "Defense in Burden-Sharing," in David Holloway and Jane Sharp, eds., *The Warsaw Pact: Alliance in Transition* (London: 1984); Jonathan Dean, "The Warsaw Pact in the International System," in Holloway and Sharp; Roger E. Kanet, "Military Relations between Eastern European and Africa," in Bruce E. Arlinghams ed., *Arms for Africa* (Lexington, MA: 1983); Melvin Croan, "A New Africa Corps," in *The Washington Quarterly*, vol. 3, no. 1, (Winter: 1980); Peer Lange, *Perspektiven der Militärhilfe der Staaten des Warschauer Paktes and die Dritte Welt* (Ebenhausen: 1979); Thomas H. Snitch, "East European Involvement in the World's Arms Market," in U.S. Arms Control and Disarmament Agency (ACDA), *World Military Expenditures and Arms Transfers 1972-1982* (Washington, D.C.: April 1984).

2. Cf. Joachim Krause, *Sowjetische Militärhilfepolitik gegenüber Entwicklungsländern*, Baden Baden, 1985; Roger Pajak, "Soviet Arms Transfers as an Instrument of Influence," *Survival*, vol. 23, no. 4, July/August 1981.

3. Cf. Snitch, "East European Involvement," p. 117f.

4. Rice, "Defense in Burden-Sharing," p. 83.

5. Cf. Krause, *Sowjetische Militärhilfepolitik*, p. 92f.; see also the figures provided by ACDA, *World Military Expenditures and Arms Transfers*, 1967-1976, (Washington, D.C.: 1978), p. 158.

6. In 1967 Romania even refused to participate in a meeting of the heads of the communist parties and the governments of Eastern Europe which was held to deliberate on arms aid for Egypt and Syria; c.f. Krause, *Sowjetische Militärhilfepolitik*, p. 202.

7. Cf. Dean, "The Warsaw Pact," p. 250f.

8. Cf. Wharton Economics Forecasting Associates (Washington, D.C.), "Developments in Soviet Arms Exports and Imports 1980-83," *Centrally Planned Economies Current Analysis*, vol. iv, no. 62, August 1984, p. 4.

9. International Institute of Strategic Studies, *The Military Balance 1987-1988* (London: 1987), p. 50.

10. These CIA data exclude arms deliveries to Cuba, Vietnam, Laos, Cambodia, China, North Korea and liberation movements.

11. Cf. the article by Wolfgang Pfeiler in this volume.

9

SOME ASPECTS OF COMECON'S CLOSED-DOOR POLICY: DEAD-END FOR LDCS COMMITTED TO A "SOCIALIST ORIENTATION"

Wolfgang W. Berner

M ost Soviet and Western analysts agree that the expansionist Third World strategy pursued by the Kremlin during the period 1975-1980 was remarkably successful in spreading "socialist" precepts for political, social, and economic development in Asia, Africa, and Latin America. In those years the Soviet empire, by a series of vigorous moves combined with circumspect exploitation of a spell of American weakness and general Western irresolution, gained numerous peripheral and shaky, although militarily important, outposts in the shape of LDCs ruled by quasi-communist regimes. This group of new glacis provinces of the Moscow-controlled Socialist Commonwealth includes Angola, Mozambique, Ethiopia, South Yemen, Afghanistan, and Nicaragua.

The main body of this "socialist camp" under Soviet hegemony is made up of the ten full members of the Moscow-dominated Council of Mutual Economic Assistance (CMEA or Comecon). At the core are the seven members of the Warsaw Treaty Organization--the USSR, Poland, East Germany, Czechoslovakia, Hungary, Romania, and Bulgaria--plus Mongolia, Cuba, and Vietnam. Since the late 1970s admittance to full CMEA membership has been a major foreign policy goal for most of the pro-Soviet LDC regimes which joined the "socialist camp" after 1975. What these LDCs of "socialist orientation" have really sought, of course, is acquisition--along with full CMEA membership--of the concomitant claim to comprehensive Soviet and CMEA development aid, in judicious emulation of the Cuban and

Vietnamese precedents.

In the late 1970s and early 1980s the Kremlin leaders tended to consider a redefinition of Comecon's original organizational scope and political aims in favor of its enlargement by additional Third World members. The Soviet reasons commending such a course were mainly rooted in global power politics and military strategy. The principal objections reflected serious economic concerns, motivated in part by the unsatisfactory situation prevailing at the time, due to poor economic performance of most of the member countries within the entire Comecon system. Before admission was granted to ("socialist") Vietnam in the summer of 1978, the issue had apparently been discussed in similar terms with the result that in this case the "opposition" both inside the Soviet leadership and among CMEA club members in general had been defeated.[1] Subsequently, however, a change of mood took place. By the end of 1980 the "economists," or at least their arguments, had clearly gained the upper hand. The Comecon associates decided henceforth to embrace a strict closed-door policy with regard to the whole group of quasi-communist, "socialist-oriented" LDCs because of the many complicated problems which admittance of applicants from that group of countries would have entailed.

This chapter analyzes some of the perplexities which contributed to that momentous change of strategy. It sizes up the practical implications this shift may have for the Soviet Union's future approach to the problem of reconciling exaggerated expectations on the part of prospective Third World allies with the actual limitations of Soviet and CMEA capabilities. It also discusses some of the political, ideological, and economic issues underlying the special relationship existing between the Comecon countries and the LDCs characterized by their "socialist orientation."

The Drive for Comecon Expansion in the Late 1970s

Although much of the historical and political background to this drive remains shrouded in secrecy, the available evidence suggests that for a while the issue was a subject of intense internal debate. The most substantial piece of information on candidacies formally presented by "socialist-oriented"--and similar--LDCs in late 1978 or early 1979 was published, at the time, by the Italian communist party's newspaper *l'Unità*. In a report from Moscow on the presumable inception of a new "fifth stage" in the Comecon's history, the official PCI daily told its readers in April 1979:

At present the Comecon...is facing a period of novel and vast enrollments. In Moscow applications are cited which apparently have been submitted already by Ethiopia, Laos, Afghanistan, and South Yemen, appealing for 'full membership' status. In the event the Community's area would be considerably enlarged, and it would have not only to accommodate 'diverse' countries but also to tackle economic realities pregnant with far-reaching transformations. If we add that references to membership applications by Mozambique, Benin, and Angola are circulating with increasing insistence, the impression is clearly that the Comecon is headed for a considerable amplification.[2]

We may safely assume that the PCI's Moscow correspondent had been able to draw upon quite reliable sources. The wording of this report even suggests that he wanted to distinguish between news items belonging to different categories of credibility. He started by communicating information concerning a series of applications filed by Ethiopia, Laos, Afghanistan, and South Yemen presumably obtained from knowledgeable officials, while referring separately, in a later sentence, to a spate of less authoritative indications pertaining to comparable moves announced or undertaken by Mozambique, Angola, and Benin. As disclosed by Soviet and other Comecon insiders, some of these countries--specifically Ethiopia, South Yemen, and Afghanistan--were visited in the same context by CMEA commissions for the purpose of collecting more complete data relating to the economic prospects of these particular "vanguard" LDCs uppermost on the list of applicants for full Comecon membership.[3]

Not surprisingly, therefore, the 33rd CMEA Council session held in Moscow in June 1979 was marked by particularly optimistic expectations on the part of those LDC delegates who felt that their countries could safely rely for the eventual success of their applications on earlier assurances of Soviet patronage. An exceptionally large number of observer delegations had come to participate in the proceedings. Laos, Angola, Ethiopia, Afghanistan, and Mozambique were represented, upon invitation, with provisional observer status.[4] South Yemen also had sent observers to whom the council granted permanent status at the beginning of the session, by "special decision".[5] Mexico, Iraq, and Finland participated with delegations distinguished by another type of permanent observer status reflecting the specific ties existing between the CMEA and these countries in the shape of special cooperation agreements.[6] Finally, Yugoslavia was represented as an associated CMEA member with a qualified (but in some respects rather privileged) semi-member status.[7]

Observer delegations listed on occasion of the next four council sessions (Prague--1980; Sofia--1981; Budapest--1982; East Berlin--1983) regularly included Laos, Angola, Ethiopia, South Yemen, Afghanistan, and

Mozambique (in addition to Yugoslavia). Nicaragua was represented for the first time, presumably with permanent observer status,[8] at the East Berlin session in October 1983, while Finland, Iraq, and Mexico habitually preferred to stay away.[9]

Why were some of the aspirants for full CMEA membership so overconfident in 1979? Their hopes had been boosted in particular by the recent promotion of Vietnam (acknowledged as a "socialist" republic by Soviet standards since January 1970) from observer to full CMEA member status at the 32nd Council session in June 1978. Apparently they were also misled by explicit Soviet assurances to the effect that other--not yet "socialist"--candidates could similarly expect to be granted admittance, upon request, at one of the next CMEA Council sessions.[10] The upgrading of Vietnam in disregard of massive economic objections[11] was widely seen as a prelude to a wave of further promotions awaiting several other Third World countries provided they were both "socialist-oriented" and of military-strategic interest for the Soviet Union.

Ethiopia and South Yemen figured most prominently among the applicants claiming overt Soviet backing.[12] Laos (reckoned among the "socialist" countries by the Soviets officially since mid-1979)[13] reportedly failed to obtain full CMEA membership in 1978 when it had been prompted by Vietnam's application to start a parallel initiative.[14] But given the generally favorable climate for such candidacies during the following period, the Vientiane government certainly would have reapplied in 1979.

Before the 33rd CMEA session in Moscow, whose program also included special functions commemorative of the CMEA's 30th anniversary, provisional or permanent observer status had been granted to the following LDCs: China (1956, terminated in 1961); Yugoslavia (1956, associated member since 1964); North Korea (1957); Mongolia (1958, full member since 1962); Vietnam (1958, full member since 1978); Cuba (1965, full member since 1972); Iraq (1975); Mexico (1975); Laos (1976); Angola (1976); Ethiopia (1978). South Yemen, Afghanistan, and Mozambique obtained it in 1979, at the 33rd CMEA Council session, Nicaragua in 1983, at the 37th session. Invitations to participate, with observer status, in CMEA conferences and other activities may be extended to non-members by the CMEA Secretariat in conformity with Article XI of the CMEA statue.

That the idea of admitting selected "socialist-oriented" LDCs to the CMEA with full membership privileges was under discussion in early 1979 is evidenced not only by the *l'Unità* article quoted above. It was also confirmed by other reports mainly from Ethiopian and Mozambican sources published by Yugoslavian or British media.[15] The tug of war between advocates and opponents over the issue of Comecon expansion not only touched off a very far-reaching controversy within the organization's policy-making bodies, but also provoked a parallel discussion among Soviet "operators" and policy advisers, with participants ranging from members of the top Soviet leadership and key functionaries of the CPSU foreign policy apparatus to various categories of experts associated either with the Ministry of Foreign Affairs and other government agencies or with apposite research institutes connected with the USSR Academy of Sciences. The anti-expansionist Soviet "economists" and their foreign allies, in particular the six lesser East European CMEA members, relying heavily on advice and arguments supplied by the Moscow based Institute for the Economics of the World Socialist System (IEMSS)[16] finally prevailed over their antagonists--a coalition composed of Soviet "empire-builders" and Castro's Cuba.

After the fray, when the matter had been settled, enforcement of the rules of "democratic centralism" ensured strict adherence by every Soviet party functionary, government official, or Academy expert to the Kremlin's option against Comecon expansion. This negative outcome made it necessary, however, to interpret the new policy line to pro-Soviet Third World regimes whose hopes for early acceptance as full CMEA members had to be dispelled, and to the interested public in general. In doing so, spokesmen of the Soviet leadership and scholarly authors tended to emphasize the tremendous backwardness of the "socialist oriented" LDCs, the wide chasm of political, social and economic underdevelopment which separates them from the majority of the "socialist" CMEA member countries. Under the same heading they severely censured the voluntaristic approach allegedly characteristic of the Third World regimes' commitment to "scientific socialism" (i.e. Marxism-Leninism) which, although very commendable in itself, could not exempt anyone from soberly assessing the real quality of these countries' development: their encumbrance by tribalism and indigenous feudalism, their pre-capitalist social and economic structures, the contingent absence of an industrial proletariat also accounting for the lack of firmly established (communist) working-class parties, and the lamentable lack of experienced administrative, technical, and party cadres.

Thus the uncertain prospects for the success of "socialist-oriented" LDCs in setting up a sufficiently solid "material-technological foundation" for the envisaged construction of and transition to "socialism" became a staple subject for discussions hinging on the feasibility problem. Complementary arguments focused on the possibility of sudden political reversals, as effected in the past by several countries previously committed to a "noncapitalist path of development" (e.g. Egypt, Somalia, Guinea, Ghana, Mali etc.). It was recalled that such shifts had frequently led up to dissociation from the "socialist camp" together with the repudiation of "socialist" principles of government and socio-economic development.

While Soviet pundits carefully avoided reference to the critical economic reasons behind the decision against CMEA enlargement rooted in that community's own internal situation, in general they concurred in attributing Moscow's change of mind mainly to the Third World applicants' economic weakness, primordial social structures, and political instability. The precarious nature of these countries' "socialist orientation" and of their alignment with the "socialist commonwealth" was seized upon to set up unquestionable "irreversibility" with regard to these parameters as the ultimate touchstone of eligibility for admittance to the hard-core components of this commonwealth--i.e. to CMEA and/or Warsaw Pact membership. In an attempt to bring this debate to a positive conclusion, the CPSU leadership invited top representatives of all pro-Soviet communist parties, Third World client regimes, and "national liberation movements" to a conference devoted to the smoke-screen subject of anti-imperialistic cooperation and solidarity.

This conference, nominally hosted by the East German party leadership, took place in East Berlin in October 1980. It was used by the head of the Soviet delegation, Politburo Candidate and Central Committee Secretary B.N. Ponomarev, as a platform for a detailed exposition of the official Soviet strategy for that particular sector, based on a thorough analysis of the main deficiencies attributable, from the Soviet point of view, to most "socialist-oriented" LDCs, but also on a rather realistic assessment of the contemporary "international correlation of forces."[17] Ponomarev's lecture combined guidance for pro-Soviet Third World regimes on how to tackle political priority tasks on their agenda with advice on how to adjust their economic programs to the prospect that--due to the impracticability of their countries' incorporation into the "socialist world-economic system"--they would have to brace themselves for long-term survival as "socialist-oriented" economic components not of the "socialist commonwealth" but of the "capitalist world market."[18]

Decisions of 1979 and After: Winners and Losers

The defeat of the advocates of Comecon enlargement inside and outside the Soviet Union became obvious on the occasion of the CMEA sessions scheduled for 1979, 1980, and 1981. At the 33rd session, which took place in Moscow, six of the seven countries registered as candidates for full membership, according to the *l'Unità* report, in late 1978 and early 1979--Laos, Afghanistan, Angola, Ethiopia, Mozambique, and South Yemen--had been invited to participate. The conference opened on 26 June 1979 with a ceremonial meeting in honor of the 30th CMEA anniversary, highlighted by a verbose special Declaration which deserves particular attention because it contains several relevant statements not taken up by the official communique published at the end of the session.[19]

The final part of this Declaration consisted of half a dozen paragraphs devoted to questions of international CMEA cooperation with non-member countries, as well as to CMEA external relations in general. Most significantly, no reference was made in this text to the "socialist-oriented countries" (or "countries with a socialist orientation")[20] as a separate category while "all socialist states" outside the CMEA (e.g. China, North Korea, Laos, Albania etc.) were labeled as a group of preferential, or privileged, cooperation partners. Obviously the quasi-communist, pro-Soviet "vanguard" regimes of the Third World had been bracketed with the large majority of the other "developing countries."

For good measure, three "socialist" semi-member and non-member states were singled out in the Declaration as models for collective CMEA cooperation (Yugoslavia) or of cooperation on a country-to-country basis (North Korea and Laos). The next sentence adds that "multilateral economic relations" with Angola and Ethiopia[21] were being established. The paragraph concludes this list of samples by citing Iraq, Mexico, and Finland as countries cooperating with the CMEA on the basis of special agreements. The Declaration does not mention any membership applications filed by Third World aspirants, nor is any other aspect of the enlargement debate perceptible. But such secrecy corresponds to a long-standing CMEA practice.

The final communique was even less communicative with regard to former or future candidacies than the Declaration. It announced, however, a CMEA decision to extend the "measures envisaged by the Comprehensive Program for the acceleration of the economic development of the Mongolian People's Republic and the Republic of Cuba, also to the Socialist Republic of Vietnam." This need to provide assistance to full CMEA members became a standard argument against the promotion of additional LDCs to full-member status. After the accession of Vietnam (population estimate for 1978/79: 50 million) to the Community, by which Poland (35.2 million) was downgraded to third place among the most populous CMEA members,[22] the major CMEA goal of leveling-up economic performance, technological standards, and average incomes of extra-European and European members by "measures" enabling the former to catch up, necessarily prohibited the enrollment of additional LDCs on the same basis as Mongolia, Cuba, and Vietnam. Finally, the communique announced that observer status had been granted to South Yemen "upon request."[23] The head of the delegation of the People's Democratic Republic of Yemen, Prime Minister and Politburo member Ali Nasser Mohammad, used his sojourn in Moscow also for an exchange of views with Ponomarev, the Chief of the CPSU Central

Committee's International Department, and Karen Brutents, Deputy Chief and area expert of the same CC department.[24]

Among the main topics discussed by them must have been the new closed-door policy adopted by the CMEA toward "socialist-oriented" LDCs as well as the most appropriate way for the disappointed aspirant regimes to react. Presumably, the visitors from South Yemen and other "vanguard" LDCs were advised to avoid dramatic initiatives and to simply cling on. Available evidence suggests that the Yemenis immediately renewed their application for Comecon membership: when the 34th CMEA session was held in Prague in June 1980, the chief PDRY representative declared that South Yemen had not given up its intention "of becoming a CMEA member" with the aim "of attaining the same high level of economic and social development achieved by the CMEA countries."[25] He further announced that South Yemen was prepared to coordinate its economic plans with plans and programs adopted by the CMEA countries.[26] In March 1981 a PDRY observer delegation participated, in fact, in a meeting of the CMEA Commission for Economic Planning, and in October of the same year PDRY observers joined a meeting of the permanent CMEA Commission for the Food Supply Industry.[27]

Several other regimes of the original group of six "socialist" or "socialist-oriented" aspirant countries have opted for a similar course. Laos and Mozambique apparently repeated their applications for CMEA membership at least twice, in 1980 and 1981.[28] Economic cooperation between North Korea and Laos and various CMEA countries was developing satisfactorily by mid-1979, as we learned from the Declaration published on the occasion of the 30th Comecon anniversary. Beyond that, considerable economic assistance, supplied primarily by the Soviet Union, went to Laos (often via Hanoi) since 1975, and to North Korea since 1978.[29] Urgent requests for development assistance addressed to the CMEA Secretariat by Ethiopia and Angola were submitted to the Community's Executive Committee in the fall of 1978, when it met in Ulan Bator, and acted upon positively. Subsequent negotiations led to the establishment of "multilateral relations" with both countries--also mentioned by the CMEA Declaration of June 1979--based on protocols concerning specific aid projects which were realized step by step, beginning in 1979, mainly with Soviet, East German, Hungarian, and Bulgarian support.[30] A separate program had been launched for Afghanistan which received multilateral economic and technological assistance on the basis of commitments made by several CMEA member countries in 1978, after Taraki's crypto-communist PDPA had seized power in Kabul, and in 1979.[31]

This incomplete survey indicates that as early as in mid-1979 a multitude of projects and programs, of pledges and assurances, of claims and obligations had begun to accumulate which could be utilized by the various "vanguard" regimes of "socialist" or "socialist-oriented" complexion gradually to widen their influence within the Comecon's institutional framework. This capability, combined with this awareness of the huge importance attributed by Soviet "empire-builders" and "global strategists" to alliance-like relations with their countries, enabled the respective regimes to build up a series of common positions, and sometimes even to act as a pressure group prodding at the CPSU foreign policy apparatus and the Soviet Ministry of Foreign Affairs as their main targets. They always could count, moreover, on unfailing Cuban support within both the Comecon organization and the worldwide system of ruling communist parties. But also among Soviet party functionaries, government officials, and academic experts, there were many undeclared "expansionists" favoring a more vigorous and much more generous strategy of alliances with regard to Third World partners.

The chief Soviet representative at the 35th CMEA session held at Sofia in July 1981, Prime Minister N.A. Tikhonov, presumably was prompted by this convergence of political pressures, hegemonial interests, and partisan criticisms concerning political strategy, when he declared in his opening statement:

> Three developing countries, having chosen the path of socialist construction--Mongolia, Cuba, and Vietnam--have become members of the CMEA...The CMEA countries are also endeavoring by all available means to broaden their economic relations with Laos, Cambodia, Afghanistan, the PDR Yemen, Angola, Ethiopia, and Mozambique. In its relations to all developing counties the Socialist Community is trying to create the prerequisites for an independent development of their respective economies.[32]

In other words: the CMEA will not concentrate its future development assistance exclusively on the less developed CMEA members, Mongolia, Cuba, and Vietnam, but proposes instead to dedicate a certain part of available resources also to the broadening of economic (and political) relations with Laos, Cambodia, Afghanistan, South Yemen, Angola, Ethiopia, and Mozambique. The goal envisaged for these latter countries is not, however, eventual integration into the CMEA with full member status. They should be assisted rather in their efforts to achieve economic autonomy within the "capitalist world market" in view of the CMEA's limited capacity to accommodate additional LDCs on the basis of conditions equal to those granted to Cuba, Mongolia, and Vietnam.

The order in which the aspirant countries were listed by Tikhonov may be read as a catalogue of Soviet preferences. First place is logically given to

Laos, considered to be a "socialist" state. That Cambodia surprisingly appears as second in line indicates a Soviet inclination to facilitate Cambodia's rehabilitation--under Vietnamese supervision--as a "socialist" country. Afghanistan's third place is as significant as are positions four (South Yemen), five (Angola), and six (Ethiopia) or the assignment to Mozambique of the bottom rung. Although this list was compiled in mid-1981, it seems remarkable that the line-up of the seven countries according to Soviet preferences has remained as valid as it was six years ago.

The Case of Nicaragua and the
1983-1987 Makeshift Agreements

Circumstantial evidence, partly confirmed by Soviet and Cuban insiders in private conversation,[33] suggests that in early 1983 a resumption of the debate over the Comecon's closed-door policy was brought about by the urgency of Nicaraguan appeals addressed to Havana and Moscow as well as by Castro's intercession in favor of the Sandinistas. Nicaragua's FSLN comandantes had triumphed over Somoza in July 1979, but they had to wait until 1983 before they were invited to send observers to a CMEA Council session. These stalling tactics were resented by the Managua leadership and their Cuban patrons also in view of the fact that the Sandinista movement (Frente Sandinista de Liberaciòn Nacional/FSLN) had been represented much earlier at the October, 1980, East Berlin conference of communist and pro-Soviet Third World "vanguard" parties. At the same time, B.N. Ponomarev, the CPSU Central Committee Secretary in charge of relations with Third World regimes, had indeed begun to reckon Nicaragua among the "countries of socialist orientation."[34]

Apparently Nicaragua also submitted a petition for full CMEA memberships[35] which was turned down, as a matter of course, in keeping with the official policy line. Under Cuban pressure, the Sandinistas were, however, offered negotiations for an agreement on economic and scientific-technical cooperation modeled on similar agreements concluded by the Comecon with Finland (in 1973), Iraq (in 1975), and Mexico (in 1975). Agreements of this type envisage the establishment of a joint government commission responsible for the elaboration of an outline program, and for creating the organizational framework required for that program's realization. The commission is expected to produce recommendations or joint resolutions which may lead, upon approval by the governments addressed, to the conclusion of multilateral or bilateral agreements between the respective governments, government agencies or other authorities.

A Nicaraguan-CMEA agreement based on that formula was signed in September 1983. After confirmation by the 37th CMEA Council session, held in East Berlin in October 1983, it became effective in February 1984.[36] But if Managua had expected it to be a magic instrument which could be used for tapping locked-away Comecon emergency funds, disenchantment was quickly to follow. No sooner had Nicaragua put in for a sizable loan than its request was coolly turned down by the proper CMEA bodies. Although Nicaragua's Daniel Ortega tried had to have this decision reversed during a hurried visit to Moscow in June 1984, or to obtain a stop-gap credit of similar proportions from the Soviet Union, all his endeavors failed, and he had to return empty-handed. These tribulations imposed on Cuba's Sandinista satellite aggravated Cuban-Soviet tensions, which had become acute after the October 1983 overthrow and execution of Castro's Grenadian protégé and personal friend Maurice Bishop with Soviet connivance, if not complicity, as perceived from Havana.

When Castro boycotted the important June 1984 CMEA summit for which the Soviet party leadership had convoked the party chiefs of the ten member countries to Moscow, this was immediately understood inside and outside the Comecon area as a signal of opposition against the Community's general policy line of keeping out any additional LDCs volunteering for CMEA membership, regardless of their pro-Soviet or pro-Cuban "socialist orientation," above all on the grounds of their socio-economic backwardness. Simultaneously it was interpreted as a more specific demonstration of protest against high-handed Soviet global-power politics, too often inconsiderate toward the interests of beleaguered minor allies as, for instance, Castro's Cuba, the Nicaraguan Sandinistas, or the Grenadian NJM regime of the early 1980s. It should be remembered that originally Cuba also had been at best a "socialist-oriented" LDC when it was admitted by Khrushchev to the communist camp in February 1963, shortly after the "missile crisis," and had continued as such into 1972 when it was granted full CMEA membership. Cuba, too, had been kept on short commons for seven years (since 1965), assuaged initially with the sop of the almost meaningless title of a CMEA observer country. This experience proved so frustrating for the Cubans that after only two years of playing the role of mere spectators and underprivileged, pathetic petitioners they preferred to stay away from CMEA Council sessions or Executive Committee meetings until they were granted full CMEA membership, as the result of another five years of incessant prodding.

Subsequently, Castro has been bent upon getting more LDCs admitted because in his view such an "amplification" is necessary to balance the preponderance of the East European member countries, and to offset the impact of their often quite selfish political as well as economic interests. But as his own position within the Community never was strong enough to warrant a course of open, public contention, he had learned to rely on patient tenacity and clever tactics aiming at gradual step-by-step gains. So it may not have been a mere coincidence that Havana was destined to host the next "ordinary" CMEA Council session following the Moscow summit meeting of June 1984 boycotted by Cuba's "màximo lìder." This 39th council session was the first one ever to be convened at Havana--a decision which in fact changed the established order governing the succession of Moscow and the other six East European capitals as meeting places for the CMEA Council, obviously in compliance with Cuban requests.

The novelty of a Third World venue for this purpose raised fresh, overoptimistic hopes among the regimes of many of the "socialist-oriented" LDCs concerned in consideration not only of the particular aura of the locality but also of the prospect that Castro would act, in line with standing procedures, as chairman of the entire conference. The impressive list of observer delegations which were assembled when the 39th Council session opened on 29 October 1984 included emissaries from Laos, Afghanistan, Angola, Mozambique, Ethiopia, South Yemen, Nicaragua, Mexico, the United Nations' Economic Commission for Latin American (ECLA), and the Latin American Economic Community (Sistema Econòmico Latino Americano/SELA). Mexico and Nicaragua were enumerated as a group apart by the official communique,[37] obviously on the grounds that they represented a distinct category of "permanent observers" whose attendance was based on "contractual legitimation." CMEA cooperation with Yugoslavia and the four other partner countries coupled to the Community by special agreements--Finland, Iraq, Mexico, and Nicaragua--was positively recorded in a separate paragraph.

If judged by the major policy statements contained in the communique, the results of this CMEA Council session must have been extremely disappointing for the Cubans as well as for most of the observer delegations. The main emphasis was placed on recapitulating the directives issued at the end of the summit meeting of party chiefs held four month before. In this context, the task of accelerating the overall development of Cuba, Vietnam, and Mongolia with the target of raising these countries' economic performance to the average level of the European CMEA member states was not only confirmed as a pivotal commitment but given added urgency by pledges to speed up project realization in close relation with concerted efforts toward more expedited overall Comecon integration. Cuba reaped (unmerited) praise for its alleged economic achievements--a cheap verbal sop, certainly, but also an important acknowledgement for the record. Finally, Cuba and Nicaragua were promised solidarity in support of their efforts to defend themselves against imperialist aggression and counterrevolution.[38]

But those who had been waiting for a substantial, comprehensive, multilateral program of economic assistance for "socialist-oriented" LDCs were deeply disappointed. Also missing was any allusion to a more general concept for future extension of CMEA cooperation with privileged "socialist-oriented" LDCs patterned on the CMEA-Nicaraguan special agreement. Not even the slightest hint presaging CMEA initiatives in favor of individual observer countries, if not of the whole group of "socialist-oriented" LDCs, could be discovered which might have tinged the looming clouds of hopelessness surrounding these paupers with a silver lining.

Several months later it became evident that some really tough bargaining must have been going on behind this outward facade of inflexibility--negotiations which apparently continued after the end of the Havana conference. Finally compromise was reached. On the one hand the doors were kept as tightly bolted as before; on the other hand a decision was reached to offer special cooperation agreements modeled upon the one concluded with Nicaragua to all "socialist-oriented" LDCs in a comparable position.

It was a makeshift solution, of course, which did not evoke much enthusiasm. Most the of the addressees hedged a bit, but only for a while. Not surprisingly, Mozambique was the first country of the group to accept the offer. Although the Frelimo regime had been under heavy economic, political, and military pressure ever since the country became independent in June 1975, Moscow always tended to keep its own commitments at a minimum level. In other words, because Mozambique was considered relatively unimportant for Soviet global strategy, the Frelimo regime had to be more obliging vis-à-vis the Soviet Union and the Comecon if it wanted to be assured of their willingness to assist Mozambique's Afro-Marxist rulers on a long-term basis. Burgeoning mistrust had been heightened in Maputo even by Soviet indulgence when Mozambique accepted the inclusion of West Berlin in two minor aid agreements with the Federal Republic of Germany (over considerable East German opposition) in June and July 1982[39]--a move which also opened the way for Mozambique's adherence to the Lomè III Convention on development cooperation between the European Community and 65 African, Caribbean and Pacific (ACP) states signed on 8 December 1984. On closer examination, however, the Soviet attitude regarding both the Mozambican concessions to Bonn over the issue of West Berlin and the acceptance of the corresponding clauses of the Lomè Convention easily squares with Moscow's policy, developed under the impact of growing international isolation following upon the invasion of Afghanistan, of encouraging Third World clients to improve their relations with "capitalist" trading partners and to draw economic aid, wherever possible without giving up essential positions, increasingly from "capitalist" resources.[40]

The special agreement concluded between the CMEA and Mozambique was approved by the CMEA Council in June 1985, half a year after Maputo's adherence to the Lomè III Convention, during the 40th Council session held in Warsaw.[41] Not much later Angola,[42] Ethiopia and South Yemen followed suit. The respective agreements were confirmed in November 1986 by the 42nd CMEA Council session.[43] Afghanistan completed the series in the following year; this agreement came up for confirmation at the 43rd Council session held in Moscow in October 1987.[44] Thus of the seven "socialist" or "socialist-oriented" membership aspirants with CMEA observer status, only Laos has remained unresponsive so far, and there is good reason to suspect this solitary stance to be closely linked with specific Soviet as well as Comecon majority interest.

Judging the improvements obtained by the CMEA's partners on the basis of the substance of the new cooperation agreements, their immediate gains seem to be rather insignificant. The main benefit offered by these agreements may consist of the broadening of the individual signatories' opportunities for elaborating, over the years, in close contact with CMEA experts, cooperation and development programs tailored to meet their real needs and more effectively to exploit available resources. Ultimately, success or failure of these agreements will depend very much on the professional competence, the diplomatic skills, and the goodwill of key members of the joint commission responsible for drawing up plans, determining projects, and setting up machinery for the realization of such programs.

It is one of life's ironies that the basic concept for the CMEA special agreements on economic and scientific-technical cooperation was originally conceived as a standard formula for cooperation with "capitalist" and other "non-socialist" states. The first partner to an agreement of this type with the CMEA was indeed Finland (1973), followed by Iraq and Mexico (both in 1975). Iraq is considered by ranking functionaries of the Soviet CP's International Department a "socialist-oriented" LDC of the "non-vanguard" variety in view of its Ba'thist, inherently anticommunist regime; Mexico, on the other hand, is bracketed with the LDCs of "capitalist orientation."

In the case of the CMEA agreement with Finland, the experiment proved satisfactory for both sides, mainly because contingent projects have been handled in practice as parts of a bilateral, Soviet-Finnish program. By contrast the CMEA agreements with Iraq and Mexico did not produce any positive results worth mentioning, above all due to the inadequate performance of the respective joint commissions responsible for programming and for the creation of suitable administrative machinery. As for the new CMEA agreements with pro-Soviet, "socialist-oriented" LDCs, their operationalization might be facilitated, in the take-off phase, by the circumstance that most of the signatories--with the sole exception of Nicaragua--have been accumulating for some time ample experience in practical economic and development cooperation with the Soviet Union on the basis of a series of "treaties on friendship and cooperation"[45] contracted between 1976 and 1979. All these treaties covering a wide range of activities provide not only for political, cultural and military, but also for economic and scientific-technical cooperation.

Lessons and Prospects

The six special cooperation agreements concluded by Comecon with Nicaragua (1983), Mozambique (1985), Angola (1986), Ethiopia (1986), South Yemen (1986), and Afghanistan (1987) have to be understood, in the first place, as a makeshift scheme devised by the CMEA majority to fulfill several purposes at the same time. They were aimed, on the one hand, at easing strains existing inside the Community where the Cubans, backed by sympathizers in the Soviet leadership and among the foreign policy establishments of several other Comecon members, acted as spokesmen for the "socialist-oriented vanguard regimes" in particular, but also as champions of a more aggressive, expansionist, revolutionary Third World strategy in general. On the other hand, the agreements were intended to defuse accumulated resentment among the observer countries which, although still considering themselves candidates for full CMEA member status, had become more and more exasperated by Comecon's stonewalling tactics. The Soviet leadership felt confronted with a politically significant dilemma which threatened to throw the entire "socialist camp" into disarray. It risked losing most of the quasi-communist regimes with CMEA observer status as strategic allies in the global superpower competition if the CMEA continued to cold-shoulder them, but admittance of so many LDCs from the "poorest nations of the world" category[46] to full CMEA membership would have meant jeopardizing the community's political and economic viability. It is evident therefore that, in the final analysis, the new overture was a ruse mainly motivated by the CMEA majority's desire in some way to cushion the inevitable consequences of their persistent refusal to relax the club's rigorous closed-door policy.

In all probability, this harsh policy line will remain effective for many years to come, an indispensable element of the present Soviet administration's "grand design" for economic reform both in the USSR and in the East European provinces of the Soviet empire--a program for economic rehabilitation and modernization separate from Gorbachev's personal fortunes and forced upon the Soviet collective leadership by necessity. In other words, the economists, after becoming influential at the highest level, will continue to argue that the entire CMEA structure might collapse if additional LDCs were admitted to the Community with full membership rights. They also will continue to be very strict in defending the non-enlargement principle against infringements, motivated by considerations of military or political strategy, on the grounds that it would become impossible to keep other countries out if a single exception were made.

With typical circumspection, the Soviet "operators" in charge--most likely positioned in the CPSU Secretariat's International Department--even devised a subtle ploy forestalling unwelcome future applications for CMEA membership. Apparently a special barrier function has been assigned to Laos which remains excluded from full member status although officially recognized by Moscow as an authentic "socialist" country and ruled by a communist party committed to an incontestably pro-Vietnam and pro-Soviet posture. Accordingly, "socialist-oriented" candidates seeking full CMEA member status are obliged to wait for Laos to move up first, as none of them can hope to leap-frog "socialist" Laos given their own clearly inferior qualifications and credentials. It will suffice to point to "socialist" Laos at the head of the queue to silence impatient candidates from the group of "socialist-oriented" aspirants. On the other hand Laos (with an estimated population of 4.3 million)[47] need not complain insofar as it is receiving, in compensation for this tactical lock-out, considerable Soviet and CMEA development assistance, the bulk of which reaches Vientiane through Vietnamese channels.

But even those Soviet leaders who do not share the apprehension that enlargement might cause the entire Comecon system to collapse have sound reasons to support the Community's closed-door policy. Many of them are simply afraid that admittance of additional LDCs would paralyze the laborious process of economic integration envisaged primarily for the European part of the Soviet empire. This concern has also surfaced in many passages of the revised version of the CPSU program adopted in March 1986 by the XXVII party congress.

According to this program, "the CPSU stands for a further deepening of socialist economic integration as the material foundation for drawing the socialist countries closer together." It goes on to announce that the CPSU "will help enhance the role of the CMEA and broaden economic, scientific and technical cooperation," stressing its conviction "that the development of socialist integration should enhance the technical and economic invulnerability of the community."[48]

The program does not conceal the fact that every major stage of the road to socialist integration "sets new complex tasks, whose accomplishment

involves struggle, search and the overcoming of contractions and difficulties."
It alerts the party members that all along this road "utmost attention" is
required to to avoid wasteful setbacks. They are admonished that in
consideration of the many existing differences of actual living conditions and
development levels it is particularly important to face up to future challenges
on the basis of a "profound understanding of both national interests" (of the
various WTO and CMEA member states) "and of common, international
interests" (of the Community as a whole) "in their organic interconnection."[49]

This process of integration is not only a priority task, it is dictated--in the
view of the program's authors--by the "general laws of socialism." They are
persuaded that "the objective requirement of the socialist countries' drawing
ever closer together stems from the very essence of socialism," and they
finally proclaim: "The higher and the more similar the levels of socialist
development of socialist countries, the richer and deeper their cooperation,
the more organic the process of their drawing together."[50]

The Soviet party program's pronouncements on East European and
CMEA integration can be summed up in the statement that acceleration of
the political, economic and military integration of the Warsaw Treaty and
CMEA member states must be rated as a Soviet national and
"internationalist" commitment of crucial importance. But the same program
also tenders a very significant promise--although announced in cautious
terms--to the minor WTO and CMEA partners of the Soviet Union. It
contains the message that accelerated progress towards higher levels of
integration would lead, on the strength of the "general laws of socialism,"
inevitably to the establishment of "more organic" relations between the Soviet
Union and the other bloc members. Since all East European governments,
including the communist functional elites of these countries, are seriously
committed to the same goal of "more organic" intra-bloc relations, they will
certainly respond to the Soviet quid-pro-quo proposal positively, but
emphasizing at the same time their firm stand against Comecon enlargement.

In the final analysis, Soviet foreign policy priorities and vital interests of
most East European Comecon members converge on this matter. The likely
result is that the CMEA's closed-door policy will perpetuate itself as a long-
term strategy, because the alternative course--expansion--would dramatically
aggravate the many problems which have been hampering East European
economic integration since Comecon's founding days in early 1949 up to the
present. What is more, most of the East European CMEA members are
deeply worried by the prospect that the inevitable consequences of Comecon
enlargement might severely compromise the prospects of WTO-CMEA
evolution into a "more organic" commonwealth of socialist nations, a
transformation strongly desired by them all.

Notes

1. Bräker, Hans, "Die Aufnahme Vietnams in den RGW" *Berichte des Dundesinstituts für ostwissenschaftliche und internationale Studien (BIOst)*, Cologne, no. 7, 1979.

2. *l'Unità*, Rome, 5 April 1979.

3. Cf. Bräker, op. cit., pp. 7, 56 (ref: Ethiopia, South Yemen); private communications to the author by a Central Committee member of the Yemen Socialist Party, March 1989 (ref: South Yemen), by East European and Soviet sources, May 1981 (ref: Afghanistan). It should be noted that South Yemen and Afghanistan were the first "socialist-oriented" LDCs to obtain "permanent" CMEA observer status in 1979 and 1980, respectively (for more detailed information on this point see notes 4 and 5 below).

4. Cf. Tiraspolsky, Anita, "Les relations économiques de l'URSS et de l'Europe de l'Est avec les pays observateurs au CAEM," *le courrier des pays de l'est*, Paris, no. 314, January 1987, pp. 3-41. The Soviet author Danilov distinguishes two types of CMEA observer status: For delegations with provisional observer status, participation in CMEA events and activities is subject, on each occasion, to a specific formal invitation, while there is no such restriction curbing governments with permanent observer status; cf. Danilov, E.S., *SEV i tret'i strany. Iuridicheskie predposylki i formy sotrudnichestva*, Moscow, 1982, p. 103. Laos and Angola were represented for the first time, with provisional observer status, at the 30th Council session (July 1976), Ethiopia at the 32nd session (June 1978), Afghanistan and Mozambique at the 33rd session (June 1979); cf. Tiraspolsky, op. cit., p. 27.

5. South Yemen had been asking for CMEA association since September 1973 (see note 32 below). It attended a CMEA Council session for the first time in June 1979, but obtained permanent observer status immediately by a "special" Council decision. Afghanistan's position was upgraded to permanent observer status "by special decision" of the 34th Council session (cf. the official communiques in *Pravda*, Moscow, 30 June 1979, and 20 June 1980, respectively).

6. Finland and the CMEA signed a special cooperation agreement on 16 May 1973; corresponding agreements were concluded by the CMEA

with Iraq on 4 July 1975, and with Mexico on 13 August 1975. The countries involved hold permanent observer status granted to them presumably in acknowledgement of the existing "contractual" partnership relations, although the agreements do not contain pertinent provisions. Text of the agreement with Finland in *International Affairs*, Moscow, vol. 19, no. 10 (Oct. 1973), pp. 122-125.

7. Yugoslavia's CMEA association is determined by a special agreement dated 17 September 1964 which also bestowed permanent observer status upon the Yugoslav government.

8. The Nicaragua observer delegation participated, according to the communique, "in connection with the confirmation of the agreement on cooperation between the CMEA and the Republic of Nicaragua" (cf. *Pravda*, 21 October 1983). The wording of this communication supports the conjectured linkage between the establishment of a "contractual" partnership relation and the bestowal of a specific type of permanent observer status.

9. Tiraspolsky, op. cit., p. 27.

10. Arguments to the same effect were repeated by Danilov, op. cit., p. 123, whose book, although published in 1982, reflects in many instances Soviet positions dominant during the preceding five-year period.

11. Cf. Bràker, op. cit., pp. 6-7, 50-53.

12. Wolde-Kidak Gessese, the head of the Ethiopian delegation which participated in the 32nd CMEA Council session of late June 1978, declared after his return from Bucharest that his country "would get a chance soon to acquire full CMEA membership," according to a *Tanjug* report from Addis Ababa, dated 3 July 1978 and reprinted by the Belgrade party daily *Borba* next day. It further said that a CMEA commission, in conclusion of an on-site survey conducted in Ethiopia in early 1978, had "supported the idea of a closer CMEA association of this African country" (see also note 15 below). As for South Yemen, there were indications "in late 1980...that the Soviet Union had reached a secret agreement with South Yemen whereby Aden would permit the Soviets liberal access to its military facilities in exchange for a Soviet guarantee to protect South Yemen. The PDRY in turn would be granted full membership in the CMEA and eventual observer status in the Warsaw Pact"; cf. Foreign Affairs Committee of the U.S. House of Representatives, *The Soviet Union in the Third World, 1980-85: An Imperial Burden or Political Asset?* Committee Print (Washington D.C.: U.S. Government Printing Office, 23 September 1985), p. 170.

13. In early July 1979 the ruling Lao People's Revolutionary Party (LPRP) was listed for the first time officially among the participants of a meeting of Central Committee Secretaries of the communist parties "of the socialist countries," held in East Berlin (cf. the report in *Pravda*, 7 July 1979). The LPRP has been throughout considered by the Soviet party leadership a full-fledged communist "brother party" descended from the former Indochinese Communist Party (ICP) founded in 1930. After the ICP's dissolution in 1951, its Laotian branch established the new clandestine LPRP which in 1955 was reorganized to become the Laotian People's Party, but renamed itself LPRP in February 1972. The inauguration, in December 1975, of an LPRP-controlled Lao People's Democratic Republic marked, in the party's official terminology, both the end of the "national-democratic" phase of the Lao revolution and the beginning, for Laos, of the "period of transition to socialism."

14. Laos was "the failed candidate of June 1978," according to the postscript author of *The New Communist Third World* (edited by Peter Wiles, London: Croom Helm, 1982); this statement is tagged to the suggestion that Laos may have reapplied, without success, for full CMEA membership some time before the 35th Council session held in July 1981 (p. 364).

15. According to newspaper reports (e.g. in *The Guardian*, London, 18 November 1980; *Le Monde*, Paris, 5 December 1980; *The Times*, London, 7 December 1980) the fact that Mozambican observers had attended two consecutive CMEA Council sessions in June 1979 and June 1980 led to a spate of official claims voiced in Maputo in late 1980 that full CMEA membership would follow soon. Allegedly, President Samora Machel had hoped to secure a binding Soviet commitment during a visit to Moscow in November 1980 but with a negative result. Undaunted, Mozambique filed another application in 1981, and although it was turned down by the following 35th Council session (Sofia-July 1981), Machel "seems to have instantly and publicly re-applied"; cf. *The New Communist Third World*, loc. cit., pp. 158, 364, and *The Guardian*, 14 July 1981. As for Ethiopia see note 12 above. A survey by Heinrich Machowski and Siegfried Schultz ("RGW-Staaten und Dritte Welt," *Arbeitspapeire zur Internationalen Politik*, DGAP series no. 18, Bonn, November 1981, p. 60) cites East German reports on a CMEA delegation's visit to Ethiopia in March 1978 and on other CMEA activities in that country (*Neues Deutschland*, East Berlin, 13 March, 19 March, 16 November 1978). Another CMEA delegation toured Angola as early as in December 1976. Similar CMEA "contacts" with Afghanistan apparently had been established before the end of

1978. Late in 1980 the Polish party daily (*Trybuna Ludu*, Warsaw, 1 December 1980) quoted the Mozambican foreign minister with statements on his country's prospects to obtain CMEA membership (cf. Machowski/Schultz, loc. cit., p. 60).

16. Arguments employed by Soviet authors during the late seventies and early eighties in advocating economic reforms at home, better adaptation of domestic and foreign policies to economic capabilities, and more prudence in drafting development programs for Third World countries (although evasive with regard to the CMEA expansion issue) are well exemplified by Thomas J. Zamostny in his survey "Moscow and the Third World: Recent Trends in Soviet Thinking," *Soviet Studies*, Glasgow, vol. 36, no. 2, 1984, pp. 223-235. Most of the articles cited appeared in print after 1981 but reflect earlier non-public debates. The IEMSS is represented, among the disputants, by Anatoliy Butenko, Yuriy Novopashin, and Evgeniy Ambartsumov. This institute, under its influential director Oleg T. Bogomolov, is mainly concerned with problems of USSR-Comecon relations, coordination of Comecon programs, and Soviet bloc integration. Indispensable as a guide to the complex system of interrelations between Soviet Third World policy concepts and academic expertise, between ideology and political pragmatism, between priority perceptions and economic constraints, between rivaling schools of thought and political leadership is Elisabeth Kridl Valkenier's book *The Soviet Union and the Third World: An Economic Bind*, (New York: Praeger, 1983); see also her articles "Inside Russia: Globalists vs. Ideologues," *The Christian Science Monitor*, Boston, 24 December 1982, and "Revolutionary Change in the Third World: Recent Soviet Assessments," *World Politics*, Princeton, vol. 38, no. 3, April 1986, pp. 415-434.

17. Cf. "Sovmestnaya bor'ba rabochego i natsional 'no-osvoboditel 'nogo dvizhenii protiv imperializma, za sotsial'nyi progress," *Kommunist*, Moscow, no. 16, 1980, pp. 30-44. A slightly differing German language version was published in *Neues Deutschland*, East Berlin, 21 October 1980. The text of Ponomarev's address had been drafted by Rostislav A. Ulianovsky, at the time Deputy Chief of the CPSU Secretariat's International Department (ID) in charge of "socialist-oriented" LDCs and "revolutionary-democratic" organizations of the Third World. While he could not attend the conference due to illness, the Soviet delegation included Oleg B. Rakhmanin (First Deputy Chief of the Department for Liaison with ruling communist parties), Karen N. Brutents (ID Deputy Chief in charge of "capitalist-oriented" LDCs), Ivan I. Kovalenko (ID Deputy Chief in charge of Far Eastern affairs),

Anatoliy A. Gromyko and Evgeniy M. Primakov (directors of the African and Oriental institutes of the USSR Academy of Sciences, respectively); cf. *Pravda*, 20 October 1980.

18. During an extensive interview granted to the author in May 1981, Ulianovsky explicitly confirmed that this proposition had been one of the principal messages of Ponomarev's address delivered in East Berlin six months before. He also emphasized that many "socialist-oriented" LDCs had been clamoring for full integration into the "socialist world-economic system" as a result of widespread misconceptions grossly overestimating this system's limited capabilities. To illustrate the Soviet response to such requests, he claimed that Angola had been prompted by Soviet advice to turn to American firms for investment capital, joint exploitation of mineral oil deposits, and sales promotion for Angolan commodities on the "capitalist" world market.

19. *Pravda*, 30 June 1979.

20. For a detailed discussion of this concept see Berner, Wolfgang, "States With a Socialist Orientation: A Soviet Partnership Model," *The Soviet Union 1984/85*, BIOst series no. 8 (Boulder: Westview Press, 1986), pp. 300-308; also Valkenier, *The Soviet Union and the Third World: An Economic Bind*, op. cit., pp. 97-103; idem, "Revolutionary Change in the Third World: Recent Soviet Assessments," loc. cit., pp. 416-422.

21. CMEA assistance for Angola started in 1979 with a large-scale vaccination campaign against cattle diseases after a protocol on cooperation had been signed by the CMEA Secretariat; several CMEA countries sent 79 specialists, three mobile laboratories, 22 other motor vehicles, considerable quantities of equipment and medicines, all free of cost. Multilateral CMEA cooperation with Ethiopia was established likewise in 1979, with the USSR, Bulgaria, Hungary and the GDR participating. Cf. Tiraspolsky, op. cit., p. 28.

22. A recent statistical survey provides the following population estimates for 1987: USSR-282,550,000; Vietnam-61,532,000; Poland-37,839,000; Romania-23,500,000; East Germany-16,783,000; Czechoslovakia-15,631,000; Hungary-10,789,000; Cuba-10,262,000; Bulgaria-8,996,000; Mongolia-1,966,000; cf. *The Military Balance 1987-1988* (London: IISS, 1987), pp. 212-214.

23. *Pravda*, 30 June 1979 (communique). Efrat, Moshe, "The PDRY: Scientific Socialism on Trial in an Arab Country," *The New Communist Third World*, op. cit., p. 170, reports that South Yemen had applied for CMEA association as early as in September 1973, omitting, however, to

attribute this isolated communication.

24. *Bulletin d'Information*, Prague, vol. 17, no. 16-17, 1979, p. 74.

25. Cf. Danilov, op. cit., p. 123.

26. Cf. Tiraspolsky, op. cit., p. 28.

27. *Pravda*, 19 March 1981, 15 October 1981.

28. Cf. *The New Communist World*, loc. cit., pp. 158, 364. Negative CMEA decisions on Mozambican applications for full membership are reported variously for 1980 or for 1981 by many different sources.

29. Cf. Williams, Michael C., "North Korea: Tilting Toward Moscow?" *The World Today*, London, vol. 40. no. 10 (Oct. 1984), pp. 399-400.

30. Cf. *Pravda*, 4 October 1978, for report on the 87th meeting of the CMEA Executive Committee (27 Sept. - 1 Oct. 1978); op. cit., p. 28 (see also note 21 above).

31. Cf. Tiraspolsky, ibidem.

32. *Pravda*, 3 July 1981.

33. Personal communications to the author obtained during a visit to Moscow in June 1984.

34. Cf. Boris N. Ponomarev, "The Cause of Freedom and Socialism Is Invincible," *World Marxist Review*, Prague, vol. 24, no. 1 (Jan. 1981), p. 13 (editorial work on this issue was terminated on 1 December 1980). The FSLN delegation attending the East Berlin conference held in October 1980 was headed by comandante Marcos Somarriba; cf. *Neues Deutschland*, 23 October 1980.

35. Robert S. Leiken, "Fantasies and Facts: The Soviet Union and Nicaragua," *Current History*, Philadelphia, vol. 83, no. 495 (Oct. 1984), pp. 314-317, 344-345, cf. p. 344.

36. *Pravda*, 21 October 1983 and 3 November 1984 (communiques of the 37th and 39th CMEA Council sessions, respectively); cf. Leiken, op. cit., p. 344.

37. *Pravda*, 3 November 1984 (communique).

38. Ibidem.

39. Macqueen, Norman, "Mozambique's Widening Foreign Policy," *The World Today*, vol. 40, no. 1 (Jan. 1984), p. 22-28, cf. p. 26. In swallowing the "Land" designation for West Berlin as a term used in the agreements, the Mozambican government went beyond acceptance of the hazier Frank-Falin formula sometimes applied by Bonn to snaggy

cases; this formula stipulates "extension to Berlin (West)" of the agreements concerned "in conformity with the Four-Powers-Agreement of September 3, 1971, and in compliance with established proceedings." The Soviet Union and the GDR object to the inclusion of West Berlin as "Land" no. 11 among the ten other "Länder" (i.e. self-administrated regions) of which the Federal Republic of Germany is composed.

40. Cf. Valkenier, *The Soviet Union and the Third World: An Economic Bind*, op. cit., pp. 97-103, 122-127; see also note 18 above.

41. *Pravda*, 29 June 1985 (communique).

42. Angola signed the Lomé III Convention as a solitary latecomer on 30 April 1985. Here too the Berlin clause had been the main hitch, although removed from Article 283 concerning the territorial expanse covered by the Convention to a correlated Annex XLVII referring to the "Land Berlin" as a part of that domain to be represented, moreover, by the government of the Federal Republic of Germany.

43, *Pravda*, 6 November 1986 (communique).

44, *Pravda*, 15 October 1987 (communique).

45. Such "treaties of patronage" were concluded by the USSR with Angola on 8 October 1976, Mozambique on 31 March 1977, Ethiopia on 20 November 1978, Afghanistan on 5 December 1978, South Yemen on 25 October 1979; cf. Berner, Wolfgang, "The Soviet Treaties of Friendship and Cooperation With Developing Countries," *The Soviet Union 1980-81*, BIOst series no. 6, New York: Holmes & Meier Publishers, New York and London, 1983, pp. 296-305.

46. In a statistical classification for 1983 covering a total of 203 countries (based on per capita GNP) Ethiopia held 199th place, Afghanistan 192nd place, Mozambique 160th place, South Yemen 153rd place, Angola 128th place (cf. Tiraspolsky, op. cit., p. 4). Nicaragua presumably kept a position between places 95 and 100, while Laos held 197th or 198th place, always calculated on the basis of their 1983 GNP.

47. Population figure for 1987 (4,228,000) from *The Military Balance 1987-1988* (London: IISS 1987), p. 165. Comparable figures cited by the same source for "socialist-oriented" LDCs with CMEA observer status are: Ethiopia-42,555,000; Afghanistan-15,531,000; Mozambique-13,126,000; Angola-8,435,000; Nicaragua-3,408,000; South Yemen-2,300,000 (all estimates for 1987).

48. Cf. "Programme of the Communist Party of the Soviet Union. A New

Edition," *Information Bulletin*, Prague, vol. 24, no. 9, 1986, pp. 5-91; ref. pp. 71-72.

49. Ibid. pp. 72-73.
50. Ibid. pp. 17-18.

CONTINUITY AND CHANGE IN SOVIET-EAST EUROPEAN RELATIONS: RECENT TRENDS AND IMPLICATIONS FOR THE WEST

Marco Carnovale

Gorbachev and Eastern Europe

Three years into the Gorbachev era, there is reason to believe that the Kremlin is taking stock of Soviet/East European relations from an increasingly pragmatic standpoint. While nothing indicates a dramatic redefinition of fundamental Soviet interests in the region, Moscow seems to be more concerned with the economic aspect of the relationship and less with the previously all-important ideological issues and ritualistic demonstrations of loyalty.[1] The chapter by Keith Crane in this volume has argued in this context that while there is a perceived trade-off in Moscow between pursuing profitable trade and avoiding political instability, the latter remains a more important goal than the former.

Aggressively looking for resources to implement its perestroika at home, the Kremlin seems to be less willing to shoulder the costs of its economic support of the troubled East European economies, and it is therefore vigorously prompting the fraternal parties to increase productivity and economic efficiency as a matter of top priority. For the same reason, as Wolfgang Berner notes in his chapter, both the Soviets and the East Europeans have been wary of admitting to the CMEA new Third World members, which would have represented an economic burden in terms of both aid and trade.

As a general indication of this trend, one might note how during 1986 and 1987 the targets of the most pungent Soviet criticism have been economically stagnant Rumania and Czechoslovakia, while relatively more dynamic Poland and Hungary have been repeatedly praised and encouraged in their efforts. This line was paralleled at the political level during the debate in the USSR over the reform of the party's electoral systems, when Soviet leaders referred to the Polish and Hungarian systems as positive precedents in multi-candidate elections.[2]

Successful economic reform in Eastern Europe would allow the Soviets to reduce their economic subsidies to their allies and redirect the savings to domestic investment, which is sorely needed for the success of the process of perestroika. Nonetheless, one should remember that what prompted past Soviet economic subsidies to Eastern Europe was Soviet concerns about the social and political stability of the East European allies. This stability was considered by Moscow to be more important than the marginal improvements which the resources devoted to those subsidies would have generated in its own domestic economy. There is no reason to think this has changed. Thus, an increasingly pragmatic USSR will continue to look with favor at East European reforms to the extent that they can substitute for Soviet subsidies. Reforms in Eastern Europe might however generate concern even in a reformed Soviet Union if they feed excessive popular expectations and generate destabilizing domestic political repercussions. This concern is clearly justified by past experience.

A longer-term Soviet concern might be to avoid an excessive East European dependency on Western credits and technology which, if extensive enough, might generate some undesirable Western leverage as well. This might provide an additional motivation for Moscow to incur the costs of its subsidies.[3] In this sense, as Keith Crane points out in his chapter, Moscow's overriding desire to retain control over the region still outweighs its obvious desire to make the countries in the region economically viable. At this time there is not much reason for the Soviets to be concerned about this potential problem: the West no longer has the massive availability of capital which made the soft loans of the 1970s possible, and Eastern Europe can hardly afford to buy expensive high technology to the extent that it would make it vulnerably dependent on Western know-how.

In fact, East European trade has recently been rather re-directed *toward* the Soviet Union, whose trade with the junior allies has risen from 52.9% in 1985 to 61.5% in 1986.[4] The European CMEA members continue to be dependent on the USSR for the energy raw materials which they can not afford to buy in the world market for hard currency, despite the recent lowering both of energy prices and of the value of the dollar. Even Romania, which used to be the most self-sufficient in energy, is increasingly forced to resort to energy imports from the Soviet Union. This forces the USSR to continue to sell more oil, and at less favorable terms, than it would prefer to do, particularly at this time, since serious problems deriving from years of over-exploitation of national hydrocarbon reserves are becoming apparent and are threatening the future of the Soviets' main source of hard currency.[5] In light of this, it is not surprising that for several years the Soviets have been doing their utmost to exhort the East Europeans to increase productivity, and particularly to improve their energy efficiency.

In the institutional framework of the CMEA, the Soviets have aired proposals to improve efficiency by selectively introducing competitive market mechanisms--including some sort of convertibility for the ruble--in intra-bloc trade. This might help to overcome the current trade inflexibility owed to the widespread counter-trade practices and to the lack of incentives for producers to compete with better products from outside the bloc--and indeed from within the bloc as well.[6] As I note in my chapter on the Warsaw Pact, over time the Soviets have allowed greater room for political maneuver in their institutionalized security framework as well.

Concomitantly with their increasing pragmatism in the economic and security policies, the Soviets have reduced the ideological emphasis in their relationship with the allies. In particular, references to "socialist internationalism"--the long-time catch-phrase indicating that the interests of the socialist community, as defined by the community's Soviet leaders, must have precedence over those of each individual socialist state--have since the inception of Gorbachev become increasingly rare. Ever since his first speech as General Secretary to the Central Committee in 1985, Gorbachev has used few ideological slogans and catchwords.[7] Significantly, he has not renewed his predecessors' calls for a world-wide conference of the international communist movement. In this respect, as Wolfgang Pfeiler notes in his chapter, the Soviets have followed in the wake of the East Europeans.

Yet, memories are still recent from the incandescent days of 1968 when Brezhnev stated that under no circumstances may the interest of socialist countries conflict with those of world socialism, thus stigmatizing with his name the theory of limited sovereignty for the junior allies--though it obviously had long preceded his coming to power.[8] Indeed, while Gorbachev has referred to socialist internationalism most sparingly, the debate in the Soviet Union is clearly far from settled on this score. At least three positions can be singled out among authoritative Soviet spokesmen.

The first position is that of those who both flatly deny the contention that the interests of individual socialist states can not be different and even contradictory, and are also opposed to "hegemonic" and "domineering" temptations by the most powerful among them over the weaker ones.[9]

The second group includes those, at the other extreme, who continue to uphold the validity of socialist internationalism in essentially the same form as did the Brezhnev Politburo.[10]

The third group is trying to square the circle by placing more emphasis on the possible contribution of initiatives on the part of the small socialist states both to peace in Europe and to better superpowers relations.[11] This formula might afford them more latitude for independent foreign policy initiatives, while reserving for the USSR the ideological "right" to stop them should the threshold of "acceptability"--however defined by the Soviets--be crossed.

As Wolfgang Pfeiler points out, Gorbachev appears to belong to the third group, but this may be due as much to his current need to keep his balance in Politburo politics as to his genuine conviction about the desirability for reform in Soviet/East European relations. In any case, it is still too early to judge which of the three groups will eventually prevail in the Kremlin.

East European Responses to Gorbachev's Policies

The above discussion on the conflict between national and international interests in the context of Soviet-East European relations suggests that some novel aspects have emerged in the East Europeans' reactions to the policy changes and to the proposals emanating from Moscow. While East European responses to Gorbachev's initiatives have varied significantly from country to country, they exhibit interesting common denominators. This section will outline them individually, while the next one will use these reactions as a basis to examine prospects for Soviet-East European relations.

One general point to note with respect to all of the regions is a rather paradoxical one. For the first time ever a Soviet leader draws enthusiastic responses from East European dissidents--including a portion of the population at large--while the national leaderships generally are very ambiguous about economic restructuring and political democratization, both of which are at the core of the "new thinking" in Moscow. By the same token, it is now the East European reformers who tend to emphasize "socialist internationalism" to strengthen their case in favor of emulating Soviet reforms, while it is the opponents of such change who now stress the right of each country to pursue a "national way to socialism."[12]

Another general point is that the East Europeans, so far, have responded more on the economic than on the political plane. This may be due to several reasons. First, the Soviets have better defined their economic plans for restructuring than their schemes for political reform. Second, in light of the objective needs of the Soviet economy, there is a lesser danger of a sudden reversal of perestroika than is the case for glasnost. Third, the East

Europeans had already been doing some of the things Gorbachev proposes to do in the economic sphere. Fourth, economic reforms are less dangerous domestically and are more predictable than are political ones. Finally, economic reforms are more badly needed and much less controversial domestically than are political transformations.

When Gorbachev launched his drive for economic restructuring, Hungary was the CMEA ally which had already done the most to improve economic efficiency, beginning with the introduction of the New Economic Mechanism in 1968. The Hungarian response to Moscow's attempt at economic perestroika has therefore predictably been a positive one. New economic legislation has been enacted which continues and strengthens Budapest's drive for greater decentralization and increased room for market mechanisms and individual enterprise.[13]

Yet, the possibility looms large that further economic liberalization might fuel higher expectations of political freedom as well, particularly should such widening economic liberalizations fail to raise productivity and to create the basis for a permanent increase in the average standards of living. This is what happened in Poland in the late 1970s, and the result was the well-known social turmoil and ensuing political crackdown. Thus, while obviously agreeing with Gorbachev's emphasis on the right of each socialist country to pursue its own model of economic and social organization, the current Hungarian leadership seeks to to avoid dangerous excesses by restating--and thus reminding itself and the populace--the continuing applicability of the "general laws" of socialism, something they were brusquely reminded of by Soviet ideologue Suslov thirty years ago.[14] In sum, Budapest is trying to continue on its course of reform without providing ammunition to the maximalists who might be inclined to do too much too fast.

The Gorbachev era finds Bulgaria in relatively good economic health. The recent record of economic growth and technological progress of the country is generally recognized as satisfactory. The government has therefore little reason to be critical of its own recent past, and it has welcomed Soviet exhortations toward greater efficiency without, however, reneging the course of action followed so far.[15]

In particular, the party headed by the Todor Zhivkov, the doyen of all socialist rulers in Eastern Europe with 33 years of uninterrupted power behind him, has followed a duplicitous course. It has been careful to distinguish between its support for the advisability of further *economic* improvements and reforms and any connection whatsoever between it and even the most limited form of *political* liberalization.

Overall, one may conclude that the Bulgarian response to Gorbachev's innovations has been cautious, with much more emphasis on economic perestroika than on political glasnost. The success of this policy will largely depend on the outcome of the post-Zhivkov transition.[16]

Poland has wholeheartedly welcomed Moscow's economic initiatives. This is hardly a surprise in light of the fact that since 1983 Jaruzelski had been pursuing essentially the same moderate economic reforms that Gorbachev is advocating. Thus, there is more than a kernel of truth in the general's statements about how the two countries have never experienced such a convergence of interests as they do today in all of their past common history.[17]

Aside from the prevailing convergence of the pragmatic economic outlooks in both countries, Poland's economic efforts require good relations with the Soviet Union because help from the latter will be instrumental to its success at economic revival--or perhaps one should say resurrection. In fact, after the lesson of the seventies Warsaw is unlikely to once again become overly dependent on Western technological and financial inputs, which have proven to be expensive and difficult to absorb and properly utilize.

For all its support for economic perestroika, Poland welcomes perhaps even more the Soviet drive toward political glasnost, particularly with respect to Gorbachev's call for more transparency in Soviet-Polish relations. Specifically, Gorbachev has underlined the necessity to finally fill in the "blank spots" in the historical record of the two countries' relations. In that context, both leaders have stressed the need for a re-foundation of bilateral relations on more solid grounds after decades of mistrust. The first sign of this effort has been the re-opening in the fall of 1987 of public discussion in both countries on the question of the infamous World War II massacre at Katyn, which remains a bleeding wound in Polish memories.[18]

An additional novel aspect in Soviet-Polish relations is the increasingly open recognition by the Soviets of the role of the Church in Poland. Given the recent warming of relations between the Jaruzelski government and the Church, it is conceivable that the former has successfully persuaded Moscow to recognize the importance of the latter in terms of the positive contribution which it can provide to social stability through its pervasive influence in the country.

The government of East Germany has reason to be satisfied with Gorbachev's initiatives. Honecker can point to the success of his own economic reforms during the past decade, and thus resist domestic and international pressure to emulate the Soviet trend toward increasing political openings.

Moreover, he can avail himself of the new Soviet overtures to the West to pursue the inter-German detente which Gorbachev's predecessors had persistently stifled. In fact, the renewed Soviet dynamism in East-West relations allows Honecker to better resist Soviet-type political reforms at home by displaying positions which are fundamentally identical to the

Soviets' in foreign policy. This had not been the case in the last years of the pre-Gorbachev era, when Moscow restrained the GDR's overtures to the West.

At the heart of East German efforts toward better East-West relations is the well-known goal of *de jure* political recognition of the East German state by Bonn. For this reason, there probably is a structural limit to the extent to which the Soviets can approve of better inter-German relations.[19] If Bonn should eventually come to recognize the East German state, this would undoubtedly increase the international standing of the latter and, with it, diminish its subordination to the USSR. Moreover, Moscow would see its post-war official authority over *all* of Germany undermined.[20]

In Czechoslovakia, the similarities between Gorbachev's economic and political initiatives and those which led to the tragedy of 1968 are evident. While there are also important differences between Gorbachev's goals and those which animated Dubcek two decades ago, the perception in Czechoslovakia tends to stress the similarities.[21]

During his visit to Czechoslovakia in the spring of 1987, Gorbachev praised the accomplishments of the Husàk leadership, but prior to and during the visit he repeatedly emphasized the need for Czechoslovakia to move on with economic restructuring. On the eve of the visit there was some speculation that he would also meet with Dubcek. The meeting did not take place. At the end of the trip, however a Soviet spokesman when questioned about the differences between Dubcek's reforms and those of Gorbachev, he could only reply "nineteen years"--an implicit acknowledgment that timing rather than the substance of reform had been Dubcek's main error.[22]

In sum, the Czechoslovak reply to Gorbachev's prompting in the economic sphere has been cautious and the future of reforms there remains uncertain. The Czechoslovak leadership appears to be divided. The new Party leader Jakes was seen by some as a supporter of reform, but his first few speeches as party leader have been extremely cautious on the subject.

Ceaucescu's Romania has expressed the stiffest resistance to the new course in the USSR. What used to be Bucharest's maverick behavior in foreign policy is now becoming the norm in domestic policy as well. Ceaucescu has repeatedly gone on record with statements about how a truly revolutionary party will, under no circumstances, give up its role in guiding all the economic entities of the society. He insists that any form of either free enterprise or of self-management is incompatible with such a role because it would allow for conflicts of choices outside of the party's reach. Ceaucescu is steadfast in his position against any suggestion of perestroika, let alone glasnost, in his country.

To make Soviet-Romanian relations worse, he continues to energetically reject any notion of socialist internationalism, no matter how veiled. This reduces Soviet readiness to help Romania at a time when its economic difficulties and its inability to attract help from the West have produced a rise in the volume of Soviet-Romanian trade.[23]

One can only speculate about Ceaucescu's motives in opposing Moscow on most issues.[24] Be that as it may, the current course may create serious problems for Romania's dealings with the West as well. For twenty years Ceaucescu was able to woo the West into granting him various kinds of preferential economic treatment thanks to his maverick foreign policy. Being out of tune with the current reforms in the USSR however, may threaten the continuation of such favorable treatments, especially if Romania is increasingly identified with neo-stalinist orthodoxy while the prevailing forces in the USSR project an image of increasing openness and reform.

Such an image could hardly come at a worse time for Romania. Bucharest is in the process of repaying its massive debt to the West at the cost of draconian reductions in its standard of living. These cuts have produced the first serious social disturbances in a major urban center under Ceaucescu's rule.[25] Soon Ceaucescu will have to look for new capital abroad in order to restart industrial and other investment which is now being cut along with everything else. It is unlikely that he will be able to find this capital without at least some Western help. To make matters worse, improvements in Soviet-Western relations might act synergically and become a factor for a further worsening of both Soviet-Romanian and Western-Romanian relations, as parties in East and West have more and more serious reasons to object to Bucharest's domestic and foreign policies.

Prospects in Soviet/East European Relations

Soviet-East European relations are slowly entering uncharted waters. The Soviet leadership is seemingly abandoning some of the old guiding principles in inter-socialist relations, but it is not clear yet that it has formulated new ones to replace them. In particular, past references to the subordination of the national sovereignty of the individual socialist countries to the interests of international socialism--as defined by Moscow--have become increasingly rare. At the same time, open discussion about the importance of, and even the divergences among, national interests of the various socialist countries has expanded. However, it is at this time unclear how such recognition of national interests will, in the long run, be reconciled on the one hand with the ideological guidelines which continue to shape the official policies and positions of the bloc, and on the other with the imperatives of Soviet realpolitik interests in the region.

Except for Romania, all the East European allies praise Gorbachev's reform attempts,[26] but only Poland has shown a determined attempt to follow suit. Even there the outcome is in doubt, particularly after the November 1987 referendum which has confirmed a fundamental distrust by the population of *any* initiative coming from Jaruzelski's government, even political and economic reforms.

The East Europeans have two main possible motives for being reluctant to follow Gorbachev's line too closely. While the relative importance of each will vary from country to country, they are likely to play a role in all. First, East European leaders must be anxious to see whether and how fast Gorbachev's power and his political line become consolidated at the apex of the Soviet polity. Inner struggles in the Politburo and in the Central Committee of the Communist Party of the Soviet Union continue. As the dismissal of Moscow's Party chief Boris Yeltsin--an erstwhile staunch supporter of Gorbachev's--demonstrates, the general secretary has won important battles but not yet the war. In light of this uncertainty, East European leaders may want to be cautious about becoming irrevocably committed to his line, lest they become alienated from potential successors, who might well hold different and more conservative views.

Second, East European leaders know full well that in the past economic and political reforms have fueled social instability, and may therefore fear for their political survival should the reforms result into uncontrollable social transformations.[27]

Thus, Eastern Europe continues to represent a cause of both concern and embarrassment for the Soviets. Concern, both because of its sluggishness to improve economic performance, with the consequent economic burden placed on the USSR; and because of the potential social and political time bomb which any reform would represent. Embarrassment, because with the last remnants of the myth of socialist internationalism quickly withering away, it becomes harder for Moscow to justify its pervasive role in East European affairs. This embarrassment also translates into a foreign policy handicap to the extent that it continues to portray an image of the USSR as an imperial power in the eyes of neutral and Third World countries and, most importantly, many West Europeans.[28] This embarrassment is not new. It may however, soon become more serious if continued Soviet overt interference in Eastern Europe disappoints the currently rising Western expectations for a relaxation of tensions in the continent.

One author has suggested that to solve this problem Gorbachev needs to find a "Greek solution" to the East European question. In other words, the junior allies should be allowed more political room for maneuver while remaining associated with the USSR for their security arrangements.[29] This would not quite be "Finlandization" which many--including many in Eastern

Europe--see as Eastern Europe's ultimate foreign policy goal. However, according to this view, it would be the minimum requirement for the West to somehow acknowledge the unavoidability of a heavily unequal Soviet/East European relationship and remove it as a permanent obstacle to improved Soviet/Western European relations.

The problem with this parallel with Greece is that the latter is a rather isolated example in Western Europe of a country with strong neo-nationalist feelings, a recent memory of American collusion with an oppressive regime and an on-going conflict with another alliance member who is believed, rightly or wrongly, to enjoy a privileged status vis-à-vis the alliance's superpower. All of these conditions make it possible for Athens to pursue its maverick foreign policy without much of a problem for the rest of the alliance. In Eastern Europe, Romania has been pursuing a comparably deviant foreign policy course, but it might be difficult to predict (and for the Soviet Union to control) the synergetic effect that East European "Greek-type" foreign policies might have on the general geopolitical equilibrium in the region.

Be that as it may, there is little reason to believe that the Soviets are at all inclined to underwrite such a "Greek" solution. As Andrej Korbonski argues in his chapter in this volume, the most likely path for Soviet-East European relations in the future is that of a continuation of the present pattern.

Thus, the status of Eastern Europe will remain an obstacle to the improvement of Soviet-Western relations. Most West Europeans are not reconciled to what they consider the heritage of Yalta. While they are unable to clearly formulate, let alone credibly propose, a workable alternative, West Europeans are not resigned to the perpetuation of overt Soviet domination of the region. In fact, to formulate a realistic alternative would be a formidable task, since any workable proposition would have to be one which at the same time should: impede the resurgence, under whatever form, of Germany as a predominant power in Central Europe; prevent the birth of any German ambition, however veiled, to that effect; impede the rekindling of the now dormant inter-East European conflicts; respect Soviet security interests, as perceived by the Soviets; and, last but not least, be implemented gradually and peacefully.

Implications for the West

The development of Soviet-East European relations under Gorbachev carries both important economic and political opportunities and potentially serious challenges and risks for the West.

In the economic sphere, the Soviet trend toward greater liberalization and availability for cooperation with the West is widely perceived as a signal to the East Europeans that they, too, can and perhaps should do more themselves. But in light of the huge diversities between the two economic systems, great obstacles will have to be overcome before any positive results will become manifest.

For example, the new Soviet propensity to establish joint ventures is unprecedented and might turn out to be an important path-breaking development, all the more so if imitated throughout Eastern Europe.[30] However, several problems must be solved before the joint venture initiatives will yield concrete results. First, there will be a problem with the organization of the local management, which will not be integrated into the state plan, but will not be able to adopt capitalist management criteria either. There is a danger that some sort of a hybrid and unworkable management system will result. In particular, there might arise problems in accounting and in wage differentiations between local and imported personnel, using rubles and convertible currency. Second, the Soviet and Western partners might find themselves moved by contradictory motivations: the main economic rationale for the Soviets is to produce quality products so as to increase exports and raise hard currency revenues, whereas for the Western partners it is to penetrate the potentially enormous Soviet market and repatriate profits.

More broadly, there is a risk that, as in the past, the West, and particularly the United States, will oscillate between a pragmatic look at economic relations with the East and policies of linkage of this trade with political issues. Without entering into the merits or the desirability of such linkage, it is a potentially disruptive political factor of economic cooperation that must be reckoned with.

In fact, if economic opportunities for East-West cooperation are uncertain, political prospects are more volatile and even less clearly definable. In the political sphere, the major issue that confronts the West is whether prospective developments in Soviet-East European relations will lead to a less antagonistic East-West relationship. Most agree that increased relaxation of the Soviet grip over its junior partners, coupled with greater liberalization at home, will indeed contribute to East-West detente. This, according to the argument, is because the Soviet regime's oppression of its own people as well as of Eastern Europe has always been a major political irritant in Western-Soviet relations. Moreover, the argument continues, if liberalization brings about better standards of living, the Soviet government will be less inclined to use foreign policy expansionism to suppress potential social unrest at home.

Yet, there is ground to be skeptical about this line of reasoning. The fact is that Russia was more expansionist, rather than less, at times of greater enlightenment and internal and international openness--for example, during the reigns of Tsars Peter I and Catherine the Great. Evidence to prove that Soviet enlightenment would have different foreign policy implications than did Tsarist enlightenment is wanting. Be that as it may, and quite aside from speculations about the intentions of the Soviet leadership, opportunities for an expansion of Soviet influence abroad will increase if the domestic reforms succeed, for military, political and economic reasons.

From a military point of view, clearly in the medium and long run the Soviets will have more resources to devote to military purposes if the performance of their economy improves than if it continues to stagnate or deteriorates further. It is not surprising that the 1970s witnessed both a Soviet military build-up and a relatively good performance of the Soviet economy. Also, East European military spending has in the recent past been closely related to fluctuations in national income.[31] Again, this does not mean that Soviet leaders intend to devote larger economic resources to military purposes, but they would have the capability to do so.

Economically, the Soviets and the East Europeans would be able to resume a more widespread use of economic aid to strengthen their presence in the Third World. In fact, while in the 1960s and 1970s the Soviet were expanding their influence in the Third World also through economic aid, in the 1980s they have been less and less able to to do so. The case of Mozambique is a good example of this reversal. This was a revolutionary country which during the 1970s had strong Marxist leanings and a growing Soviet and Cuban influence. It gradually began to turn to the West when the leaders in Maputo perceived that the Soviets were unable to provide what they needed more urgently than ideology or even arms--development aid. With respect to the latter, as pointed out in Wolfgang Berner's chapter, both the Soviets and the East Europeans have been increasingly reluctant to make a serious effort.

The inflow of Western aid, though limited for now, has brought Soviet influence in Mozambique to an ebb, and the trend is unlikely to be reversed, despite frequent Western collusion with racist South Africa, which remains Mozambique's main security threat. In the future, however, if the Soviets and the East Europeans were able to resume substantial economic aid, it is not at all inconceivable that Maputo will again move politically closer to them.

Finally, if Gorbachev's *glasnost* restores some of the appeal that the Soviet system once held but which it lost over decades of ideological disillusionment and economic failures, the USSR might recuperate part of its erstwhile ideological and political attractiveness in the eyes of both East Europeans and of the Western left. In particular, the Communist parties of

Western Europe--and specifically the more orthodox and pro-Soviet factions within them--might regain some of the dynamism of the mid-1970s, particularly if a revival of the USSR should at some point be accompanied by a serious economic recession in the West.

One other issue which deserves a separate treatment in the context of the political implications for the West of Soviet-East European relations is the German question. Impolitic as it is to explicitly say so, to prevent the resurgence of a predominant German entity in Central Europe remains an imperative for all other European states, in both East and West.[32] While this fact of course poses agonizing political and ethical dilemmas for the nations which are friends and allies of the two German states, nonetheless it will remain true for the foreseeable future.

The GDR, for its part, strives for a rather ambiguous policy. As noted in the chapter by Wolfgang Pfeiler, it insists on *Abgrenzung* while pursuing intense economic ties with the West Europeans in general and, of course, with the FRG in particular.

Recognizing this, one author has recently suggested that the only way to reconcile German aspirations for closer ties without political unity with the concerns which such aspirations generate for the rest of the Europeans is to favor "the gradual emergence of a much less threatening loose confederation of the existing two states."[33] The problem with this view is that for such a confederation to be conceivable, it would have to be preceded by a dramatic change in the two Germanies' relations with their respective military alliances and economic communities. But if this were the case, a formidable political momentum would inevitably be generated, and it is difficult to imagine how the rest of the Europeans--or, for that matter, the two superpowers--could prevent it from developing into a drive toward an ever more complete unification.

In the shorter run, it is probably in the interest of inter-German rapprochement that Gorbachev's drive toward better relations with the West succeed. In particular, good Soviet-West German relations have recently proven to be a pre-condition for good inter-German relations.[34] Because of this, many in Western Europe worry about the prospect of Soviet-West German relations becoming too close. But since improved Soviet-West German relations are unlikely to raise Soviet propensity to accept a reunified German political entity--of whatever kind--a permanent Soviet-West German detente should be welcome by all in the West who look for a lessening of overall East-West tensions in the continent. At the same time, it will be up to the Germans, both in the East but especially in the West, to ensure that inter-German detente fuels sympathy but not suspicion in the West. As Wolfgang Pfeiler notes in his chapter, the Federal Republic's *Ostpolitik* is and must remain a part of its *Westpolitik*.

In conclusion, one notices how the West is sometimes confused over the definition of its political goals in East-West relations. What is it that we are striving to achieve? Most would probably agree that it is first and foremost the preservation of peace, and secondly quantitatively and qualitatively improved political, economic, cultural and human contacts between East and West. The current roughly bipolar political division of the continent has arguably served the former goal well, but not the latter.

As far as the goal of peace is concerned, the division of Europe into two blocs, together with the inception of the nuclear era, has contributed to freeze many actual and potential conflicts among the states and the nations of Europe--particularly of central Europe. It has repressed--though by no means erased--divisive nationalist tendencies across the continent. In this respect, it has served a useful purpose.

However, that same division has prevented all Europeans from taking full advantage of the enormous potential which exists for greater exchanges and integration, which would be to the benefit of all. For this reason, many in Europe today are uneasy with the division which is commonly referred to as the "heritage of Yalta." French president Mitterrand in 1982 went as far as saying that anything that will contribute to escape from the divisions resulting from Yalta will be welcome.

With all the due respect for the authoritativeness of that position, it is a rather simplistic one. To move in the direction of an abandonment of the post-Yalta settlement would be desirable only if it resulted in a more united and less conflictual Europe. But there is no guarantee that steps toward overcoming Yalta would, ipso facto, contribute to that goal. They might, instead, result into a more fragmented Europe, reviving dormant but still creeping and potentially explosive nationalism. A Europe of "fatherlands" might well become one where the single East-West divide of our times would yield to a whole net of newly stiffened international borders--with all the undesirable political and economic consequences that would signify.

Another authoritative writer argued that escaping from Yalta is desirable because it would allow for the "spiritual and moral recovery" of Europe.[35] Again, this seems a rather blurred goal for which to strive. There is no doubt that many Europeans today feel frustrated that they cannot overcome a political division whose guarantors are the two superpowers. Yet, one is left to wonder what "spiritual and moral" values Europeans have lost, because of the post-war political division settled at Yalta, which they enjoyed before. Was pre-Yalta Europe a "spiritual and moral" model worth recovering? Hardly so.

In sum, while all in East and West have an interest in building a safer Europe in which to live, a safer Europe does not need to be a Europe without the two blocs. On the contrary, the withering away of the latter might well bring about increasing divisions and dangers for peace. This does not mean that the best we can do is passively accept the status quo. It is by no means true that we should assume a "if it ain't broke don't fix it" attitude. The current arrangement has its merits, but it is certainly perfectible. Moreover, there is no sense in striving to somehow freeze history: The current geopolitical arrangement in Europe, like all others before it, will change. But we in the West should strive to "fix" the division of Europe only if and when we can be reasonably sure that we *can* do it, and that the unavoidable risks involved are absolutely minimized, for a failure might well have catastrophic results.[36]

Europeans, both East and West, should strive for the dissolution of the blocs only after sufficient East-West ties have been developed at all levels to ensure that it would indeed result in a less divided continent. For the foreseeable future, however, lingering nationalism makes such a pre-condition unimaginable, although this might change and hopefully will.

In this light, Western interests lie in a continuing effort toward concrete improvement in economic, cultural, technological and above all security cooperation both between and within the blocs. In particular, arms control agreements to increase crisis stability, minimize the possibility of misperceptions and accidental conflicts and redirect precious economic and human resources away from the defense industry should be pursued with energy. Increased economic cooperation between East and West should be developed both for its value *per se* and as a means to increase East-West interdependence, which, even if somewhat imponderable, remains a stabilizing factor of common interests. Easier human contacts should be favored throughout the continent and in both directions, and recent developments in Eastern Europe seem to indicate an increasing willingness on the part of those governments to lower past barriers to such contacts.

The West should energetically encourage such developments, while however refraining from using human rights in Eastern Europe as an instrument for political rhetoric to be conveniently manipulated in particular political contingencies--as it sometimes did in the past. To this end, as pointed out in my chapter on the Warsaw Pact, a fine balance between overtures and restraint toward Eastern Europe will be required. Overtures should help the East Europeans to increase their say vis-à-vis the Soviet Union, while restraint should be aimed at avoiding any process of fundamental change that is not both gradual and peaceful.

These are concrete, realistic and this writer believes unequivocally positive steps. However, to leap to more abstract visions of a post-Yalta transition which *ipso facto* would unify the continent and somehow eliminate all the conflicts of interests among the various nations and states is unjustified, might be counterproductive, and should therefore be avoided.

Notes

1. Karen Dawisha and Jonathan Valdez, "Socialist Internationalism in Eastern Europe," *Problems of Communism*, vol. xxxvi, March-April 1987, p. 13.

2. During the course of the debate over party electoral reforms at the CC Plenum of January 1987 Hungary and Poland were even praised by the usually conservative Ligachev. Werner G. Hahn, "Electoral Choice in the Soviet Bloc," *Problems of Communism*, vol. xxxvi, March-April 1987, p. 32.

3. Vladimir V. Kusin, "Gorbachev and Eastern Europe," *Problems of Communism*, vol. xxxv, January-February 1986, p. 46.

4. Data provided by the Soviet-Italian Chamber of Commerce.

5. Kramer and T. Gustafson, "Energy and the Soviet Bloc," *International Security*, vol. 6, no. 3, Winter 1981/82. As is known, intra-CMEA oil prices are calculated yearly on the basis of a five-year moving average. This of course favored the East European buyers when world market prices were rising, but the same mechanism turns against the buyers when world prices fall for a prolonged period of time. In fact, what was a subsidy *from* the Soviet seller might become a premium. But since not all energy trade is settled in hard currency, the degree to which the Soviets are making the East European shoulder the financial burden represented by the fact that Soviet prices have been declining more slowly than world prices depends on the *degree to which Moscow demands that energy be paid back either in hard currency on in "hard goods."* So far Moscow has avoided pressing for "hard" payments too strongly.

6. Jackson Diehl, "Soviet Rewriting East Bloc Economic Rules," *International Herald Tribune*, 14 October 1987.

7. Vladimir Kusin, "Gorbachev and Eastern Europe," op. cit., p. 40.

8. Reported in *Pravda*, 26 September 1968.

9. Karen Dawisha and Jonathan Valdez "Socialist Internationalism ...," op. cit., p. 2.

10. Ibid.

11. Vladimir Kusin, "Gorbachev and Eastern Europe," op. cit.,p. 44.

12. Michael Kraus, "Soviet Policy Toward East Europe," *Current History*, vol. 86, no. 523, November 1987, p. 354.

13. Private enterprises are now allowed to have up to 24 employees, twice as many as before. Since March 1987 Hungary is the first socialist country in Eastern Europe with a law on bankruptcy, enacted amidst growing dissatisfaction with the mismanagement of large sums of foreign hard currency credits on the part of several major enterprises. In 1987 Hungary has also introduced the first value added tax and personal income tax. Federigo Argentieri, "I Paesi Europei del Blocco Sovietico e la Politica di Gorbaciov," *Note & Ricerche CeSPI, #* 14, Rome, September 1987, pp. 26ff.

14. Dawisha and Valdez, "Socialist Internationalism...," op. cit., p. 5.

15. Charles Gati, "Gorbachev and Eastern Europe," *Foreign Affairs*, vol. 65, no. 5, Summer 1987, p. 963.

16. Federigo Argentieri, op. cit., p. 37.

17. Gati, "Gorbachev and Eastern Europe," op. cit., p. 968.

18. The socialist government of Poland, unlike the government in exile at the time, has supported the Soviet version which, contrary to the findings of the Red Cross during World War II, attributed the responsibility for the execution of thousands of Polish officers to the Nazis, however, many in Poland have never been convinced and the memory of Katyn has fueled considerable anti-Soviet resentment.

19. As Eberhard Schulz argues in this volume, the East Europeans have long balanced their desire for better relations with Bonn with Soviet pressure to limit such relations. In this light, Gorbachev's "green light" to improve FRG-GDR relations may have long-lasting consequences for Bonn's ties with the rest of Eastern Europe as well.

20. The Kremlin still considers it important to maintain a *de jure* recognition of its presence in Germany as guarantor of one of four occupation sectors rather than host of one of two German states. This status maintains a Soviet right of say in West German affairs which would be lost should the two German states become fully sovereign again. That the Soviets place much value on this legal nuance was highlighted in the famous incident in 1985 when the SED's newspaper *Neues Deutschland* once referred to the "Soviet forces in the German Democratic Republic" only to be promptly rebuked by the Soviet commander of those units, who emphasized that he was the head of the "Soviet forces in Germany". See Vladimir Kusin, op. cit., p. 48, and Wolfgang Pfeiler's chapter in this volume.

21. To some extent this perception is present also at the apex of the Soviet leadership, as testified by the open consideration which was given in the

fall of 1987 to a re-evaluation of the events which had led to the invasion of 1968. The consequences of the recent dramatic and unprecedented interview granted to the Italian CP's daily *l'Unità*, in which Dubcek praised Gorbachev's ideas and stressed the similarities with those which his government tried to implement 20 years earlier, remain to be seen. For the text of the interview, see *l'Unità*, 9 and 10 January, 1988.

22. In November, Georgi Smirnov, Director of the Institute for Marxism-Leninism, went on record saying that the time had come to review the decisions of 1968 about the Czechoslovak intervention. See *la Republica* (Rome), 5 November 1987.

23. Gati, "Gorbachev and Eastern Europe," op. cit., p. 962.

24. Several non-exclusive explanations are possible. First, Ceaucescu may fear that to take positions closer to those of Moscow would endanger his family rule over the country by facilitating the rise of more reform-minded leaders. Second, he may fear that opening his society, even slightly, through economic reforms and glasnost would dilute the nationalist cement which has provided some badly-needed social cohesion during the long period of economic hardships. Third, he may fear that even limited economic liberalization, with the accompanying rationalization and international division of labor would accelerate the process of CMEA integration, which he has resisted for twenty years.

25. On 15 November 1987 riots broke out in Brasov during local elections, and Ceaucescu portraits were burned while crowds sang anti-regime slogans and invaded public offices. See press reports in most Western newspapers of the following days.

26. Gati, "Gorbachev and Eastern Europe," op. cit., p. 959.

27. This concern might be made worse by the fact that most of them are at the end of their political lives, and therefore not interested in restructuring the systems which has served them well for so long. Zhivkov has been in power since 1954, Ceaucescu since 1965, and Honecker since 1971.

28. Gati, "Gorbachev and Eastern Europe," op. cit., p. 972.

29. Ibid, p. 975.

30. The Soviet laws with respect to this initiative are still being perfected, but the main points can be summarized as follows. The Soviet partner will retain a quota of 51 percent or more in the venture; the president and the director general must be Soviet citizens, as must 51 percent or more of the work force; profits can be exported if the joint venture still

retains residual hard currency after having paid all personnel--they will be taxed at a fixed 20 percent rate, but will be exempt for the first two years; the amount of the foreign input into the joint venture will be calculated on the basis of international prices at the official Soviet exchange rate; the joint ventures will operate out of the plan, and must therefore be geared to producing for foreign markets. See G. Salvini, "Fare Affari Con Gorbaciov," *Mondo Economico*, 20 April 1987; Natalia Karpova, (of the foreign trade commission at the Soviet Council of Ministers) "Compagni Pronti alle Joint Ventures," *Il Sole-24 Ore*, 9 September 1987.)

31. Keith Crane, *Military Spending in Eastern Europe* (Santa Monica, CA: Rand Corporation, 1987), passim, and especially p. 55.

32. This point is discussed in some detail in Peter Bender, "The Superpower Squeeze," *Foreign Policy*, no. 65, Winter 1986-87, passim, and especially p. 109.

33. Zbigniew Brzezinski, "The Future of Yalta," *Foreign Affairs*, vol. 63, no. 2, Winter 1984/85, p. 296.

34. One will recall how Honecker's long-awaited visit to the FRG was twice postponed during the chill in Soviet-West German relations at the time of the NATO INF deployments in 1983-84, while it finally took place in September of 1987, a few weeks after the Bonn government had acceded to the Soviet request that its Pershing-1 missiles be dismantled as a part of the overall INF settlement, though they would not be in the actual U.S.-Soviet treaty.

35. Zbigniew Brzezinski, "The Future of Yalta," op. cit., p. 295.

36. Some identify a less divided Europe with a "safer" one, but no evidence has been provided to prove this thesis. See William H. Luers, "The U.S. and Eastern Europe," *Foreign Affairs*, vol. 68, no. 5 Summer 1987, p. 994.

Books in the CISA Series, Studies in International and Strategic Affairs

1. William C. Potter, Editor, *Verification and SALT* (Westview Press, 1980).
2. Bennett Ramberg, *Destruction of Nuclear Energy Facilities in War: The Problems and Implications* (Lexington Books, 1980); revised and reissued as *Nuclear Power Plants as Weapons for the Enemy: An Unrecognized Military Peril* (University of California Press, 1984).
3. Paul Jabber, *Not by War Alone: Security and Arms Control in the Middle East* (University of California Press, 1981).
4. Roman Kolkowicz and Andrzej Korbonski, Editors, *Soldiers, Peasants, and Bureaucrats* (Allen & Unwin, 1982).
5. William C. Potter, *Nuclear Power and Nonproliferation: An Interdisciplinary Perspective* (Oelgeschlager, Gunn and Hain, 1982).
6. Steven L. Spiegel, Editor, *The Middle East and the Western Alliance* (Allen & Unwin, 1984).
7. Dagobert L. Brito, Michael D. Intriligator, and Adele E. Wick, Editors, *Strategies for Managing Nuclear Proliferation-Economic and Political Issues* (Lexington Books, 1983).
8. Bernard Brodie, Michael D. Intriligator, and Roman Kolkowicz, Editors, *National Security and International Stability* (Oelgeschlager, Gunn and Hain, 1983).
9. Raju G.C. Thomas, Editor, *The Great Power Triangle and Asian Security* (Lexington Books, 1983).
10. R.D. Tschirgi, *The Politics of Indecision: Origins and Implications of American Involvement with the Palestine Problem* (Praeger, 1983).
11. Giacomo Luciani, Editor, *The Mediterranean Region: Economic Inter-dependence and the Future of Society* (Croom Helm (London & Canberra) and St. Martin's Press (NY), 1984).
12. Roman Kolkowicz and Neil Joeck, Editors, *Arms Control and International Security* (Westview Press, 1984).
13. Jiri Valenta and William C. Potter, Editors, *Soviet Decision-making for National Security* (Allen & Unwin, 1984).
14. William C. Potter, Editor, *Verification and Arms Control*, (Lexington Books, 1985).
15. Rodney Jones, Joseph Pilat, Cesare Merlini, and William C. Potter,

Editors, the *Nuclear Suppliers and Nonproliferation: Dilemmas and Policy Choices* (Lexington Books, 1985).

16.   Gerald Bender, James Coleman, and Richard Sklar, Editors, *African Crisis Areas and U.S. Foreign Policy* (University of California Press, 1985).

17.   Bennett Ramberg, *Global Nuclear Energy Risks: The Search for Preventive Medicine* (Westview Press, 1986).

18.   Neil Joeck, Editor, *The Logic of Nuclear Deterrence* (Frank Cass, 1987).

19.   Raju G.C. Thomas, *Indian Security Policy* (Princeton University Press, 1986).

20.   Steven Spiegel, Mark Heller, and Jacob Goldberg, Editors, *Soviet-American Competition in the Middle East* (Lexington Books, 1987).

21.   Roman Kolkowicz, Editor, *The Logic of Nuclear Terror* (Allen & Unwin, 1987).

22.   Roman Kolkowicz, Editor, *Dilemmas of Nuclear Deterrence* (Frank Cass, 1987).

23.   Michael D. Intriligator and Hans-Adolf Jacobsen, Editors, *East-West Conflict: Elite Perceptions and Political Options*, (Westview Press, 1988).

24.   Marco Carnovale and William C. Potter, Editors, *Continuity and Change in Soviet-East European Relations: Implications for the West* (Westview Press, 1988).

25.   William C. Potter, Editor, *The Emerging Nuclear Suppliers and Nonproliferation* (forthcoming).